T0291209

Real-World Shocks and Retirement System Resiliency

Real-World Shocks and Retirement System Resiliency

Edited by

Olivia S. Mitchell
John Sabelhaus
and
Stephen P. Utkus

OXFORD
UNIVERSITY PRESS

UNIVERSITY PRESS

Great Clarendon Street, Oxford, OX2 6DP,
United Kingdom

Oxford University Press is a department of the University of Oxford.
It furthers the University's objective of excellence in research, scholarship,
and education by publishing worldwide. Oxford is a registered trade mark of
Oxford University Press in the UK and in certain other countries

Enquiries concerning reproduction outside the scope of this licence
should be sent to the Rights Department, Oxford University Press, at the address above

Published in the United States of America by Oxford University Press
198 Madison Avenue, New York, NY 10016, United States of America

British Library Cataloguing in Publication Data

Data available

Library of Congress Control Number: 2023948510

ISBN 9780198894131

DOI: 10.1093/oso/9780198894131.001.0001

Printed and bound by
CPI Group (UK) Ltd, Croydon, CR0 4YY

Links to third party websites are provided by Oxford in good faith and
for information only. Oxford disclaims any responsibility for the materials
contained in any third party website referenced in this work.

Preface

The past decade has wreaked labor market, health, and financial shocks on the entire world, calling into question the roles of social insurance and old-age retirement schemes. This volume explores how these shocks are driving the need for new policy to meet these challenges, along with the need for adaptive changes by households, in an effort to enhance retirement resilience. The volume will be informative to researchers, plan sponsors, policymakers, and investment experts working to enhance retirement plan offerings.

In preparing this book, many people and institutions played key roles. Our co-editors, John Sabelhaus and Stephen P. Utkus, were invaluable in identifying topics to be considered, as well as experts who contributed to this endeavor by examining novel datasets. We remain deeply grateful to our Advisory Board and Members of the Pension Research Council for their intellectual and research support. Additional funding was provided by the Boettner Center for Pensions and Retirement Research, the Pension Research Council, and the Ralph H. Blanchard Memorial Endowment at the Wharton School of the University of Pennsylvania. We also are delighted to continue our long-term association with Oxford University Press, which publishes our series on global retirement security. The manuscript was expertly prepared by Sarah Kate Sanders and Natalie Gerich Brabson.

Our work at the Pension Research Council and the Boettner Center for Pensions and Retirement Security of the Wharton School of the University of Pennsylvania has focused on aspects of pensions and retirement wellbeing for 70 years. This volume reflects our ongoing commitment to generate useful research on and engage debate around policy for retirement security.

Olivia S. Mitchell
Executive Director, Pension Research Council
Director, Boettner Center for Pensions and Retirement Research
The Wharton School, University of Pennsylvania

Contents

List of Figures   ix
List of Tables   xi
Notes on Contributors   xiii

1. Retirement System Resiliency in the Face of Real-World
   Shocks: Introduction   1
   Olivia S. Mitchell, John Sabelhaus, and Stephen P. Utkus

Part I. Labor Market Shocks: Scarring the Future?

2. How Gloomy Is the Retirement Outlook for Millennials?   11
   Richard W. Johnson and Karen E. Smith

3. Older Workers, Retirement, and Macroeconomic Shocks   36
   Erika McEntarfer

4. Recessions and Retirement: New Evidence from the
   COVID-19 Pandemic   52
   Courtney Coile and Haiyi Zhang

Part II. The Changing Financial Environment and Retirement Security

5. Wealth Inequality and Retirement Preparedness: A
   Cross-Cohort Perspective   73
   John Sabelhaus and Alice Henriques Volz

6. Changes in Retirement Savings during the COVID Pandemic   97
   *Elena Derby, Lucas Goodman, Kathleen Mackie, and Jacob
   Mortenson*

7. Saving and Wealth Accumulation among Student Loan
   Borrowers: Implications for Retirement Preparedness   120
   Lisa J. Dettling, Sarena F. Goodman, and Sarah J. Reber

Part III. Real-World Shocks and Policy Developments

8. The Safety Net Response to the COVID-19 Pandemic
   Recession and the Older Population   155
   Robert A. Moffitt and James P. Ziliak

9. Retirement Security and Health Costs   180
   Glenn Follette and Louise Sheiner

10. Economic Conditions, the COVID-19 Pandemic
   Recession, and Implications for Disability Insurance in the US   211
   Nicole Maestas and Kathleen J. Mullen

The Pension Research Council   222
Index   226

List of Figures

3.1 Flows into and out of retirement, and retirement status static flows   41

3.2 (a) Recessions and flows into retirement at age 55, 60, and 62   43

3.2 (b) Recessions and returns to the labor market from retirement at age 60   44

4.1 Monthly retirement probability, relative to reference month   63

5.1 Relative rank distributions at age 60   83

5.2 Relative rank distributions at age 50   85

5.3 Relative rank distributions at age 40   87

5.4 10th percentile of cross-cohort wealth distributions   89

5.5 25th percentile of cross-cohort wealth distributions   90

5.6 50th percentile of cross-cohort wealth distributions   91

5.7 75th percentile of cross-cohort wealth distributions   92

5.8 90th percentile of cross-cohort wealth distributions   92

6.1 Aggregate DC and IRA contributions by year   102

6.2 Employee DC contributions by income groups   104

6.3 IRAs and other retirement withdrawals, by year   106

6.4 Mean withdrawals from IRAs and other retirement accounts, by age   107

6.5 Counts of IRA withdrawals as a percent of prior year balance for 75-year-olds   109

6.6 Total IRA withdrawals and penalized withdrawals by those under age 59½   110

6.7 Total IRA withdrawals close to a $100,000 threshold, 2019–2020   111

6.8 Probability of taking retirement plan withdrawals by age, close to age 59½   114

7.1 Income and wealth by current student debt-holding status and education   126

7.2 Share of families with student debt by age   130

7.3 Borrowing by college-educated families: imputed versus actual share   136

7.4 Wealth and retirement preparation for college-educated families, by imputed student borrower status   138

7.5 Credit report characteristics by student borrower status   140

8.1   Transfer program participation rates of men age 50–61   162

8.2   Transfer program participation rates of women age 50–61   163

8.3   Transfer program participation rates of men age 62–74   164

8.4   Transfer program participation rates of women age 62–74   165

9.1   Medicare spending, projected as of 2009, and actual   184

9.2   Real health expenditures by income quintile (2021 $), age adjusted   191

9.3   (a) Private spending as share of income by income quintile. (b) Premiums as a share of income by income quintile. (c) Cost burdened share of beneficiaries by income quintile (private spending > 20% income). (d) Cost burdened share of beneficiaries by income quintile (private spending > 50% income)   192

9.4   Out-of-pocket spending by age as a share of income in 2016   193

9.5   Increase in non-health consumption by 2019 from slower growth of Medicare savings since 2009, by income quintile   195

10.1   Awards into and exits from the DI program   213

10.2   Number of DI beneficiaries with successful return to work   213

10.3   Employment rate by disability status   214

10.4   Rise in unemployment rate during COVID more pronounced than Great Recession   215

10.5   Number of SSDI applications and beneficiaries May 2019–May 2022   217

10.6   Percent reporting disability among civilian non-institutionalized population age 18–64, June 2008–April 2022   218

List of Tables

2.1 Projected mean and distribution of per capita annual family income at age 70 by birth cohort ($)   20

2.2 Projected annual per capita family income at age 70 by birth cohort, income source, and income quintile   21

2.3 Projected median annual per capita family income at age 70 by birth cohort and personal characteristics ($)   23

2.4 Projected percentage of adults with inadequate income at age 70 by birth cohort and personal characteristics   25

2.5 Projected percentage of Pre-Boomers and Early Millennials with inadequate income at age 70 under alternative scenarios about how social security benefits will be paid after the trust funds run out, by personal characteristics   27

2.6 Projected percentage of Pre-Boomers and Early Millennials with inadequate income at age 70 under alternative adequacy measures, by personal characteristics   28

3.1 Initial retirement spells   42

3.2 Cyclical regressions: Retirements and partial retirement   46

3.3 Cyclical regressions: Labor market returns   48

4.1 Summary statistics   59

4.2 Retirement regressions   61

4.3 Retirement regressions, by age and gender   64

4.4 Retirement regressions, by education   66

6.1 Characteristics of those taking retirement plan distributions close to $100,000 in 2020   112

7.1 Student debt and college attendance by age group   132

7.2 Characteristics of families, by presence of student debt   133

8.1 Marginal effects of transfers: male age 50–61 Probit models   166

8.2 Marginal effects of transfers: Female age 50–61 Probit models   168

8.3 Marginal effects of transfers: Male age 62–74 Probit models   170

8.4 Marginal effects of transfers: Female age 62–74 Probit models   171

9.1 Decomposition of health spending 1980–2019   185

9.2 Relative health care inflation   187

9.3   Difference in real non-health consumption share of income
      relative to baseline scenario where Medicare costs increase
      with inflation   197
9.4   Difference in non-health consumption share of income
      compared to 2016 cohort   199

Notes on Contributors

Courtney Coile is Professor of Economics at Wellesley College; she is also a NBER Research Associate where she co-directs the NBER Retirement and Disability Research Center and the International Social Security project. She is also a member of the Committee on Population at the National Academy of Sciences and of the Data Monitoring Committee of the Health and Retirement Study. Her research focuses on the economics of aging and health, with a focus on retirement decisions, health trends, and public programs used by older and disabled populations. She earned her PhD in economics from MIT and her AB from Harvard University.

Elena Derby is an economist at the United States Congressional Joint Committee on Taxation where her research focuses on retirement savings behavior and low-income housing, automatic enrollment in retirement plans, and the long-run effects of living in tax-subsidized housing. She earned her MA and PhD in economics from Georgetown University; her MA in international conflict studies at the School of Science and Public Policy, King's College London; and her BA in economics/international relations at the Claremont McKenna College.

Lisa J. Dettling is a principal economist in the Division of Research and Statistics at the Federal Reserve Board, where she forecasts economic effects of fiscal policy. Her academic research focuses on issues in household finance, especially how public policies affect family finances. Previously, she served on the team tasked with administering and disseminating the Survey of Consumer Finances. She earned her PhD in economics from the University of Maryland, and her BS in mathematics and economics from the Ohio State University.

Glenn Follette oversees the group of economists that examines the effects of fiscal policy actions on the economy and produces and presents the staff's economic outlook to the Federal Reserve Board. His research interests include the macroeconomic effects of fiscal policy actions, the effects of the economy on government budgets, and health economics. Previously, he advised the Federal Reserve Board Governor Jerome Powell on macroeconomic issues. He received his PhD from Georgetown University, and his BSE from the University of Connecticut.

Lucas Goodman is an economist at the US Department of the Treasury, Office of Tax Analysis. His research interests include the tax-advantaged retirement system, and how firms respond to changes in tax incentives for investment and other activities. Previously he worked at the United States Congressional Joint Committee on Taxation. He obtained his PhD in economics from the University of Maryland, and his BS in economics and mathematics from MIT.

Sarena F. Goodman is a principal economist in the Division of Research and Statistics at the Federal Reserve Board, where she administers and disseminates the Survey of Consumer Finances. Her research covers labor economics and household finance, with an emphasis on the identification of causal pathways that give rise to inequality and intergenerational mobility. Previously, she worked on the team that monitored developments in consumer lending, and she also served as a staff economist and research assistant at the White House Council of Economic Advisers. She earned her PhD in economics from Columbia University, and her AB in economics from Dartmouth College.

Richard W. Johnson is a senior fellow at the Urban Institute where he directs the Program on Retirement Policy. His research focuses on health and income security at older ages, older Americans' employment, retirement preparedness, social security reform, retirement decisions, and occupational change at older ages. He received his PhD in economics from the University of Pennsylvania, and his BA in economics from Princeton.

Kathleen Mackie is a senior economist at the United States Congressional Joint Committee on Taxation where her research interests focus on retirement savings. Previously she worked at the Office of Tax Analysis at the US Department of Treasury. She earned her PhD in economics from the University of Kentucky.

Nicole Maestas is an Associate Professor of Health Care Policy at Harvard Medical School and a Research Associate of the National Bureau of Economic Research where she directs the NBER's Retirement and Disability Research Center. She studies the economics of disability insurance, labor markets, health care systems, and population aging, as well as labor supply and the use of medical care. She is also investigating the causes of the opioid epidemic and its impact on employment and participation in the federal disability programs, as well as the effects of state Medicaid policies on the health care and wellbeing of people receiving Supplemental Security Income benefits. She received her MPP in public policy from the Goldman School of Public Policy, and her PhD in economics, both from UC Berkeley.

Erika McEntarfer is the lead economist for the US Census Bureau's Longitudinal Employer-Household Dynamics data program. Her research uses US linked employer-employee data to examine the business cycle dynamics of labor markets, worker mobility, and wage stickiness. She has an undergraduate degree from Bard College and a PhD in economics from Virginia Tech.

Olivia S. Mitchell is the International Foundation of Employee Benefit Plans Professor; Professor of Insurance/Risk Management and Business Economics/Policy; Executive Director of the Pension Research Council; and Director of the Boettner Center on Pensions and Retirement Research; all at the Wharton School of the University of Pennsylvania. Her research focuses on pensions, risk management, financial literacy, household finance, and public finance. She is also Research Associate at the NBER; Independent Director on the Allspring Mutual Fund Boards; and Executive Board member for the Michigan Retirement Research Center. She received her MA and PhD in economics from the University of Wisconsin-Madison, and her BA in economics from Harvard University.

Robert A. Moffitt is the Krieger-Eisenhower Professor of Economics at Johns Hopkins University, where his research focuses on the economics of the labor market, the family, and welfare systems for the poor. He has also studied statistical, econometric, and methodological issues in economics. He is a Fellow of the Econometric Society, a Fellow of the Society of Labor Economists, a National Associate of the National Academy of Sciences, a recipient of a MERIT Award from the National Institutes of Health, and a recipient of a Guggenheim Fellowship. He also is a past President of the Population Association of America, and past President of the Society of Labor Economists. He received his BA in economics from Rice University, and his MA and PhD in economics from Brown University.

Jacob Mortenson is an economist at the United States Congressional Joint Committee on Taxation, US House of Representatives, where he researches retirement economics, individual and corporate responses to income taxation, and measurement of income inequality. He received his PhD and MA in economics from Georgetown University, and his BA in economics and political science from the University of South Dakota.

Kathleen J. Mullen is a senior economist at the RAND Corporation and director of the RAND Center for Disability Research; she also directs the RAND Postdoctoral Training Program in the Study of Aging and the annual RAND Summer Institute Workshop on Aging. Her work addresses the economics of disability, health, and retirement, with an emphasis on intersections with social insurance programs such as Social Security and Social Security Disability Insurance. She earned her PhD in economics from the University of Chicago and her BA in economics from the University of Virginia.

Sarah J. Reber is a Lead Financial Analyst in Microeconomic Surveys Section at the Federal Reserve Board. She works on production of the Survey of Consumer Finances and focuses on survey methodology and household finance. She received her MS in applied economics from Johns Hopkins University and her BA in economics from the University of Maryland.

John Sabelhaus is a Non-Resident Senior Fellow at the Brookings Institution in Washington DC and Adjunct Research Professor at the University of Michigan. Previously he was a Visiting Scholar at the Washington Center for Equitable Growth and served as Assistant Director in the Division of Research and Statistics at the Board of Governors of the Federal Reserve System. There he oversaw the Microeconomic Surveys and Household and Business Spending sections, including primary responsibility for the Survey of Consumer Finances. He also was a Senior Economist at the Investment Company Institute and Chief of Long Term Modeling at the Congressional Budget Office, where he oversaw the development of an integrated micro/macro model of Social Security and Medicare. He received his PhD, MA, and BA in economics from the University of Maryland.

Louise Sheiner is the Robert S. Kerr Senior Fellow in Economic Studies and policy director for the Hutchins Center on Fiscal and Monetary Policy. Her research topics include issues related to health spending, federal, state, and local fiscal policy, productivity measurement, and the effects of COVID-19 on the macroeconomy. Previously she served as an economist with the Board of Governors of the Federal Reserve System, most recently as senior economist in the Fiscal Analysis Section for the Research and Statistics Division; she was also deputy assistant secretary for economic policy at the US Department of the Treasury, and as senior staff economist for the Council of Economic Advisers. Before joining the Fed, Sheiner was an economist at the Joint Committee on Taxation. She received her PhD in economics and her BA in biology from Harvard University.

Karen E. Smith is a Senior Fellow in the Income and Benefits Policy Center at the Urban Institute, where her work focuses on economic microsimulation models for evaluating social security, pensions, taxation, wealth and savings, labor supply, charitable giving, health expenditure, student aid, and welfare reform. She writes on demographic and economic trends, and their implications for the retirement wellbeing of current and future cohorts. She has a dual degree in economics and computer science from the University of Michigan.

Stephen P. Utkus previously worked as an officer and researcher at Vanguard, where he directed retirement security and investor behavior research teams. He is currently a visiting scholar at the University of Pennsylvania and

Georgetown University. He received a bachelor's degree from MIT and an MBA from the Wharton School of the University of Pennsylvania.

Alice Henriques Volz is a section chief of the Microeconomic Surveys section at the Federal Reserve Board, which oversees the Survey of Consumer Finances. Her research interests focus on inequality and retirement, retirement preparation across cohorts, and the wealth distribution, and measuring and understanding trends in wealth and income inequality. She earned her PhD in economics at Columbia University and a BA from the University of California at Berkeley.

Haiyi Zhang is currently a Master of Finance student at MIT Sloan School of Management. She was a research assistant at Wellesley College and MIT. She received her BA in economics and mathematics from Wellesley College.

James P. Ziliak holds the Carol Martin Gatton Endowed Chair in Microeconomics and University Research Professor in the Department of Economics at the University of Kentucky, where he serves as Department Chair and is also the Founding Director of the Center for Poverty Research. His research focuses on labor economics, poverty, food insecurity, and tax and transfer policy. Previously he was Founding Executive Director of the Kentucky Federal Statistical Research Data Center, and he taught economics at the University of Oregon. He currently chairs the National Academies of Sciences CNSTAT Study on Panel on Evaluation and Improvements to the Supplemental Poverty Measure, and previously he chaired the Board of Overseers of the Panel Study of Income Dynamics. He received his BS degree in economics and in sociology from Purdue University, and his PhD in economics from Indiana University.

Chapter 1

Retirement System Resiliency in the Face of Real-World Shocks

Introduction

Olivia S. Mitchell, John Sabelhaus, and Stephen P. Utkus

Labor market shocks and financial stresses are shaping how older workers fare as they head into retirement, as well as how younger workers are preparing financially for their future. These shocks come on top of long-standing concerns surrounding increasing longevity and the adequacy and sustainability of public and private benefit systems. Drawing on exciting new datasets and the perspectives of old as well as new researchers to the field, this volume explores how financial and labor markets, and social as well as private insurance programs, are driving the need for new policy to meet these challenges, along with the need for adaptive changes by households, in an effort to enhance retirement resilience.

Are Recent Labor Market Shocks Scarring the Future of Retirement?

Important labor market shocks include declining attachment to work among middle-aged men, as well as stagnant earnings among lower- and moderate-income men, as noted in the chapter by Richard W. Johnson and Karen E. Smith. The authors emphasize that, in the US, retirement preparedness depends heavily on how much people earn and save during their working lives, as well as the government retirement and health policy environment. Particular challenges confront Millennials or Americans born in the 1980s and 1990s, now in their late 20s and early 30s.

Millennials are still decades away from retirement, so there remains uncertainty about their eventual outcomes in later life. The method used by Johnson and Smith to project retirement outcomes relies on looking at earnings and savings patterns for the cohorts that precede the Millennials

Olivia S. Mitchell, John Sabelhaus, and Stephen P. Utkus, *Retirement System Resiliency in the Face of Real-World Shocks*. In: *Real-World Shocks and Retirement System Resiliency*. Edited by: Olivia S. Mitchell, John Sabelhaus, and Stephen P. Utkus, Oxford University Press. © Pension Research Council (2024). DOI: 10.1093/oso/9780198894131.003.0001 when they were at the same ages, and then extrapolating evolving trends. This approach captures factors like rising real wages and greater women's labor force participation that will contribute to higher retirement incomes for Millennials, but also factors like changes in employer-sponsored pensions and declining men's labor force participation that will likely work in the other direction.

In terms of expected retirement incomes, the news is generally good. The authors' projections indicate that the median income for Millennials at age 70 will be $44,700 (in today's dollars), representing a 75 percent replacement rate of their preretirement incomes. This will be above that received by any previous generation, and it is 22 percent more than projected income for pre-Baby Boomers (born between 1941 and 1945). Other encouraging signs include the fact that people are working longer than earlier generations; higher average wage levels are boosting social security payments; women are working longer and earning more than previous generations; and the shrinking gender gap in life expectancy and labor market participation will mean fewer older-age widows with high poverty levels.

There are, however, substantial risks for Millennials along the path to retirement. For example, benefit uncertainty is high, as the Social Security Trust Fund faces insolvency in the mid-2030s. In addition, private-sector corporations have shifted away from defined benefit (DB) plans to defined contribution (DC) plans over the past 40 years. In turn, this places responsibility for retirement saving on workers' shoulders, as employers have stepped back from guaranteeing retirees' old age security. Johnson and Smith also report evidence of other disquieting trends when comparing the outlook for Millennials with those of prior generations. Marriage and homeownership rates have fallen over time, labor force participation of middle-aged men has fallen, and debt levels have risen. Millennials will also confront higher health care costs in retirement, and their rising life expectancy will imply that their retirement savings must last longer.

Taking all of this into consideration, there does not appear to be a looming crisis in average retirement preparedness among Millennials, but there is likely greater risk to living standards for some future retirees. In addition, uncertainties remain on other fronts: stock market volatility, rising interest rates and housing prices, skyrocketing inflation, slow wage growth, whether people's health will allow them to work longer, and policymakers' lack of response on addressing gaps in health care financing.

Data show that retirements rise in recessions, and this was also true in COVID times, reports Erika McEntarfer using a novel administrative dataset called the Longitudinal Employer-Household Dynamics (LEHD). Her chapter focuses in part on 'unretirement,' by which she means people returning to work after retiring. This behavior also proves to be cyclical albeit less cyclically sensitive than retirement. Moreover, unretirement is more prevalent for younger workers and higher-income workers. The question of unretirement is first-order in the wake of COVID-related labor market exits. Will the older workers who exited the labor market during the pandemic return to work or remain retired?

McEntarfer's analysis indicates that retirement is quite 'sticky,' in that 70 percent of older workers who have a retirement spell are never seen to work again in her data. In the US, retirement flows tend to peak at ages 62 and 65. The first is dominated by flows into partial retirement when social security benefits first become available, and the peak at age 65 mostly reflects transitions into full retirement. Some retirees also take up 'bridge' jobs after leaving their career employment, but those jobs tend to be transitory. For instance, the average length of a partial retirement spell is just a little over a year, and most spells—over 65 percent—end in a permanent retirement.

Interestingly, the COVID economic recession differed from past recessions, since the massive and sharp employment decline did not fully translate into higher unemployment. Rather, many people dropped out of the labor force. Nevertheless, social security benefit claims did not rise appreciably following the pandemic, highlighting the importance of the government's stimulus programs in helping people cope with the recession that followed.

In their chapter, Courtney Coile and Haiyi Zhang also study the impact of the COVID recession on workers age 55+, showing that older workers accounted for 5.7 million of the record 23 million American jobs lost in the first two months of the pandemic (March and April 2020). Fortunately, most of those jobs have since returned, and the unemployment rate has returned to pre-pandemic levels. Unemployment rates for older workers have also declined, though their labor force participation rates remain below pre-pandemic levels. Previously, being an older worker was somewhat protective of the risk of job loss, but that has become less true in recent years. The labor market during the pandemic also differed in that the service sector was hardest hit, and older workers made up one-fifth of those jobs. Moreover, once older workers lose their jobs, they run the risk of facing age discrimination.

The New Financial Environment and Retirement Security

John Sabelhaus and Alice Henriques Volz use three measures of household wealth in the US to compare three generations' retirement preparedness when they were at the same ages. A first is 'base wealth' or marketable assets minus liabilities ($96.1 trillion in 2019, per the Survey of Consumer Finances) and defined benefit (DB) pension claims ($19.1 trillion). The second adds 'scheduled' social security wealth, or the present value of future scheduled social security benefits after taxes ($23.9 trillion) assuming that revenue can be raised to meet benefit projections. The third adds only 'payable' social security benefits, or what beneficiaries could expect to receive after a 24 percent cut when the Social Security Trust Fund runs out of money in 2034 as projected.

Using these data, the authors compare retirement preparedness across cohorts, to determine how wealth inequality and retirement preparedness have changed over time. They note that early Baby Boomers' wealth (born 1946–1964) at age 60 was generally on par with or above the wealth of those born in the 1930s. By contrast, relative wealth declined for mid-late Boomers and Gen Xers (born mid-1960s–early 1980s) at the bottom of the wealth distribution, relative to prior cohorts. This, they argue, is consistent with rising wealth inequality across and within generations. Their comparison of younger cohorts' wealth distributions at the same ages leads them to conclude that rising wealth inequality will undermine future retirement preparedness for those in the bottom half of the distribution.

Unsurprisingly, social security income is relatively most important to those at the bottom of the wealth distribution. Nevertheless, the youngest cohorts are unlikely to receive full scheduled benefits because of the impending shortfall in social security finances. Therefore, how well today's young people at the bottom of the wealth distribution fare in retirement will depend critically on how policymakers address expected social security shortfalls.

Workers' vulnerability in tough economic times was also visible in terms of their retirement account behavior, as reported in the chapter by Elena Derby, Lucas Goodman, Kathleen Mackie, and Jacob Mortenson. Unlike during the Great Recession of 2008, when contributions dropped, there was little change in contributions in 2020. This may have been because the pandemic was heavily borne by workers at the bottom of the income distribution who are less likely to participate in retirement accounts, and when they do, save at much lower rates than middle- and high-income earners. Moreover, the policy actions taken by Congress in response to the pandemic could have helped.

By contrast, withdrawal patterns from retirement plans during the pandemic did differ from those of prior years, falling for older individuals and increasing for younger people. Both patterns were influenced by Congress' policy moves. Thus, a requirement for older individuals to take required minimum distributions was suspended in 2020, and many responded by sharply reducing their withdrawals. Additionally, Congress granted broad (but not complete) relief from the 10 percent penalty on withdrawals by people below the age of 59.5 years. Younger people impacted by the downturn did withdraw some of their retirement savings, particularly from workplace defined contribution accounts. In other countries, particularly the UK, the recent bond market crisis has exposed risks to defined benefit pensions of derivatives-based liability-driven investment (LDI) strategies. It is unclear whether there would be similar effects in the US in the event of a sharp rise in long rates. Nevertheless, this experience has raised regulators' level of concern regarding the lack of transparency in pension investment portfolios.

Particular segments of the population have also been the subject of concern, including student loan borrowers. In the US, student debt has risen rapidly in recent decades, and it is now the largest component of non-housing debt, with $1.5 trillion outstanding according to Lisa J. Dettling, Sarena F. Goodman, and Sarah J. Reber. In their chapter, the authors report that families holding student loan debt later in life have less savings than their similarly-educated peers without such debt. Yet such comparisons fail to account for student borrowers who have already paid off their loans, requiring a more fulsome analysis.

To more accurately capture the experience of student borrowers, the authors develop strategies to identify families that ever financed their educations with student loans using two large and novel datasets. Their main finding is that households with student loans are similar to other college-educated families near retirement, and both are much better off financially than those who did not attend college. Concluding that student loans do allow students to make valuable investments that earn them a return on the labor market, the authors conclude that student loans on average do not present a threat to the retirement system, and access to student loans also probably decreases inequality.

Real-World Shocks and Safety Nets

US retirees weathered the pandemic recession better than some had expected. One reason is that safety nets cushioned the impact for many. A second factor was that health care costs stayed relatively stable, although some increases did disproportionately hurt lower-income people. And third, disability insurance claims and new applications that accompanied prior recessions did not spike during the COVID pandemic. These trends offer lessons to help bolster those safety net cushions for future downturns, note Robert A. Moffitt and James P. Ziliak in their chapter. In particular, the authors explore how specific safety net programs shaped older workers' and early retirees' wellbeing, measured by changes in benefit receipt in these populations using data from 2000 to 2020, including the first year of the pandemic.

Government safety net and social insurance programs were highly responsive to the needs of the older population (age 51–74) during the pandemic recession. The Supplemental Nutrition Assistance Program (SNAP) which provides food stamps, and the unemployment insurance (UI) program, were critical to these groups' financial standing. UI and SNAP during the pandemic [have] provided the most support—astronomically more than anything else. Other programs the authors cover included social security retirement, disability insurance, Supplemental Security Income, and Medicaid, in addition to direct cash transfer programs provided during the pandemic. (The authors did not consider tax system-based benefits such as the earned income tax credit.)

These safety net programs also helped contain the poverty rate, which was 13 percent before the pandemic but had touched 16 percent during the 2008 Great Recession. Cash transfer payments were also very important in reducing poverty among the older (as well as the younger) population. The authors conclude that social security is actually the largest anti-poverty program in the country in terms of numbers of individuals moved over the poverty line. This observation reflects how many retirees have almost nothing other than social security benefits.

The safety net—which the authors see as including tax benefits as well as transfers, though they evaluate only the latter—had a major impact on reducing the volatility of household income during the pandemic for those age 50–61, albeit less so for those age 62–74. During a recession, income volatility goes up meaning that some people's earnings and incomes fall while others' do not. While recessions tend to hurt people more at the bottom of the income distribution, the US safety net, including transfer programs, cushioned the pandemic shock well so that the impact of the recession on volatility remained small.

Recessions also render the elderly vulnerable to larger health care costs, but those can be mitigated with the right approaches. Thus, greater public transfers can improve health care affordability, but controlling costs is also valuable, note Glenn Follette and Louise Sheiner. Their chapter documents significant progress made since 2010 in controlling US health care costs, attributed to changes made by the 2010 Affordable Care Act to reimbursement rates for providers and other costs, as well as slower growth in physician payments. They highlight, however, that such provider cost control is likely not sustainable over the long term.

Older households tend to be particularly vulnerable to high health care costs, especially when they crowd out other consumption. Out-of-pocket health care expenses (including premiums) comprise a large share of the elderly's total spending: 14 percent for those above age 65 versus 9 percent overall in 2021. The authors point out that a 10 percent increase in health costs has much larger effects on income net of health expenses when the share of health spending in income is 50 percent, versus when it is 5 percent. Moreover, health costs are quite burdensome for the low-income elderly, often amounting to 25–30 percent of their total income.

While health shocks triggered by the pandemic might have been expected to show up in applications for Social Security Disability Insurance (SSDI) benefits, they did not, according to Nicole Maestas and Kathleen J. Mullen in their chapter. Moreover, there was no discernible increase in DI applications during 2020–2021, and the number of beneficiaries actually fell in those two years. One explanation could be that Social Security Administration (SSA) field offices closed due to COVID. Yet the number of Google searches for DI benefits also fell during the period, which is a bit of a mystery.

The recent SSDI caseload decline began before the pandemic, driven both by fewer new awards and more exits from the program. The authors reason that the number of new awards likely dropped due to a combination of improving economic conditions after the Great Recession leading up to the strong labor market before the pandemic, as well as policy changes that effectively tightened standards for disability determination. More SSDI exits could have been because of a small but rising number of beneficiaries who returned to work. Debates continue over whether that downturn in applications and beneficiaries is a blip or the new normal. A small uptick in SSDI applications noticed in the last few months of 2021 may indicate that these are now rebounding. A spurt in morbidities during the pandemic could also trigger more applications down the road.

Conclusions

Managing longevity risk in the modern era has become more difficult, and more difficult to plan for, than in the past. Not only are lifespans potentially increasing, but health care costs, debt, and morbidity pose challenges for retirement savers as well as retirees. Macroeconomic shocks, including those due to the recent pandemic, have created cohorts of workers who think about retirement saving and investment differently from their earlier counterparts, and government policy and private pension design are playing a key role in both encouraging and undermining retirement preparedness. At the same time, it remains to be seen to what extent these risks will be mitigated at the margin by household behavioral change, most notably through delayed retirement and increased labor force participation at older ages, but also perhaps through earlier participation and greater risk taking in private pension accounts due to federal automatic enrollment policy.

If there is one thing we have learned from the COVID shock, it is that plan sponsors, financial advisors, investment managers, policymakers, and the broader population must remain alert for the future 'unknown unknowns' that could undermine the best-laid plans for retirement security. As with COVID, what matters is not only the nature of a given shock, but also how system participants respond to that shock over time, and whether their responses enhance or undermine retirement resilience.

References

Coile, C. and H. Zhang (2024). 'Recessions and Retirement: New Evidence from the COVID-19 Pandemic.' In O. S. Mitchell, J. Sabelhaus, and S. Utkus, eds., *Real-World Shocks and Retirement System Resiliency*. Oxford, UK: Oxford University Press, pp. 52–70.

Derby, E., L. Goodman, K. Mackie, and J. Mortenson (2024). 'Changes in Retirement Savings During the COVID Pandemic.' In O. S. Mitchell, J. Sabelhaus, and S. Utkus, eds., *Real-World Shocks and Retirement System Resiliency*. Oxford, UK: Oxford University Press, pp. 97–119.

Dettling, L. J., S. F. Goodman, and S. J. Reber (2024). 'Saving and Wealth Accumulation among Student Borrowers: Implications for Retirement Preparedness.' In O. S. Mitchell, J. Sabelhaus, and S. Utkus, eds., *Real-World Shocks and Retirement System Resiliency*. Oxford, UK: Oxford University Press, pp. 120–151.

Follette, G. and L. Sheiner (2024). 'Retirement Security and Health Costs.' In O. S. Mitchell, J. Sabelhaus, and S. Utkus, eds., *Real-World Shocks and Retirement System Resiliency*. Oxford, UK: Oxford University Press, pp. 180–210.

Johnson, R. J. and K. E. Smith (2024). 'How Gloomy Is the Retirement Outlook for Millennials?' In O. S. Mitchell, J. Sabelhaus, and S. Utkus, eds., *Real-World Shocks and Retirement System Resiliency*. Oxford, UK: Oxford University Press, pp. 11–35.

Maestas, N. and K. J. Mullen (2024). 'Economic Conditions, the COVID-19 Pandemic Recession, and Implications for Disability Insurance in the US' In O. S. Mitchell, J. Sabelhaus, and S. Utkus, eds., *Real-World Shocks and Retirement System Resiliency*. Oxford, UK: Oxford University Press, pp. 211–221.

McEntarfer, E. (2024). 'Older Workers, Retirement, and Macroeconomic Shocks.' In O. S. Mitchell, J. Sabelhaus, and S. Utkus, eds., *Real-World Shocks and Retirement System Resiliency*. Oxford, UK: Oxford University Press, pp. 36–51.

Moffitt, R. A. and J. P. Ziliak (2024). 'The Safety Net Response to the Covid-19 Pandemic Recession and the Older Population.' In O. S. Mitchell, J. Sabelhaus, and S. Utkus, eds., *Real-World Shocks and Retirement System Resiliency*. Oxford, UK: Oxford University Press, pp. 155–179.

Sabelhaus, J. and A. H. Volz (2024). 'Wealth Inequality and Retirement Preparedness: A Cross-Cohort Perspective.' In O. S. Mitchell, J. Sabelhaus, and S. Utkus, eds., *Real-World Shocks and Retirement System Resiliency*. Oxford, UK: Oxford University Press, pp. 73–96.

Part I
Labor Market Shocks

Scarring the Future?

Chapter 2

How Gloomy Is the Retirement Outlook for Millennials?

Richard W. Johnson and Karen E. Smith

Changes in retirement programs and ongoing economic, social, and health care trends raise worrisome questions about the future financial security of American retirees. The increase in social security's full retirement age will reduce benefits for future retirees, and the system's long-term financing problems could lead to additional benefit cuts within the next few years unless policymakers address the funding shortfall. Private-sector employers have moved away from defined benefit (DB) pensions to defined contribution (DC) retirement plans over the past four decades, shifting much of the responsibility for retirement saving from employers to employees and reducing future retirement income flows for many workers (Morrissey 2016; Munnell 2014). Falling labor supply among middle-aged men (Council of Economic Advisers 2016) and stagnant earnings for lower- and moderate-income men (Mishel 2015) also threaten future retirement security, because social security benefits and the capacity to save for retirement depend on lifetime earnings. Future retirees will need more money than earlier generations, as health care costs and indebtedness rise (Hatfield et al. 2018; Karamcheva 2013), and retirement savings must last longer as retirees' life expectancy grows.

Nevertheless, other economic and demographic trends are more encouraging. Women who retire in coming decades will have worked in paid employment longer and earned more than previous generations (Goldin and Mitchell 2017), thus accumulating more social security benefits and retirement savings under their own names. National average wage increases will boost social security payments for all beneficiaries, even for those with relatively low earnings. Widows are especially likely to be impoverished (Sevak et al. 2003/2004), but the shrinking gender gap in life expectancy (Trovato and Heyen 2006) will reduce future widowhood rates. In addition, people are working longer than previous generations (Johnson and Wang 2017), increasing their lifetime earnings, future social security benefits, and capacity to save for retirement.

Richard W. Johnson and Karen E. Smith, *How Gloomy Is the Retirement Outlook for Millennials?*. In: *Real-World Shocks and Retirement System Resiliency*. Edited by: Olivia S. Mitchell, John Sabelhaus, and Stephen P. Utkus, Oxford University Press. © Pension Research Council (2024). DOI: 10.1093/oso/9780198894131.003.0002

Given these conflicting trends, it is not surprising that there is little consensus about how future generations will likely fare in retirement. Some studies warn of a looming retirement crisis, predicting that in coming decades many older adults will live in or near poverty, and a majority will be unable to maintain their preretirement living standards (Munnell et al. 2014; Rhee 2013). Other studies are more sanguine, concluding that most people are saving adequately, and that economic growth will boost future retirement incomes (Biggs and Schieber 2014; Butrica et al. 2012; Scholz et al. 2006).

This study uses a dynamic microsimulation model to assess retirement prospects for future generations, with a special focus on the Millennial generation. We project future incomes to age 70, accounting for working-age outcomes that have already occurred. The analysis compares outcomes for adults born 1980–1989, labeled Early Millennials, with outcomes for earlier cohorts. We project inflation-adjusted per capita family income levels and the share of adults with inadequate income, both measured at age 70. The analysis classifies age-70 income as inadequate if it falls below 25 percent of the annual national average wage, a level we deem necessary to cover basic needs, or if it replaces less than 75 percent of annual preretirement earnings, a commonly-assumed minimum amount needed to maintain preretirement living standards. Conversely, we classify income that equals or exceeds 100 percent of the annual national average wage as adequate, regardless of the replacement rate. Because the share of preretirement earnings needed to ensure that retirees can maintain their preretirement livings standards is uncertain, we also consider two alternative replacement rate thresholds: 60 percent and 90 percent.

Our baseline projections assume that social security will pay all benefits scheduled under current law indefinitely. Yet the program faces a long-term financial shortfall, and social security's trustees project that under current benefit and revenue schedules the Social Security Trust Fund will run out before Early Millennials reach age 70, so that they may receive less than their full scheduled benefits. To capture this possibility, we also model two scenarios that cut future social security benefits.

Our results show that inflation-adjusted age-70 incomes are projected to increase over time, yet the share of retirees with insufficient income to meet basic needs or maintain their preretirement income standards is also projected to grow. We estimate that if scheduled social security payments are fully paid, 38 percent of Early Millennials will have inadequate income at age 70 based on a 75 percent replacement rate adequacy threshold, compared with 28 percent of adults born 1937–1945. Inadequate retirement incomes are projected to be especially common among certain groups of Early Millennials, with more than half of Hispanics and those who did not complete high school projected to have inadequate age-70 income.

Retirement security will become even more precarious if policymakers do not increase social security's revenues and instead, implement across-the-board benefit cuts when the program's trust funds run out in the mid-2030s. We project that nearly half (49%) of Early Millennials will have inadequate income at age 70 if policymakers fail to shore up social security's finances.

Trends in Employment, Earnings, Wealth, and Demographic Characteristics

How Millennials fare in retirement will largely hinge on how much they earn over their lifetime, as social security retirement benefits, DB pensions, and employer contributions to retirement plans generally increase with earnings, and people are typically better able to save when they earn more. Lifetime earnings, in turn, depend on how much people work and how much they are compensated each hour.

Labor force participation. Millennial men were less likely to participate in the labor force in their 20s and early 30s compared to previous cohorts (Johnson and Smith 2022). At ages 26–30, 89 percent of men born 1986–1990 participated in the labor force, compared with 96 percent in the 1941–1945 cohort. The low participation rates for Millennials may simply reflect the high unemployment rates that existed early in their careers, which discouraged them from looking for work, or they may have been related to their high college attendance rates (which also may have resulted from the poor job market). Millennial men's market participation rates now appear to be catching up to those of earlier recent cohorts; at age 36–40, men born 1981–1985 were just about as likely to participate in the labor force as those born 10 years earlier. However, men born in the early 1970s were less likely to participate in the labor force than earlier cohorts, so the fact that Millennial men are catching up to them may not be particularly encouraging.

A more worrisome trend for future retirement security is the long-term decline in labor supply among men in their 40s and 50s. At ages 41–45, for example, male labor force participation rates fell from 94 percent for the 1941–1945 birth cohort, to 90 percent for the 1971–1975 birth cohort (Johnson and Smith 2022). This decline has been concentrated among men with a high school education or less, perhaps because technological change and increased globalization reduced employer demand for low- and middle-skilled workers (Aaronson et al. 2014; Beaudry et al. 2016; Council of Economic Advisers 2016; Juhn et al. 1991; Juhn and Potter 2006). Rising receipt of Social Security Disability Insurance (SSDI) benefits and the opioid epidemic may have also affected the rise in male labor force dropouts (Autor et al. 2016; Autor and Duggan 2003; Bound and Burkhauser 1999;

French and Song 2014; Krueger 2017). As average educational attainment has risen over time, those who fail to complete high school are increasingly disadvantaged in employment.

An encouraging sign for retirement security is the recent increase in labor force participation among older men. Men born 1951–1955 were 11 percentage points more likely to participate in the labor force at ages 61–65 than those born 20 years earlier (Johnson and Smith 2022). This recent surge reflects higher educational levels among older adults, changes in social security rules that increase work incentives, and erosion in DB pension and retiree health insurance coverage from private-sector employers (Friedberg and Webb 2005; Gustman and Steinmeier 2015; Johnson et al. 2003; Mermin et al. 2007; Song and Manchester 2007).

Working longer can significantly improve the lives of older adults, especially if workers delay social security benefit receipt until they exit the labor force. Extending the work life and delaying retirement benefit take-up can bolster financial security at older ages (Maestas and Zissimopoulos 2010), because adults who work longer can receive higher monthly social security benefits, accumulate more employer-sponsored pensions, save part of their additional earnings, and shrink the period over which their retirement savings must be spread. Working longer may also improve health and happiness at older ages by keeping people physically and mentally active, allowing them to maintain social networks and giving purpose to their lives (Calvo 2006). To date, however, employment gains after age 65 have been concentrated among college graduates (Johnson and Wang 2017). As Coile and Zhang (2024) point out, recent health concerns associated with the COVID-19 pandemic have depressed market participation among older adults more likely than younger workers to experience serious complications if they contract COVID-19. The pandemic appears not to have had long-lasting effects on Millennial workers, however, and the pandemic is likely to have ended long before Millennials reach retirement age.

Millennial women's labor force participation rates have not fallen as far behind the participation rates of previous cohorts, as they did for their male counterparts. At age 26–30, female participation rates were 73 percent for the 1981–1985 cohort, compared with 76 percent for the 1971–1975 cohort (Johnson and Smith 2022). Although Millennial women's labor force participation rates did fall in the wake of the 2007–2009 Great Recession, the downward pressure created by the weak economy was somewhat offset by the long-term generational increase in women's labor supply. Among women age 31–35, for example, those in the 1981–1985 cohort were more likely to participate in the labor force than women born before 1956. Nevertheless, generational gains in women's labor force participation have slowed over the past two decades (Blau and Kahn 2007). While women's labor supply does tend to dip when women move through their 30s while raising children, over the past two decades there is no evidence that they are more likely to leave the labor force to raise children (Goldin and Mitchell 2017). Women, like men, are also lengthening their careers, working more at older ages than earlier generations (Goldin and Katz 2016).

Earnings. Millennial men have generally earned less than men born 30 or more years earlier, but their earnings so far are roughly comparable to those in recent cohorts (Johnson and Smith 2022). Among men age 25–29 employed full time, median annual earnings for the 1981–1985 birth cohort were 23 percent lower than for the 1941–1945 cohort but only 5 percent lower than for the 1971–1975 cohort. Moreover, as Millennial men moved through their 30s, they closed and even eliminated the earnings gap.

The recent stagnation in median earnings reflects deteriorating labor market prospects for low- and middle-skilled men. Technological advancements, increasing globalization, and declining union membership have enhanced earnings for men in the top quarter of the earnings distribution, even as earnings in the bottom half of the distribution fell or remained flat (Gottschalk and Danziger 2005; Holzer and Hlavac 2012; Kopczuk et al. 2007; Mishel 2015; Rose 2016). Rising health care costs have also increased the share of compensation going to non-wage benefits, suppressing growth in cash earnings (Burtless and Milusheva 2012).

Millennial women, by contrast, have generally averaged higher earnings than previous cohorts of women employed full time, especially after they entered their 30s (Johnson and Smith 2022). Median inflation-adjusted annual earnings for full-time workers age 30–34 and age 35–39 were higher for the 1981–1985 cohort than for any other cohort over the previous 50 years. For women age 35–39 working full time, median earnings for the 1981–1985 birth cohort were 19 percent higher than for the 1971–1975 cohort, and 59 percent higher than for the 1931–1935 cohort.

Education. Educational trends affect future lifetime earnings because workers with a college education generally earn more than less-educated workers and face less physically demanding working conditions, allowing many to extend their careers. Educational attainment surged for men born in the mid-1940s and then tapered off for men born in the late 1950s and early 1960s (Johnson and Smith 2022). Among men age 31–35, 30 percent of those born 1946–1950 had a four-year college degree, compared with 20 percent of those born 10 years earlier and 25 percent of those born 10 years later. The Vietnam War draft, which many men avoided with an educational deferment, appeared responsible for the surge in college attendance for men in the 1946–1950 birth cohort, who were 20 years old in the late 1960s (Card and Lemieux 2001). For men born 1966–1980, the share with a four-year college degree fluctuated between 30 percent and 32 percent. Nevertheless, the share rose to 37 percent for men born 1981–1985, and 40 percent for those born 1986–1990, who were in their early 20s during and immediately after the Great Recession and likely pursued higher education because employment prospects were bleak (Mordechay 2017). It remains to be seen whether the recent educational surge for men will persist.

Among women, educational attainment has improved steadily over the past five decades. The share of women age 31–35 with a four-year college degree increased from 9 percent for those born 1931–1935, to 21 percent for those born 1946–1950, to 37 percent for those born 1976–1980 (Johnson and Smith 2022). This trend accelerated among Millennials, with 49 percent of women born 1986–1990 having completed college by age 31–35. Since the 1971–1975 birth cohort, women have been more likely than men to hold a four-year college degree. Millennials' high level of educational attainment bodes well for their future earnings and retirement security.

Marriage. Marriage is an important source of retirement security, because it allows spouses to pool resources, insure against risks, and qualify for spouse and survivor benefits from social security (and from employer pensions if they have them). However, the institution of marriage has been eroding for decades for both men and women (Cherlin 2010). For men, each successive cohort has postponed marriage later, and marriage rates for earlier cohorts plateaued in middle age at successively lower levels (Johnson and Smith 2022). At age 51–55, 67 percent of men in the 1961–1965 cohort were married, compared with 78 percent of men born 20 years earlier. Millennial men have continued this trend. At age 36–40, 63 percent of men born 1981–1985 were married, compared with 67 percent of men born 1971–1975, 72 percent of men born 1951–1955, and 89 percent of men 1931–1935.

Marriage patterns are similar for women, who have increasingly delayed marriage over the past four decades, to pursue education or careers (Johnson and Smith 2022). At age 26–30, 39 percent of women born 1981–1985 were married, compared with 81 percent of women born 1941–1945. Yet the share of women who were married in middle age no longer appears to be declining. Women in the 1981–1985 birth cohort were just as likely to be married at age 36–40 as those in the 1971–1975 birth cohort.

Homeownership. Homeownership is an important financial resource in retirement. Retirees can avoid rental payments by owning a home, and homeowners may tap into their housing wealth to supplement their retirement income. Millennials are less likely to own a home than people born between the early 1940s and the mid-1960s. At age 31–35, only 44 percent of people born 1981–1985 owned a home; that rate was about 10 points lower than the rate for people born 1971–1975, 1961–1965, or 1951–1955, and it was 20 points lower than for people born 1941–1945 (Johnson and Smith 2022). At age 36–40, Millennials remained 9 percentage points less likely to own a home than people born 20 years earlier, and 18 percentage points less likely than people born 30 years earlier.

Retirement accounts. The share of household heads and their spouses who hold a retirement account increases with age until it reaches about 66 percent in the mid-40s (Johnson and Smith 2022). Retirement account ownership then declines somewhat after age 60, as people retire and deplete their account holdings.

Retirement account ownership has generally increased with each successive birth cohort, although the pattern is not a smooth one, and growth has slowed recently. At age 33–38, 58 percent of Millennial household heads and their spouses held a retirement account, about the same percentage as for people born in the 1960s and early 1970s (Johnson and Smith 2022). By contrast, those born in the early 1970s were about 5 percentage points less likely to own a retirement account during their 40s than their counterparts born in the late 1940s. This pattern, if it persists, is a worrisome sign for Millennials' retirement security.

Household debt. Household debt has grown significantly over the past quarter-century. The share of household heads and spouses with debt has not changed much in midlife or at younger ages, although it has fallen somewhat over the past two decades for people in their 20s, 30s, and early 40s (Johnson and Smith 2022). Older Americans, however, are now more likely to hold debt than in the past. At age 69–74, 69 percent of people born 1945–1950 held debt, compared with 60 percent of people born 1933–1938.

Debt holdings among people with debt have risen sharply over time. At age 51–56, median per capita outstanding debt for debt holders born 1957–1962 was 51 percent higher than for people born 12 years earlier, and more than three times as high as for people born 24 years earlier (Johnson and Smith 2022). At age 33–38, median per capita debt was more than twice as high for people born 1969–1974 than for people born 1957–1962. Median per capita debt levels for Millennials were about the same as for people born in the early 1970s, well above levels for earlier generations.

Rising housing prices, financial innovations that increased access to credit, demographic shifts, and low and stagnating incomes spurred the rise in household indebtedness (Barba and Pivetti 2009; Dynan and Kohn 2007). Student loan debt has also been growing over time (Brown et al. 2014). The median debt level for debt holders declined between 2007 and 2019, but it remained at much higher levels than in the 1990s. As people enter retirement with more debt, debt service payments could strain their financial wellbeing (Butrica and Karamcheva 2013; Karamcheva 2013).

Household net worth. In each generation, household net worth (the value of household assets minus outstanding debt) grows rapidly over the life course. For people born 1957–1962, median per capita household net worth increased from $23,600 in inflation-adjusted 2021 dollars at age 27–32, to $187,900 at age 57–62 (Johnson and Smith 2022). For people born in the

1940s, 1950s, and 1960s, household net worth increased with each successive generation. At ages 45 to 50, for example, median per capita household net worth was 55 percent higher for people born in the early 1960s than for those born 15 years earlier.

By contrast, household net worth has stagnated for those born in the 1970s and 1980s. For people born in the early 1970s, median per capita household net worth has been somewhat below the level at the same age for people born 10 years earlier (Johnson and Smith 2022). At age 33–38, median net worth for Millennials roughly equaled that for people born in the early 1960s. Sabelhaus and Volz (2024) also note that household wealth has become more unequal over time. For people born in the 1960s and 1970s, wealth in the bottom of the distribution has declined relative to earlier cohorts.

Data and Methods

To assess retirement prospects for people born in the 1980s, we compare projections of retirement incomes for different birth cohorts generated by our dynamic microsimulation model. The analysis generates outcomes at the individual level, and we report all financial values in constant 2021 dollars, adjusted by the change in the consumer price index. To do so, we use the Urban Institute's Dynamic Simulation of Income Model (DYNASIM4), a dynamic microsimulation model designed to analyze the long-run distributional consequences of retirement and aging issues. The model starts with a representative sample of individuals and families from the 2004 and 2008 Surveys of Income and Program Participation (SIPP) and ages them year by year, simulating key demographic, economic, and health events. For example, DYNASIM4 projects that, each year, some people in the sample get married, have a child, or find a job. The model projects that other people become divorced or widowed, stop working, begin collecting social security, become disabled, or die. These transitions are based on probabilities generated by carefully calibrated equations estimated from nationally representative household survey data. The equations account for differences by sex, education, earnings, and other characteristics in the likelihood of various experiences.

Other equations in DYNASIM4 project annual earnings, savings, and home values. The model uses program rules—combined with projections of lifetime earnings, disability status, and household income and wealth—to project social security retirement and disability benefits and Medicaid coverage. For consistency with social security's projections about system finances, we generally use the same assumptions as the social security and Medicare trustees.[1]

Using DYNASIM4, we project outcomes for six birth cohorts: 1937–1945 (Pre-Boomers), 1946–1954 (Early Boomers), 1955–1964 (Late Boomers), 1965–1972 (Early Gen Xers), 1973–1979 (Late Gen Xers), and 1980–1989 (Early Millennials). The analysis compares inflation-adjusted per capita family income levels and the share of adults with inadequate income, both measured as of age 70. We focus on age 70 because most people have stopped working by then. Our income measure includes social security payments, earnings, DB pension benefits, Supplemental Security Income (SSI), and other government cash benefits, plus the income stream that retirees would receive if they annuitized 80 percent of their retirement accounts and other financial assets under actuarially fair terms. Excluding the annuitized value of financial assets from our income measure would understate the financial resources available to later generations of retirees, because many employers have shifted from offering workers DB pensions that provide a steady income stream to offering DC retirement plans whose balances are rarely annuitized (Lockwood 2012; Smith et al. 2009). We divide family income by two for married adults to create a per capita measure.

As noted above, we classify age-70 income as inadequate if it is less than 25 percent of the annual national average wage, or if it replaces less than 75 percent of annual preretirement earnings received from age 50–59, a commonly assumed minimum amount needed to maintain preretirement living standards (T. Rowe Price 2019). The replacement rate needed to maintain preretirement living standards is deemed less than 100 percent because retirees do not generally pay payroll taxes or save for retirement, and expenses usually fall after children leave the home. Of course, how much income retirees actually need is uncertain, and low-income people who do not save much for retirement or pay much in taxes when they are working may need more than 75 percent of their preretirement earnings to maintain their living standards (Benz 2010). To test the sensitivity of our adequacy estimates to our replacement rate threshold, we also consider two alternative replacement rates: 60 percent and 90 percent.

Social security's long-term financing gap complicates our income projections. The social security trustees' 2022 intermediate projections indicate that the program will be able to finance full benefits under existing revenue forecasts only until 2035 (Social Security Trustees 2022), 15 years before the oldest Millennials reach age 70. Unless the system receives additional revenue, the trustees project that the program will be able to pay only about 75 percent of scheduled benefits in later years. Our analysis considers three scenarios about future social security payments. We focus first on the *scheduled benefits* scenario, which assumes policymakers will replenish the program's revenue so that retirees receive the full payments provided under the existing benefit formula. Next, because policymakers' response to social security's financial problems is uncertain, we also consider two alternative scenarios. The *payable benefits* scenario assumes that the program receives no additional financing, and benefits are cut across the board to close the financing gap once social security's trust fund is depleted. The *balanced benefits* scenario assumes that Congress implements a balanced reform that closes half the financing shortfall through benefit cuts and half through revenue increases.[2]

Results

The model projects that per capita family income at age 70 will increase over time (see Table 2.1). Average age-70 income is projected to reach $80,300 for Early Millennials in 2021 inflation-adjusted dollars, 35 percent higher than the $59,400 average for Pre-Boomers and 23 percent higher than the $65,400 for Late Boomers. While overall incomes rise, there is also much heterogeneity. For Early Millennials, projected age-70 income ranges from $16,200 at the 10th percentile and $28,100 at the 25th percentile to $90,100 at the 75th percentile and $154,700 at the 90th percentile.

Income sources. The projected composition of age-70 income varies across income levels (see Table 2.2). Social security accounts for about three-quarters of total income in the bottom income quintile and about one-half

TABLE 2.1 Projected mean and distribution of per capita annual family income at age 70 by birth cohort ($)

Percentile of distribution	Pre-Boomers	Early Boomers	Late Boomers	Early Gen Xers	Late Gen Xers	Early Millennials
Mean	59,400	61,800	65,400	71,700	73,500	80,300
Percentile of the distribution						
10th	12,000	13,200	13,300	14,000	14,400	16,200
25th	20,800	23,200	22,800	23,900	25,100	28,100
50th (median)	38,800	42,400	42,100	43,500	45,600	50,700
75th	70,100	76,500	77,300	81,100	84,600	90,100
90th	116,500	126,600	132,800	138,000	149,400	154,700

Notes: Estimates are rounded to the nearest $100 and expressed in 2021 inflation-adjusted dollars. The analysis assumes that scheduled social security benefits are paid in full. The income measure includes social security, earnings, DB pensions, SSI, other government cash benefits, and the annual income from an actuarially fair annuity valued at 80 percent of financial assets, including retirement accounts. The analysis divides total family income by two for married adults.

Source: Authors' calculations using DYNASIM4 runid999.

TABLE 2.2 Projected annual per capita family income at age 70 by birth cohort, income source, and income quintile

	Pre-Boomers		Early Millennials		Change	
	Mean ($)	% of Total	Mean ($)	% of Total	Mean ($)	%
Bottom Quintile						
Social Security	8,700	75	10,900	75	2,200	25
Labor Market	400	3	900	6	500	125
Assets	700	6	1,900	13	1,200	171
DB Pension	500	4	200	1	−300	−60
SSI	1,100	9	400	3	−700	−64
Other income	200	2	300	2	100	50
Total	11,600	100	14,600	100	3,000	26
Middle quintile						
Social Security	17,400	45	27,100	53	9,700	56
Labor Market	4,400	11	7,100	14	2,700	61
Assets	7,700	20	12,200	24	4,500	58
DB Pension	7,900	20	2,100	4	−5,800	−73
SSI	0	0	0	0	0	na
Other income	1,200	3	2,300	5	1,100	92
Total	38,800	100	50,800	100	12,000	31
Top quintile						
Social Security	20,400	13	37,000	17	16,600	81
Labor Market	37,300	23	82,100	37	44,800	120
Assets	61,800	39	73,200	33	11,400	18
DB Pension	28,100	18	11,200	5	−16,900	−60
SSI	0	0	0	0	0	na
Other income	12,000	8	18,400	8	6,400	53
Total	159,500	100	221,800	100	62,300	39

Notes: Estimates are rounded to the nearest $100 and expressed in 2021 inflation-adjusted dollars. The analysis assumes that scheduled social security benefits are paid in full. See the notes to Table 2.1 for details on the income measure.
Source: Authors' calculations using DYNASIM4 runid999.

of income in the middle income quintile. In the top income quintile, however, it accounts for less than one-fifth of income. For Early Millennials, after claiming social security, income from assets and labor earnings are the most important income sources for older adults in the bottom and middle income quintiles. In the top income quintile, labor earnings account for more income than any other source, followed closely by income from assets. Social security is the third most important income source in the top income quintile.

Our model also projects that mean age-70 income will grow somewhat more rapidly for higher-income people than for lower-income people.

Over the roughly 45 years that separate the Pre-Boomers and the Early Millennials, projected mean income will rise 26 percent in the bottom income quintile, 31 percent in the middle income quintile, and 39 percent in the top income quintile. Growth differences are starker when we consider income levels, with mean income rising $3,000 in the bottom income quintile and $62,300 in the top quintile.

Income sources are also shifting. The importance of labor earnings at older ages is projected to rise, especially for older adults near the top of the income distribution, while the importance of DB pensions falls. SSI benefits also decline, with participation rates falling because the program does not index eligibility thresholds for income growth or inflation (Favreault 2021). We project that SSI accounts for 9 percent of income for Pre-Boomers in the bottom income quintile, compared with only 3 percent for Early Millennials.

Income differences by demographic characteristics. Age-70 projected incomes are also rising for men, non-Hispanic white adults, married adults, and people with a college education, more than for women, people of color, single adults, and people who did not attend college (see Table 2.3). Yet many of these projected differentials are likely to narrow over the coming decades, as retirement incomes grow rapidly for people of color and women, reflecting lifetime earnings gains for these groups. Comparing Pre-Boomers and Early Millennials, we project that median age-70 income will increase 97 percent for Hispanic adults and 63 percent for Black adults, but only 33 percent for white adults. Consequently, the median income advantage for non-Hispanic white adults relative to Hispanic adults will fall from 175 percent among Pre-Boomers to 87 percent for Early Millennials, and the advantage for non-Hispanic white adults relative to Black adults will fall from 78 percent to 46 percent. We project that median age-70 income for women will be 40 percent higher among Early Millennials than Pre-Boomers, whereas median income for men will be only 23 percent higher among Early Millennials. Anticipated strong income growth for women will shrink men's income advantage from 22 percent among Pre-Boomers to only 8 percent among Early Millennials.

Nevertheless, projected age-70 income differentials by lifetime earnings will also grow over time. For people in the top quintile of the lifetime earnings distribution, median age-70 income will be 51 percent higher among Early Millennials than Pre-Boomers. Median age-70 income across the six generations will grow only 22 percent for people in the middle lifetime earnings quintile and only 31 percent for people in the bottom lifetime earnings quintile. This differential largely reflects ongoing growth in earnings inequality, as earnings increase more rapidly near the top of the earnings distribution than in the middle or near the bottom (Piketty and Saez 2003).

TABLE 2.3 Projected median annual per capita family income at age 70 by birth cohort and personal characteristics ($)

	Pre-Boomers	Early Boomers	Late Boomers	Early Gen Xers	Late Gen Xers	Early Millennials
All	38,800	42,400	42,100	43,500	45,600	50,700
Gender						
Men	42,900	45,000	45,000	46,600	46,800	52,700
Women	35,100	40,500	39,900	41,200	44,500	49,000
Race and ethnicity						
Non-Hispanic White	44,900	49,000	49,400	53,800	55,300	59,900
Non-Hispanic Black	25,200	29,700	29,900	34,100	33,800	41,000
Hispanic	16,300	19,700	21,500	22,100	25,000	32,100
Other	31,000	33,300	39,300	47,200	60,000	59,900
Education						
No high school diploma	17,600	16,600	16,200	15,300	15,100	17,600
High school diploma	32,200	31,600	30,500	29,700	30,400	34,300
Some college	45,600	42,800	44,500	44,000	45,800	47,500
College +	74,700	74,700	81,000	80,900	82,500	79,900
Marital Status						
Married	43,000	47,500	48,800	50,200	52,900	56,600
Widowed	27,900	35,400	35,800	35,400	39,800	47,700
Divorced	33,200	35,100	34,500	37,400	38,200	45,500
Never married	25,700	31,000	27,700	27,200	28,500	37,000
Quintile of lifetime earnings						
Bottom	13,400	14,700	14,400	14,900	15,500	17,600
Second	25,200	28,500	27,100	27,400	28,600	33,200
Third	40,500	42,700	40,900	42,300	43,200	49,600
Fourth	53,800	61,900	61,700	65,300	68,200	73,300
Top	86,900	98,200	110,000	113,400	127,500	131,400

Notes: Estimates are rounded to the nearest $100 and expressed in 2021 inflation-adjusted dollars. The analysis assumes that scheduled social security benefits are paid in full. The income measure includes social security, earnings, DB pensions, SSI, other government cash benefits, and the annual income from an actuarially fair annuity valued at 80 percent of financial assets, including retirement accounts. The analysis divides total family income by two for married adults. The lifetime earnings measure includes annual earnings of spouses in year when married, and only one earnings in years when single.
Source: Authors' calculations using DYNASIM4 runid999.

Income adequacy at older ages. Despite the anticipated rise in age-70 income over time, the share of older adults unable to cover basic needs or maintain their preretirement living standards is also projected to grow. Defining inadequate income at age 70 as income that falls below 25 percent of the annual national average wage or that falls below 75 percent of average annual earnings received at age 50–59 (unless age-70 income equals or exceeds the annual national average wage), we project that age-70 income will be inadequate for 38 percent of Early Millennials, versus 28 percent of Pre-Boomers and Early Boomers, and 30 percent of Late Boomers (see Table 2.4). These estimates assume that social security continues to pay full scheduled benefits after the program's trust fund runs out in 2035 (Social Security Trustees 2022), before Early Gen Xers, Late Gen Xers, and Early Millennials reach age 70. Therefore the projected share of older adults with inadequate income increases over time, as retirement incomes will grow more slowly than labor market earnings.

Inadequate retirement income is especially prevalent for people of color, people who did not attend college, people who never marry, and people with limited lifetime earnings. We project that, among Early Millennials, 53 percent of Hispanic adults, 42 percent of Black adults, 66 percent of people who did not complete high school, 45 percent of people with no more than a high school diploma, and 50 percent of people who never marry, will have inadequate income to meet basic needs at age 70 or maintain their preretirement living standards. Additionally, 64 percent of people in the bottom quintile of the lifetime earnings distribution are projected to have inadequate income at age 70. Even relatively privileged groups face a meaningful financial risk at older ages. We project that 28 percent of Early Millennials with a four-year college degree and 23 percent of those in the top quintile of the lifetime earnings distribution will lack an adequate income at age 70.

Although we project that financial security in retirement will deteriorate for nearly all demographic groups, certain Early Millennial groups will not face much more financial risk compared to their Pre-Boomer counterparts. Thus the projected share of Early Millennials receiving inadequate income at age 70 is only 7 percentage points higher among Black adults and a few percentage points lower among Hispanic adults and other nonwhite adults. The share with inadequate income is forecasted to rise only 4 percentage points for widowed adults, 7 percentage points for divorced adults, and 6 percentage points for adults in the top quintile of the lifetime earnings distribution.

Impact of social security's financing gap. Thus far, the retirement income projections assume that policymakers will find the additional revenues to

TABLE 2.4 Projected percentage of adults with inadequate income at age 70 by birth cohort and personal characteristics

	Pre-Boomers	Early Boomers	Late Boomers	Early Gen Xers	Late Gen Xers	Early Millennials
All	28	28	30	35	39	38
Gender						
Men	29	28	29	33	38	38
Women	27	28	31	37	40	39
Race and ethnicity						
Non-Hispanic White	23	23	25	29	32	33
Non-Hispanic Black	35	35	37	39	45	42
Hispanic	54	50	48	54	56	53
Other	37	37	35	35	33	34
Education						
No high school diploma	49	54	54	64	70	66
High school diploma	31	31	35	42	46	45
Some college	23	27	27	32	36	38
College +	14	17	19	22	26	28
Marital Status						
Married	26	25	27	32	35	35
Widowed	29	26	28	32	34	33
Divorced	33	33	35	38	40	40
Never married	39	41	43	51	55	50
Quintile of lifetime earnings						
Bottom	50	53	61	65	67	64
Second	24	25	28	34	37	35
Third	23	25	25	32	36	35
Fourth	25	22	24	28	34	36
Top	17	16	15	18	19	23

Notes: We classify adults as having inadequate income if their age-70 income falls below 25 percent of the annual average national wage or if they are unable to replace at least 75 percent of the average amount they earned from age 50–59 (unless their age-70 income equals or exceeds the annual average national wage). The analysis assumes that scheduled social security benefits are paid in full. See the notes to Table 2.3 for details on the income and lifetime earnings measures.

Source: Authors' calculations using DYNASIM4 runid999.

pay social security scheduled benefits. Next we examine both the *payable* scenario, which assumes across-the-board benefit cuts when the trust funds run out, and the *balanced* scenario which splits the difference between cutting benefits and raising payroll taxes.

Under these assumptions, the projected share of Early Millennials with insufficient income at age 70 to meet basic needs or maintain their preretirement living standards will increase to 43 percent under the balanced scenario and 49 percent under the payable scenario (see Table 2.5). Under the payable scenario, 53 percent of Black adults in the Early Millennial cohort, 62 percent of Hispanic adults, 75 percent of adults who did not complete high school, 57 percent of adults with only a high school diploma, and 74 percent of adults in the bottom quintile of the lifetime earnings distribution will receive inadequate retirement income.

Sensitivity to the definition of adequate income. Our projections of income adequacy also depend on the share of earnings that retirees are assumed to need to maintain their preretirement living standards. Thus far, we have assumed a replacement rate of 75 percent. Yet when the replacement rate is cut to 60 percent, the projected share of Early Millennials with inadequate retirement income falls from 38 percent to 29 percent (see Table 2.6). When we increase the required replacement rate to 90 percent, the share with inadequate income rises to 46 percent. Under all of these replacement rate assumptions, the projected share of financially insecure retirees is substantially higher for the Early Millennial cohort than for the Pre-Boomer cohort.

Although the projected share of adults with inadequate retirement income at age 70 is sensitive to the replacement rate assumption, the replacement rate has little impact on projected income adequacy for adults near the top and bottom of the lifetime earnings distribution. Increasing the replacement rate threshold from 60 percent to 90 percent changes the share of Early Millennials in the bottom quintile of the lifetime earnings distribution projected to have inadequate retirement income by only 2 percentage points, and the share in the top lifetime earnings quintiles with inadequate income increases only 8 percentage points. Many people with limited lifetime earnings are projected to have inadequate retirement income because their annual income falls below 25 percent of the annual national average wage, not because their projected replacement rate is too low. Many people with substantial lifetime earnings are projected to have adequate income because their income equals or exceeds 100 percent of the annual national average wage, not because they can replace a substantial portion of their preretirement earnings.

TABLE 2.5 Projected percentage of Pre-Boomers and Early Millennials with inadequate income at age 70 under alternative scenarios about how social security benefits will be paid after the trust funds run out, by personal characteristics

	Pre-Boomers		Early Millennials	
	All Scenarios	Scheduled Scenario	Payable Scenario	Balanced Scenario
All	28	38	49	43
Gender				
Men	29	38	47	43
Women	27	39	50	44
Race and ethnicity				
Non-Hispanic White	23	33	44	38
Non-Hispanic Black	35	42	53	46
Hispanic	54	53	62	56
Other	37	34	42	39
Education				
No high school diploma	49	66	75	68
High school diploma	31	45	57	50
Some college	23	38	50	43
College +	14	28	36	33
Marital Status				
Married	26	35	46	43
Widowed	29	33	45	33
Divorced	33	40	49	41
Never married	39	50	59	50
Quintile of lifetime earnings				
Bottom	50	64	74	64
Second	24	35	50	41
Third	23	35	46	41
Fourth	25	36	45	43
Top	17	23	29	28

Notes: The scheduled scenario assumes all social security benefits currently scheduled will be paid after the trust funds run out, the payable scenario assumes that only benefits that can be financed under existing revenue streams will be paid, and the balanced scenario assumes that half the financing shortfall will be closed through benefit cuts and half will be closed through revenue increases. We classify adults as having inadequate income if their age-70 income falls below 25 percent of the annual average national wage or they are unable to replace at least 75 percent of the average amount they earned from age 50–59 (unless their age 70 income equals or exceeds the annual average national wage). See the notes to Table 2.1 for details on the income and lifetime earnings measures.
Source: Authors' calculations using DYNASIM4 runid999.

TABLE 2.6 Projected percentage of Pre-Boomers and Early Millennials with inadequate income at age 70 under alternative adequacy measures, by personal characteristics

	75% Replacement Rate		60% Replacement Rate		90% Replacement Rate	
	Pre-Boomer	Early Millennial	Pre-Boomer	Early Millennial	Pre-Boomer	Early Millennial
All	28	38	21	29	34	46
Gender						
Men	29	38	22	29	34	45
Women	27	39	21	30	34	47
Race and ethnicity						
Non-Hispanic White	23	33	16	23	29	41
Non-Hispanic Black	35	42	29	34	41	50
Hispanic	54	53	49	45	58	59
Other	37	34	30	25	43	42
Education						
No high school diploma	49	66	43	64	55	70
High school diploma	31	45	22	37	39	53
Some college	23	38	17	26	29	48
College +	14	28	9	18	17	35
Marital Status						
Married	26	35	19	25	32	45
Widowed	29	33	21	25	35	39
Divorced	33	40	27	33	39	46
Never married	39	50	34	42	42	55
Quintile of lifetime earnings						
Bottom	50	64	48	64	52	66
Second	24	35	17	26	33	46
Third	23	35	14	20	32	47
Fourth	25	36	16	21	33	48
Top	17	23	13	17	20	25

Notes: We classify adults as having inadequate income if their age-70 income falls below 25 percent of the annual average national wage or the ratio of their age-70 income to the average annual earnings they received from age 50–59 falls below the specified threshold (unless their age-70 income equals or exceeds the annual average national wage). The analysis assumes that scheduled social security benefits will be paid in full. See the notes to Table 2.1 for details on the income and lifetime earnings measures.
Source: Authors' calculations using DYNASIM4 runid999.

Conclusions

Our analysis combines data from multiple high-quality sources to project how various trends in demographics, employment, earnings, savings, and other factors might play out over the next 40 years to shape future retirement incomes.

Projections show that median age-70 income will be higher for Early Millennials than previous generations, but this group still faces a higher risk of lacking sufficient retirement income to meet basic needs or maintain preretirement living standards. Classifying age-70 income as inadequate if it falls below 25 percent of the annual national average wage or if it replaces less than 75 percent of annual preretirement earnings (unless it equals or exceeds 100% of the annual national average wage), we project that 38 percent of Early Millennials will have inadequate age-70 income, compared with 28 percent of Pre-Boomers (born 1937–1945) and 30 percent of Late Boomers (born 1955–1964). Retirement security is projected to be especially precarious for Early Millennials of color, those with little education and limited lifetime earnings, and those who are not married.

These projections assume that social security will pay scheduled social security benefits. Yet because social security faces a long-term financing shortfall, benefits may be cut by one quarter, in which case we project that 48 percent of Early Millennials will have inadequate income at age 70.

Retirement is still more than two decades away for Americans born in the 1980s, and their old age financial security will hinge on several factors that have yet to play out. The future course of stock market returns, interest rates, housing prices, and inflation will affect future retirement incomes. How long people work, which depends partly on how health trajectories evolve, will surely help determine financial security for future retirees. How rapidly future wages grow will also shape future retirement security. Wage growth will depend on labor productivity which will likely continue to rise, although perhaps more slowly than in the past (Fernald 2016; Gordon 2014). Another consideration is that the relationship between wage growth and labor productivity growth has been weakening over time, reducing the share of the nation's output that goes to labor. In the past decade, productivity in the non-farm-business sector increased 12.3 percent, while real labor compensation grew only 5.1 percent (Solow 2015). Declining unionization, the shift from labor to capital, and rising employer health care costs may explain why wages have not been keeping pace with productivity growth (Ginsburg 2014; Karabarbounis and Neiman 2013).

Rising out-of-pocket spending on health care and long-term services and supports pose an additional threat to future retirees' financial security. Although Medicare covers nearly all older adults, out-of-pocket spending on Medicare premiums, premiums for supplemental private insurance, copays, and uncovered services can be financially burdensome. Hatfield et al. (2018) projected that the median share of income that adults age 65+ spend on medical care will grow from 10 to 14 percent between 2012 and 2030. Fronstin and VanDerhei (2017) estimated that a 65-year-old man would require $127,000 in savings to be 90 percent certain of covering all future medical expenses, and a 65-year-old woman would need $143,000 (exclusive of long-term care costs). Spending on long-term services and supports, which include nursing home care, residential care, and home care, can be even more burdensome for families because relatively few people have private long-term care insurance, Medicare does not usually cover them, and Medicaid pays only for people who have already depleted virtually all their wealth. Favreault and Dey (2015) projected that people turning 65 today would need $36,000 by age 65 to cover expected lifetime out-of-pocket costs for intensive long-term services and supports, and about 1 in 10 will need to set aside more than $100,000. Our projection model, DYNASIM4, now projects out-of-pocket and third-party spending on medical care and long-term services and supports, and future analyses will incorporate these estimates into our studies of retirement income adequacy.

Notes

1. For more information about DYNASIM4 and an earlier version of the model, see Urban Institute (2015) and Favreault et al. (2015).
2. We model the balanced benefit scenario after a social security reform proposal developed by the Bipartisan Policy Center's Commission on Retirement Security and Personal Savings (Bipartisan Policy Center 2016). That proposal would increase social security revenues by increasing the payroll tax rate, raising the maximum taxable earnings level, and increasing taxes on benefits for higher-income beneficiaries, and it would cut benefits by indexing the retirement age to longevity, capping the spousal benefit, reducing cost-of-living adjustments, and cutting benefits for higher income beneficiaries. The proposal would also increase payments to lower-income beneficiaries by establishing a basic minimum benefit and enhancing survivor benefits. The commission projected that social security would attain long-range solvency if the proposal had been implemented in 2016, but not if implemented later. We revised the proposal to include more revenue for social security and additional benefit cuts so that it would achieve long-range solvency if implemented in 2023.

References

Aaronson, S., T. Cajner, B. Fallick, F. Galbis-Reig, C. Smith, and W. Wascher (2014). 'Labor Force Participation: Recent Developments and Future Prospects.' *Brookings Papers on Economic Activity*, Fall 2014: 197–275.

Autor, D. H., M. Duggan, K. Greenberg, and D. S. Lyle (2016). 'The Impact of Disability Benefits on Labor Supply: Evidence from the VA's Disability Compensation Program.' *American Economic Journal: Applied Economics*, 8(3): 31–68.

Autor, D. H. and M. H. Duggan (2003). 'The Rise in the Disability Rolls and the Decline in Unemployment.' *Quarterly Journal of Economics*, 118(1): 157–206.

Barba, A. and M. Pivetti (2009). 'Rising Household Debt: Its Causes and Macroeconomic Implications—A Long-Period Analysis.' *Cambridge Journal of Economics*, 33 (1): 113–137.

Beaudry, P., D. A. Green, and B. M. Sand (2016). 'The Great Reversal in the Demand for Skill and Cognitive Tasks.' *Journal of Labor Economics*, 34(1): s199–s247.

Benz, C. (2010). 'Digging Into the 80% Rule for Income Replacement in Retirement.' *Morningstar*, (updated June 1, 2010). https://www.morningstar.com/ articles/334233/beyond-the-80-rule.

Biggs, A. G. and S. Schieber (2014). 'Is There a Retirement Crisis?' *National Affairs*, 20 (Summer): 55–75.

Bipartisan Policy Center (2016). *Securing Our Financial Future: Report of the Commission on Retirement Security and Personal Savings.* Washington, DC: Bipartisan Policy Center. https://bipartisanpolicy.org/report/retirement-security/.

Blau, F. D. and L. M. Kahn (2007). 'Changes in the Labor Supply Behavior of Married Women: 1980–2000.' *Journal of Labor Economics*, 25(3): 393–438.

Bound, J. and R. V. Burkhauser (1999). 'Economic Analysis of Transfer Programs Targeted on People with Disabilities.' In O.C. Ashenfelter and D. Card, eds., *Handbook of Labor Economics*, Volume 3. Amsterdam: Elsevier, pp. 3417–3528.

Brown, M., A. Haughwout, D. Lee, J. Scally, and W. van der Klaauw (2014). 'Measuring Student Debt and Its Performance.' *Federal Reserve Bank of New York Staff Report No. 668.* New York: Federal Reserve Bank of New York. https://www.newyorkfed. org/medialibrary/media/research/staff_reports/sr668.pdf.

Burtless, G. and S. Milusheva (2012). *Effects of Employer Health Costs on the Trend and Distribution of Social-Security-Taxable Wages.* Washington, DC: Brookings Institution. https://www.brookings.edu/wp-content/uploads/2016/06/0509_health_ wages_burtless.pdf.

Butrica, B. A. and N. S. Karamcheva (2013). 'Does Household Debt Influence the Labor Supply and Benefit Claiming Decisions of Older Americans?' CRR WP 2013-22. Chestnut Hill, MA: Center for Retirement Research at Boston College. http://crr.bc.edu/wp-content/uploads/2013/12/wp_2013-221.pdf.

Butrica, B. A., K. E. Smith, and H. M. Iams (2012). 'This Is Not Your Parents' Retirement: Comparing Retirement Income Across Generations.' *Social Security Bulletin*, 72(1): 37–58.

Calvo, E. (2006). 'Does Working Longer Make People Healthier and Happier?' *An Issue in Brief 2.* Chestnut Hill, MA: Center for Retirement Research at Boston College.

Card, D. and T. Lemieux (2001). 'Going to College to Avoid the Draft: The Unintended Legacy of the Vietnam War.' *American Economic Review: Papers and Proceedings*, 91(2): 97–102.

Cherlin, A. J. (2010). 'Demographic Trends in the United States: A Review of the Research in the 2000s.' *Journal of Marriage and Family*, 72(3): 403–419.

Coile, C. and H. Zhang (2024). 'Recessions and Retirement: New Evidence from the COVID-19 Pandemic.' In O. S. Mitchell, J. Sabelhaus, and S. Utkus, eds., *Real-World Shocks and Retirement System Resiliency*. Oxford, UK: Oxford University Press, pp. 52–70.

Council of Economic Advisers (2016). *The Long-Term Decline in Prime-Age Male Labor Force Participation*. Washington, DC: Executive Office of the President of the United States.

Dynan, K. E. and D. L. Kohn (2007). 'The Rise in U.S. Household Indebtedness: Causes and Consequence.' In C. Kent and J. Lawson, eds., *The Structure and Resilience of the Financial System*. Sydney, Australia: Pegasus Print Group, pp. 84–113.

Favreault, M. M. (2021). *Supplemental Security Income: Continuity and Change since 1974*. Washington, DC: AARP.

Favreault, M. M. and J. G. Dey (2015). 'Long-Term Services and Supports for Older Americans: Risks and Financing.' *ASPE Issue Brief*. Washington, DC: US Department of Health and Human Services, Office of the Assistant Secretary for Planning and Evaluation. https://aspe.hhs.gov/system/files/pdf/106211/ElderLTCrb-rev.pdf.

Favreault, M. M., K. E. Smith, and R.W. Johnson (2015). 'The Dynamic Simulation of Income Model (DYNASIM): An Overview.' Washington, DC: Urban Institute. http://www.urban.org/research/publication/dynamic-simulation-income-model-dynasim-overview.

Fernald, J. G. (2016). 'Reassessing Longer-Run U.S. Growth: How Low?' Working Paper Series 2016–18. San Francisco, CA: Federal Reserve Bank of San Francisco. https://ideas.repec.org/p/fip/fedfwp/2016-18.html.

French, E. and J. Song (2014). 'The Effect of Disability Insurance Receipt on Labor Supply.' *American Economic Journal: Economic Policy*, 6(2): 291–337.

Friedberg, L. and A. Webb (2005). 'Retirement and the Evolution of Pension Structure.' *Journal of Human Resources*, 40(2): 281–308.

Fronstin, P. and J. VanDerhei. (2017). 'Savings Medicare Beneficiaries Need for Health Expenses: Some Couples Could Need as Much as $350,000.' *EBRI Notes*, 38(1): 1–12. https://www.ebri.org/pdf/notespdf/EBRI_Notes_Hlth-Svgs.v38no1_31Jan17.pdf.

Ginsburg, P. B. (2014). 'Alternative Health Spending Scenarios: Implications for Employers and Working Households.' *Health Policy Issue Brief*. Washington, DC: The Brookings Institution. https://www.brookings.edu/research/health-policy-issue-brief-health-spending-implications-for-employers-and-working-households/.

Goldin, C. and L.F. Katz (2016). 'Women Working Longer: Facts and Some Explanations.' NBER Working Paper 22607. Cambridge, MA: National Bureau of Economic Research.

Goldin, C. and J. Mitchell (2017). 'The New Life Cycle of Women's Employment: Disappearing Humps, Sagging Middles, Expanding Tops.' *Journal of Economic Perspectives*, 31(1): 161–182.

Gordon, R. J. (2014). 'The Demise of U.S. Economic Growth: Restatement, Rebuttal, and Reflections.' NBER Working Paper 19895. Cambridge, MA: National Bureau of Economic Research.

Gottschalk, P. and S. Danziger (2005). 'Inequality of Wage Rates, Earnings, and Family Income in the United States, 1975–2002.' *Review of Income and Wealth*, 51(2): 231–254.

Gustman, A. and T. Steinmeier (2015). 'Effects of Social Security Policies on Benefit Claiming, Retirement and Saving.' *Journal of Public Economics*, 129: 51–62.

Hatfield, L., M. M. Favreault, T. G. McGuire, and M. E. Chernew (2018). 'Modeling Health Care Spending Growth of Older Adults.' *Health Services Research*, 53(1): 138–155.

Holzer, H. J. and M. Hlavac (2012). 'A Very Uneven Road: U.S. Labor Markets in the Past 30 Years.' New York, NY: Russell Sage Foundation. https://s4.ad.brown.edu/Projects/Diversity/Data/Report/report03082012.pdf.

Johnson, R. W., A. J. Davidoff, and K. Perese (2003). 'Health Insurance Costs and Early Retirement Decisions.' *Industrial and Labor Relations Review*, 56(4): 716–729.

Johnson, R. W. and K. E. Smith (2022). *How Might Millennials Fare in Retirement?* Washington, DC: Urban Institute.

Johnson, R. W. and C. X. Wang (2017). *Educational Differences in Employment at Older Ages*. Washington, DC: Urban Institute. http://www.urban.org/research/publication/educational-differences-employment-older-ages.

Juhn, C., K. M. Murphy, R. H. Topel, J. L. Yellen, and M. N. Baily (1991). 'Why Has the Natural Rate of Unemployment Increased over Time?' *Brookings Papers on Economic Activity*, 22(2): 75–142.

Juhn, C. and S. Potter (2006). 'Changes in Labor Force Participation in the United States.' *Journal of Economic Perspectives*, 20(3): 27–46.

Karabarbounis, L. and B. Neiman (2013). 'The Global Decline of the Labor Share.' NBER Working Paper 19136. Cambridge, MA: National Bureau of Economic Research.

Karamcheva, N. (2013). 'Is Household Debt Growing for Older Americans?' Washington, DC: Urban Institute. http://www.urban.org/research/publication/household-debt-growing-older-americans.

Kopczuk, W., E. Saez, and J. Song (2007). 'Uncovering the American Dream: Inequality and Mobility in Social Security Earnings Data since 1937.' NBER Working Paper 13345. Cambridge, MA: National Bureau of Economic Research.

Krueger, A. B. (2017). 'Where Have All the Workers Gone? An Inquiry into the Decline of the U.S. Labor Force Participation Rate.' *Brookings Papers on Economic Activity* conference draft, September 7–8. https://www.brookings.edu/wp-content/uploads/2017/09/1_krueger.pdf.

Lockwood, L. M. (2012). 'Bequest Motives and the Annuity Puzzle.' *Review of Economic Dynamics*, 15(2): 226–243.

Maestas, N. and J. Zissimopoulos (2010). 'How Longer Work Lives Ease the Crunch of Population Aging.' *Journal of Economic Perspectives*, 24(1): 139–160.

Mermin, G. B. T., R. W. Johnson, and D. Murphy (2007). 'Why Do Boomers Plan to Work Longer?' *Journal of Gerontology: Social Sciences*, 62B(5): S286–294.

Mishel, L. (2015). *Causes of Wage Stagnation*. Washington, DC: Economic Policy Institute. http://www.epi.org/publication/causes-of-wage-stagnation/.

Mordechay, K. (2017). 'The Effects of the Great Recession on Educational Attainment: Evidence from a Large Urban High School District.' *Urban Review*, 49(1): 47–71.

Morrissey, M. (2016). *The State of American Retirement: How 401(k)s Have Failed Most American Workers*. Washington, DC: Economic Policy Institute. http://www.epi. org/publication/retirement-in-america/.

Munnell, A. H. (2014). '401(k)/IRA Holdings in 2013: An Update from the SCF.' *Issue in Brief series Number 14-15*. Chestnut Hill, MA: Center for Retirement Research at Boston College. http://crr.bc.edu/wp-content/uploads/2014/09/ IB_14-151.pdf.

Munnell, A. H., W. Hou, and A. Webb (2014). 'NRRI Update Shows Half Still Falling Short.' *Issue in Brief series 14-20*. Chestnut Hill, MA: Center for Retirement Research at Boston College. http://crr.bc.edu/briefs/nrri-update-shows-half-still-falling-short/.

Piketty, T. and E. Saez (2003). 'Income Inequality in the United States, 1913–1998.' *Quarterly Journal of Economics*, 113(1): 1–39.

Rhee, N. (2013). *The Retirement Savings Crisis: Is It Worse than We Think?* Washington, DC: National Institute on Retirement Security. https://www.nirsonline.org/ reports/the-retirement-savings-crisis-is-it-worse-than-we-think/.

Rose, S. (2016). *The Growing Size and Incomes of the Upper Middle Class*. Washington, DC: Urban Institute. https://www.urban.org/research/publication/growing-size-and-incomes-upper-middle-class.

T. Rowe Price. (2019). 'Income Replacement in Retirement.' *Retirement Perspectives*, May 2019, https://www.troweprice.com/financial-intermediary/us/en/ insights/articles/2018/q2/income-replacement-inretirement.html.

Sabelhaus, J. and A. H. Volz (2024). 'Wealth Inequality and Retirement Preparedness: A Cross-Cohort Perspective.' In O. S. Mitchell, J. Sabelhaus, and S. Utkus, eds., *Real-World Shocks and Retirement System Resiliency*. Oxford, UK: Oxford University Press, pp. 73–96.

Scholz, J. K., A. Seshadri, and S. Khitatrakun (2006). 'Are Americans Saving "Optimally" for Retirement?' *Journal of Political Economy*, 114(4): 607–643.

Sevak, P., D. R. Weir, and R. J. Willis (2003/2004). 'The Economic Consequences of a Husband's Death: Evidence from the HRS and AHEAD.' *Social Security Bulletin*, 65(3): 31–44.

Smith, K. E., M. Soto, and R. G. Penner (2009). *How Seniors Change Their Asset Holdings during Retirement*. Washington, DC: Urban Institute. https://www.urban. org/research/publication/how-seniors-change-their-asset-holdings-during-retirement.

Social Security Trustees. (2022). *The 2022 Annual Report of the Board of Trustees of the Federal Old-Age and Survivors Insurance and Federal Disability Insurance Trust Funds*. Washington, DC: Social Security Trustees.

Solow, R. (2015). 'The Future of Work: Why Wages Aren't Keeping Up.' Santa Barbara, CA: Pacific Standard. https://psmag.com/the-future-of-work-why-wages-aren-t-keeping-up-6fcfac468e4.

Song, J. G. and J. Manchester (2007). 'New Evidence on Earnings and Benefit Claims Following Changes in the Retirement Earnings Test in 2000.' *Journal of Public Economics*, 91(3–4): 669–700.

Trovato, F. and N. B. Heyen. (2006). 'A Varied Pattern of Change of the Sex Differential in Survival in the G7 Countries.' *Journal of Biosocial Science*, 38(3): 391–401.

Urban Institute. (2015). 'DYNASIM: Projecting Older Americans' Future Well-Being.' Washington, DC: Urban Institute. http://www.urban.org/research/publication/dynasim-projecting-older-americans-future-well-being.

Chapter 3

Older Workers, Retirement, and Macroeconomic Shocks

Erika McEntarfer

The US population is aging rapidly, with individuals over age 45 becoming a larger share of the working-age population (US Census Bureau 2017). Over the last few decades, private-sector employer pensions have largely disappeared, and the retirement age for public pension benefits has increased. As the majority of individuals in the US do not have sufficient savings to fully support themselves in retirement, working longer has been widely proposed as the best way to boost retirement security. These factors make the labor force attachment of older workers a key question for policymakers.

In this chapter, I examine how macroeconomic conditions impact US worker retirements. Using administrative data on millions of workers, I find that worker flows to retirement increase during economic contractions. The effect is small but economically significant, with a one percentage point increase in the unemployment rate increasing flows to retirement by 0.15 percentage points. Retirements spike early in recessions when the economy is contracting, suggesting the primary mechanism is late-career job loss. I also find that retired workers are less likely to re-enter the labor market in contractions, magnifying the impact of recessions on older worker labor force participation.

While retirement decisions depend on individual factors such as health, savings, and pension eligibility, macroeconomic conditions also play an important role. Much of the literature on recessions and retirements is from the period immediately following the 2008 financial crisis. Coile and Levine (2009, 2011), using Current Population Survey (CPS) data, find that workers were more likely to leave the labor force and collect social security benefits sooner if they experience a recession late in their careers. In another closely related paper, Gordnichenko et al. (2013) use Social Security Administration administrative data to look at macroeconomic determinants of retirement transitions. They find that flows into both full and partial retirement increase during times of high unemployment.

Erika McEntarfer, *Older Workers, Retirement, and Macroeconomic Shocks*. In: *Real-World Shocks and Retirement System Resiliency*. Edited by: Olivia S. Mitchell, John Sabelhaus, and Stephen P. Utkus, Oxford University Press.
© Pension Research Council (2024). DOI: 10.1093/oso/9780198894131.003.0003

This chapter expands on the existing literature by introducing a new source of data for studying retirement transitions, by examining the cyclicality of retiree flows back into the labor market, and by providing an initial look at how the COVID-19 pandemic impacted retirements. I estimate that the pandemic increased the retirement transition rate by an excess five percentage points, much larger than the impact of the Great Recession. If these older, experienced workers do not return to the workforce, it will cause further tightening in the labor markets following the pandemic. While it is too soon to know for sure whether these workers will return, I find that flows into retirement are generally more cyclically sensitive than re-entry of retired workers, suggesting many excess retirements in recessions are permanent.

Data and Methodology

A key focus of this chapter is documenting how late-career macroeconomic shocks impact retirement transitions. To this end I use longitudinal administrative data on jobs, the US Census Bureau's Longitudinal Employer-Household Dynamics (LEHD) data, which consist of quarterly earnings records collected by state unemployment insurance (UI) programs (Abowd et al. 2009). The LEHD data are increasingly used in macroeconomic analysis to measure worker reallocation and sorting across firms over the business cycle (e.g., Haltiwanger et al. 2018; Crane et al. 2023) but are a largely untapped resource for examining retirement flows. An advantage of the LEHD data for identifying retirement transitions is that they are relatively high frequency and cover over 95 percent of workers in the US. LEHD earnings histories go back to the early 1990s for several states, allowing me to construct 30-year earnings histories for many workers. While Social Security Administration earnings data go back even further, the LEHD is more widely available to researchers through the Federal Statistical Research Data Centers.

To the best of my knowledge, I am the first to use LEHD data to identify retirement flows. As there is no established method for doing so, part of the contribution of this chapter is to outline a method for using LEHD data to identify older worker retirements and to provide some general descriptive statistics. I will first note some limitations of the LEHD data for studying retirements. First, the LEHD data contain no information on receipt of retirement benefits. So 'retirement' throughout this chapter refers to the process of exiting the labor market and not whether an individual perceives themselves as retired or is receiving social security benefits. Second, while LEHD employment coverage is broad, there are notable exclusions (particularly federal and self-employment jobs), so some late-career job transitions may be misclassified as retirement transitions. Lastly, the LEHD panel is relatively short for examining long-run trends. My cohort of older workers were relatively young during the 2001 recession, and the panel aged over the next 21 years. This shortcoming will be mitigated with time as the LEHD time-series is updated with more years of data, but presumably one reason LEHD data are not used extensively in retirement research is that the shortness of the panel was historically a serious limitation.

Identifying Retirement Transitions

I identify different stages of retirement in the LEHD data using large changes in earnings from peak lifetime earnings. Maximum lifetime earnings are defined here as the average real quarterly earnings during the three peak earning years between ages 45 and 55. Although retirement is often thought of as a permanent withdrawal from the labor force, actual retirement transitions tend to be more complicated, a job-stopping process that involves bridge jobs and occasional returns to the labor market (Ruhm 1990). To reflect this, I define retirement flows such that workers can move back to full-time work from partial retirement, and back to some meaningful labor force participation after apparently withdrawing from the labor force.

Individuals are classified as being in one of three stages each quarter: a full-time career worker (F), partially retired (P), or retired (R). Every quarter a worker can flow from one state to another, either into retirement or back into the labor market. Each state is defined as follows:

- **Full-time worker (F)**: real quarterly earnings are at least 50 percent of maximum lifetime earnings, or worker was full-time last quarter and has not entered either type of retirement spell (this allows for temporary disruption in earnings).
- **Partial retirement or bridge retirement job (P)**: a worker enters a partial retirement spell in the first quarter of a three-quarter spell where real quarterly earnings are less than 50 percent of maximum lifetime earnings. They remain in a partial retirement spell unless their earnings return to that required for full-time employment or until they enter retirement.
- **Retired (R)**: a worker enters a retirement spell the first quarter of a three-quarter spell where real quarterly earnings are less than $1,200. This figure corresponds to working approximately 13 hours per week at the federal minimum wage. They remain in a retirement spell until earnings rise above that level.

This method for identifying retirements is most similar to Gorodnichenko et al. (2013), with some key differences. The most important difference is that in my framework, retirement spells can be transitory, with flows to retirement and back to either partial or full-time work. There are two reasons for this difference. First, I am interested in whether older workers who exit the labor market return to work, and whether their post-retirement labor supply is impacted by macroeconomic conditions. A second reason for allowing retirements to be transitory is that I want to compare retirement transitions during the Great Recession and the pandemic recession. At present, data for the pandemic recession are heavily right-censored (at the time of analysis, the LEHD data available were March 2021, during the initial vaccine roll-out). So, if I define retirements as permanent exits from the labor market, I will get a much larger retirement wave in the pandemic that is largely driven by the right-censoring of the earnings histories. Allowing retirement spells to be as short as three quarters allows me to compare pandemic retirement transitions to earlier recessions. As noted in the next section, although three quarters may seem a short window for identifying a retirement spell, the vast majority who enter such spells never return to the labor market.

This method also differs from Coile and Zhang (2024) who focused on retirements during the COVID-19 pandemic. Using monthly flows in the CPS, they defined retirement as a transition out of the labor force. While retirement transitions rose sharply during the pandemic in both studies, retirements increased by more in the LEHD data. This may be because the LEHD data cannot distinguish between long unemployment spells and temporary exits from the labor market, so the LEHD measure may overstate retirement flows when long-term unemployment is high, as it was during the pandemic. But if very long unemployment spells among older workers typically end with labor market exit, Coile and Zhang might understate the retirement response to the pandemic, as many of these transitions could have been right-censored in their data. A reasonable assumption could be that the two studies represent lower and upper bound estimates on the retirement response to the pandemic.

Some final notes on the sample of older workers examined here. First, to minimize selection issues, I restrict the sample to attached workers who have seven continuous years of observed employment with annual earnings over $15,000 (constant 2020 dollars) between ages 45 and 51. The $15,000 threshold is approximately what a minimum wage worker working full-time throughout the year would have earned during the analysis period. Workers did not need to work every quarter of the year, as long as they met that minimum earnings level for the calendar year. As LEHD state coverage expanded during the 1990s, the number of workers for whom I observed seven years of earnings also increased, so the oldest cohorts of workers were smaller than later cohorts. I also drop workers with more than 100 lifetime jobs or whose average annual earnings for their highest earnings years exceed one million dollars. Worker records that match a very large number of lifetime jobs are typically due to miscoded or falsified social security numbers. Workers with very high earnings often receive large and volatile bonuses, which make it difficult to identify partial retirement transitions.

My analysis sample consists of 3.2 million older workers born between 1945 and 1965, a largely Baby Boom cohort. About 54 percent of workers in my sample were men, 74 percent white, 10 percent Black, 10 percent Hispanic, and 4.5 percent Asian. As noted earlier, this cohort of workers was relatively young during the 2000–2001 recession, with the oldest workers being only age 56 during the dot-com bust. During the Great Recession, they were mostly in their early retirement years. When the pandemic arrived in March of 2020, many workers in the sample were well beyond the traditional retirement age, although average workers in the sample were in their early 60s.

Retirement Timing

The timing of retirement and partial retirement flows using the approach described in the last section is shown in Figure 3.1. Panel (a) shows transitions into retirement, which peaked at age 62, with a second peak at age 65. This pattern is consistent with other authors who used social security earnings records to identify retirement flows. I also confirm the Deshpande et al. (2020) finding that retirement behavior remains 'sticky' at age 65, despite the rise in the social security full retirement age (FRA) from age 65 (beginning in 1983). The social security FRA was 66 for most of this cohort (and 67 for workers born 1960 or later), but there was no corresponding spike in retirements at those ages. Deshpande et al. investigated multiple sources for this stickiness and argued that it was driven by employer norms, with workers more likely to retire at the age their coworkers retired.

With respect to partial retirement flows, Ruhm (1990) first noted that most US workers leave their career jobs well before traditional retirement age, and they begin a 'job-stopping' process that combines bridge jobs, partial retirement spells, and occasional returns to career jobs. Figure 3.1 shows that this pattern also held true in the LEHD data. Panel (a) indicates that transitions to partial retirement from career employment were the most common type of retirement flow until workers reached age 62. After workers attained the social security minimum retirement age, the dominant flow became bridge retirement into full retirement. Panel (b) shows transitions back into the labor market from retirement. Early partial retirement spells for workers in their mid-50s were as likely to end with a return to career earnings as in retirement, but as workers age, flows to retirement dominate. These patterns are consistent with Ruhm's characterization that 'traditional' retirement transitions from career jobs to zero earnings were not the typical retirement path for US workers.

Panel (c) of Figure 3.1 shows the share of workers who remained either full-time, partially retired, or retired in both quarters. Interestingly, what appeared to be marked peaks and troughs in transitions to retirement in Panel (a) actually mark a relatively steady reallocation of workers from career employment to retirement in Panel (c), with a group of partially-retired workers representing a small (<10%) share of the workforce. A key takeaway from Panel (c) is that, despite increases in the social

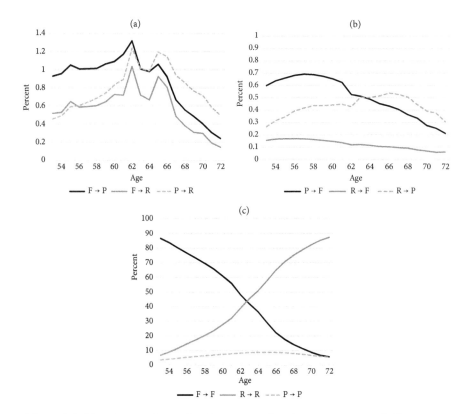

Figure 3.1 Flows into and out of retirement, and retirement status static flows

Notes: Panel (a) shows quarterly transition rates by age from full-time work to partial retirement (F → P), from full-time work to retirement (F → R) and from partial retirement to retirement (P → R). Panel (b) shows returns to the labor market after entering the job-stopping process, from retirement to partial retirement (R → P), partial retirement or retirement to at least 50 percent career level earnings (P → F and R → F. Panel (c) shows the share of workers each quarter whose status remains the same between q-1 and q (F → F, R → R, P → P).
Source: Author's calculations from US Census Bureau LEHD confidential microdata.

security maximum benefit age, a plurality of workers entered retirement by age 62.

One question arising from a comparison of the three panels of Figure 3.1 is why transition rates to bridge retirement jobs were high, yet the share of workers in partial retirement remained relatively small, peaking at just under 9 percent when workers were in their mid-60s. Table 3.1 looks into this more deeply, investigating initial transitions into retirement and partial retirement. The results indicate that, while retirement spells were long, partial retirement spells tended to be quite short. The average initial partial retirement spell began around age 60, lasted just over a year, and two-thirds of the time ended in a transition to retirement. Meanwhile, the overwhelming majority of retirement spells were permanent, with 70 percent of workers still in their initial retirement spell at the end of the time series. So, while bridge jobs appear to be a frequent part of the transition to full retirement, they are not of long duration. Meanwhile, retirement appears fairly sticky, with only a third of workers returning to some form of bridge or career employment during retirement.

Overall, Figure 3.1 and Table 3.1 provide reasonable reassurance that the method for identifying retirement flows in the LEHD data outlined above

TABLE 3.1 Initial retirement spells

Initial retirement (R) spell	
Average age at entry	61.0 years
Average length of spell	5.5 years
Working full-time at entry into spell (F → R)	50.3%
Partially retired when entered spell (P → R)	49.7%
Still retired in 2021	70.3%
Returned to partial retirement earnings	23.2%
Returned to full-time career earnings	6.5%

Initial partial retirement (P) spell	
Average age at entry	60.2 years
Average length of spell	1.2 years
Still partially retired in 2021	6.9%
Transitioned to retirement (P → R)	65.3%
Returned to full-career earnings (P → F)	**27.7%**

Notes: Initial partial retirement spells are for workers who were full-time at entry only (F → P transitions). Workers can be either full-time or partially retired when entering initial retirement (R) spell.
Source: Author's calculations from US Census Bureau LEHD confidential microdata.

produces patterns of retirement flows similar to those found in the literature. With this established, I next examine how these flows are impacted by macroeconomic conditions.

Macroeconomic Shocks and Retirement Transitions

Figure 3.2 helps evaluate whether recessions impacted retirement flows in the US. Panel (a) shows quarterly flows into retirement for workers age 55, 60, and 62, conditional on working full-time in the previous quarter. Inspection of this panel suggests that transitions into retirement spiked during all three economic downturns, with a particularly large rise during the COVID pandemic. While flows into retirement did rise during contractions, they did not noticeably decline in expansions. Consistent with later cohorts delaying retirement, there was a downward trend, but it does not appear cyclical. Transition rates to partial retirement from full-time work, not shown here,

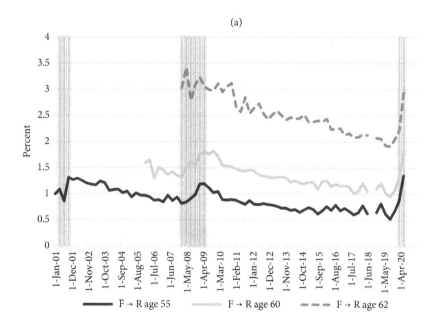

Figure 3.2(a) Recessions and flows into retirement at age 55, 60, and 62

Notes: Panel (a) shows seasonally adjusted quarterly transition rates from full-time employment to retirement (F → R) for workers aged 55, 60, and 62. Grey bars note NBER recession quarters. Flows to retirement in 2018 Q2 are suppressed as they are biased upward due to Arkansas and Mississippi withdrawing from the LEHD partnership that quarter.

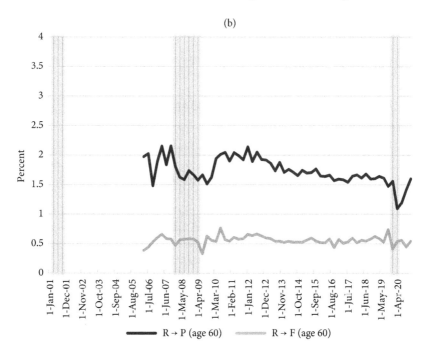

Figure 3.2(b) Recessions and returns to the labor market from retirement at age 60

Notes: Panel (b) shows flows from retirement back to the labor market at age 60 for workers who retired before age 60. Grey bars note NBER recession quarters.
Source: Author's calculations from US Census Bureau LEHD confidential microdata.

had the same general pattern: rising sharply in contractions, and otherwise evidencing a downward trend.

Panel (b) of Figure 3.2 shows returns to work at age 60, conditional on being in a retirement spell that began before age 60. The intent here is to see whether there is evidence that workers who retired early were more likely to return to the labor market when the economy improved. It does appear that flows to partial retirement from retirement declined during economic contractions, although flows to full-time work did not appear cyclical. In short, retired workers appeared less likely to return to bridge employment during downturns.

Lastly, Figure 3.2 indicates a pronounced spike in retirements at the start of the COVID-19 pandemic. While not surprising, this finding is at odds with flows in the CPS. For instance, Nie and Yang (2021) noted that the rise in retired workers in the CPS during the COVID pandemic was not driven by flows from employment into retirement, but rather by a fall in retired workers returning to the labor market during COVID. Our data also shows a drop in retired workers returning to work during the pandemic, but

Figure 3.2 shows a very sharp rise in flows from employment to retirement at the onset of the pandemic.

To more formally examine the role of macroeconomic conditions on retirement, I estimate the following regression model:

$$Prob_{it} (X \rightarrow Y) = \alpha + \beta \, cycle_t + \gamma X_{it} + \mu t_t + \varepsilon_{it} \qquad (1)$$

where the left-hand side of equation (1) is the probability that a worker who was in status X in t-1 transitions to status Y in quarter t, *cycle* is a quarterly cyclical indicator, X is a matrix of worker characteristics including worker age, and t are seasonal fixed effects and a time trend. The key parameter of interest, β, tests whether retirement flows are sensitive to cyclical indicators. In most specifications shown, the cyclical indicator is the change in unemployment rate which more precisely identifies economic contractions driving retirement flows. In unreported results, I find using the unemployment rate results in coefficients of the same sign but with effects much smaller in magnitude. In some specifications I also interact the cyclical indicator with worker characteristics to see if the cyclical sensitivity of retirement flows varies across workers.

Table 3.2 reports the results of equation 1 for full-time workers age 55–67, where the dependent variable reflects quarterly transitions into retirement ($Prob_{it} (F \rightarrow R)$) or partial retirement ($Prob_{it} (F \rightarrow P)$). Column (2) of Table 3.2 reports the results from a simple version of equation (1) with worker age controls, indicating that in 2000 Q4, about 1 percent of full-time workers age 55 transitioned to retirement, with a one percentage point increase in the unemployment rate boosting this probability by 0.16 percentage points. This is approximately equivalent to the impact of being an additional year older, which increased the probability of retiring during the quarter by 0.18 percentage points. Column (8) shows the results of the same regression with transitions to partial retirement as the dependent variable. Approximately 1.7 percent of full-time workers age 55 transitioned to partial retirement in 2000 Q4, with a one percentage point increase in the unemployment rate increasing that probability by an additional 0.22 percentage points. Again, this is approximately equal to the impact of being an additional year older, a small but economically significant effect.

Other specifications reported in Table 3.2 indicate differential retirement flows by gender and income. Women were marginally more likely to transition to retirement and much less likely to enter partial retirement, compared to men. Nevertheless, the women's transitions to retirement were not more (or less) cyclically sensitive than men's. This may be due to the inclusion of the pandemic recession in the data where, in a reverse of the usual pattern, women's employment fell relative to men's. With respect

TABLE 3.2 Cyclical regressions: Retirements and partial retirement

	Prob (F → R)						Prob (F → P)					
	(1)	(2)	(3)	(4)	(5)	(6)	(1)	(2)	(3)	(4)	(5)	(6)
Intercept	1.35	1.05	1.01	1.01	1.20	1.20	2.09	1.72	1.87	1.87	1.47	1.47
	(0.006)	(0.006)	(0.006)	(0.006)	(0.007)	(0.007)	(0.008)	(0.008)	(0.009)	(0.009)	(0.010)	(0.010)
Δ UI rate	0.15	0.16	0.16	0.16	0.16	0.25	0.21	0.22	0.22	0.23	0.22	0.24
	(0.001)	(0.001)	(0.001)	(0.001)	(0.001)	(0.003)	(0.001)	(0.001)	(0.001)	(0.002)	(0.001)	(0.003)
Age-55		0.18	0.18	0.18	0.18	0.18		0.21	0.21	0.21	0.21	0.21
		(0.001)	(0.001)	(0.001)	(0.001)	(0.001)		(0.001)	(0.001)	(0.001)	(0.001)	(0.001)
Female			0.07	0.07					-0.31	-0.31		
			(0.003)	(0.003)					(0.005)	(0.005)		
Female * Δ UI				0.00						-0.03		
				(0.002)						(0.002)		
2nd earnings quintile					-0.17	-0.17					0.11	0.11
					(0.005)	(0.005)					(0.006)	(0.006)
3rd earnings quintile					-0.16	-0.16					0.17	0.17
					(0.005)	(0.005)					(0.007)	(0.007)
4th earnings quintile					-0.18	-0.18					0.22	0.22
					(0.005)	(0.005)					(0.007)	(0.007)
5th earnings quintile					-0.24	-0.24					0.83	0.83
					(0.005)	(0.005)					(0.009)	(0.009)
2nd quintile * Δ UI						-0.09						-0.01
						(0.004)						(0.004)
3rd quintile * Δ UI						-0.11						-0.04
						(0.004)						(0.004)
4th quintile * Δ UI						-0.13						-0.05
						(0.003)						(0.004)
5th quintile * Δ UI						-0.12						0.00
						(0.003)						(0.004)

Notes: Numbers in parentheses are standard errors. Sample is individuals between age 55 and 67 working full-time in the previous quarter, quarterly observations for years 2000–2021. Earnings quintiles are calculated using the highest three earnings years between age 45 and 55. All regressions include quarter fixed effects (Q4 is omitted quarter) and a time-trend (year-2000). Data for 2018 Q3 is omitted from regressions due to bias from Arkansas and Mississippi withdrawing from LEHD in that quarter.

Source: Author's calculations from US Census Bureau LEHD confidential microdata.

to earnings, and similar to Coile and Levine (2009, 2011), I find that lower-wage workers' retirement transitions were more cyclically sensitive, with a one percentage point increase in the unemployment rate increasing the probability of retirement by 0.25 percentage points. I also find that high-wage workers were more likely to transition to partial retirement than full retirement.

Note that the estimates in Table 3.2 pool older workers age 55–67, and that the age control assumes retirement propensity increases linearly with age. In view of the retirement spikes at ages 62 and 65 in Figure 3.1, it seems likely that cyclical sensitivity was probably also nonlinear in age. Gorodnichenko et al. (2013) found that workers around normal retirement age (63–67) were more sensitive to macroeconomic conditions. In unreported results, I also find that retirement flows were more cyclically sensitive at ages with higher propensity to retire generally.

Next, I use the coefficients in Table 3.2 to estimate 'excess' retirement during the pandemic. The unemployment rate rose 9 percentage points in the second quarter of 2020, implying a 1.5 percentage point increase in the retirement rate and an additional 2.25 percent of older workers entering partial retirement. Thus, the LEHD data suggest almost 5 percent of workers over 55 may have initiated retirement sooner than planned during the pandemic. The 1.5 percentage point increase in the retirement rate in the LEHD data is quite similar to the 1.5 percentage point decline in the age 55+ labor force participation rate seen in the CPS between 2019 and 2021, which is reassuring given differences in data sources and methods.

Our finding is seemingly at odds with Coile and Zhang (2024), who found no effect of state-level labor market conditions on retirements during the pandemic. As noted earlier, however, the LEHD measure may overstate the sensitivity of retirements to macroeconomic shocks by misidentifying some long-term unemployment as labor market exit. Nevertheless, the stickiness of retirements in the LEHD data—only 6.5 percent of older workers who entered a three-quarter spell of non-employment returned to full-employment—suggests long unemployment spells among older workers are likely to end with full or partial retirement. Another possibility, suggested by Coile and Zhang, is that many retirements during the pandemic were driven by fear of the virus itself. This would explain why changes in the national unemployment rate, which tracked closely with the start of the pandemic, were more strongly correlated with pandemic retirements than changes in state-level unemployment rates.

While it is too soon to know whether older workers will eventually return to work post-pandemic, returns from retirement in the time series indicate how such returns respond to macroeconomic conditions. Our work reveals how responsive 'unretirements' were to changing labor market conditions, generally. To this end, Table 3.3 estimates a version of equation (1)

TABLE 3.3 Cyclical regressions: Labor market returns

	Prob (R → P)			Prob (P → F)			Prob (R → F)		
	(1)	(2)	(3)	(4)	(5)	(6)	(7)	(8)	(9)
Intercept	3.47	3.60	3.02	12.05	12.31	14.80	1.48	1.48	1.55
	(0.016)	(0.017)	(0.016)	(0.059)	(0.068)	(0.06)	(0.011)	(0.012)	(0.012)
Δ UI rate	−0.021		−0.022	−0.046		−0.044	0.003		0.003
	(0.001)		(0.001)	(0.005)		(0.005)	(0.001)		(0.000)
UI rate		−0.015			−0.029			−0.000	
		(0.001)			(0.005)			(0.000)	
Age–55	−0.163	−0.164	−0.167	−0.706	−0.706	−0.691	−0.096	−0.096	−0.094
	(0.001)	(0.001)	(0.001)	(0.004)	(0.004)	(0.004)	(0.001)	(0.001)	(0.001)
2nd quintile			0.330			−1.98			−0.118
			(0.009)			(0.049)			(0.006)
3rd quintile			0.462			−3.44			−0.166
			(0.009)			(0.046)			(0.006)
4th quintile			0.554			−4.15			−0.166
			(0.009)			(0.046)			(0.006)
5th quintile			0.929			−2.18			0.167
			(0.010)			(0.049)			(0.008)

Notes: Numbers in parentheses are standard errors. Sample is individuals between age 55 and 67 either retired (left panel) or partially retired (right-panel) in the previous quarter, 2000–2021. All regressions include quarter fixed effects (Q4 is omitted quarter) and a time-trend (year-2000). Data for 2018 Q3 is omitted from regressions due to bias from Arkansas and Mississippi withdrawing from LEHD in that quarter.
Source: Author's calculations from US Census Bureau LEHD confidential microdata.

where the dependent variable is the probability of returning to labor market after retirement. Generally, if workers were younger when they entered retirement, the more likely they were to return to work, and retirement was 'stickier' than partial retirement. In 2000 Q4, 3.5 percent of retired workers age 55 returned to partial employment, compared with 12 percent of partially-retired workers returning to full-time work. Higher-income workers were more likely to return to partial retirement from retirement, and the lowest quintile of workers was more likely to return to full employment earnings. A plausible interpretation of the income effects in Table 3.3 is that both the lowest- and highest-income retirees were most likely to return to the labor market, the first because they had relatively little savings, and the latter because they had more attractive opportunities for post-retirement work.

Compared to age and retirement status, Table 3.3 suggests that the impact of macroeconomic conditions on older workers returning to work was relatively modest: a one percentage point rise in the unemployment rate decreased the probability of people returning to partial retirement from retirement by 0.02 percentage points. Since such returns should plausibly be responsive to general labor market conditions, I also show results using the unemployment rate as the cyclical indicator. In other words, re-entry appears much less cyclically sensitive than flows into retirement. This relatively small cyclical effect confirms that many excess retirements in previous recessions remained permanent. Nevertheless, structural factors—particularly the general trend toward stronger labor force participation among older workers—may portend a stronger return to the labor market once the pandemic recedes.

Conclusion

Using earnings data on millions of US workers, I find that recessions caused many workers to retire earlier than they would have otherwise. Retirements spiked early in recessions, when the economy contracted, suggesting that the primary mechanism driving increased retirement flows was late-career job loss.

Retired workers were also less likely to re-enter the labor market in recessions, further depressing labor force participation rates of older workers. Generally, younger retirees tended to be more likely to return to the labor market, and retirement was a much stickier state than partial retirement. The highest-income retirees were more likely to return to partial employment, and the lowest-income retirees most likely to return to the labor market at their preretirement earnings level.

The impact of the pandemic on retirement flows was especially pronounced. I estimate that an excess 5 percent of older workers entered retirement or partial retirement in early 2020. While some of these workers may someday return to the labor market, the historical evidence suggests that excess flows into retirement in recessions tend to be quite sticky, especially for older workers, with little cyclical impact on flows back into the labor market.

A final contribution of this chapter is to illustrate the utility of LEHD data for retirement research, as well as a method for identifying retirement flows in the administrative data that may prove useful for future researchers.

Disclosure

All results have been reviewed to ensure that no confidential information is disclosed and released under Disclosure Review Board release number CBDRB-FY22-CES011-001.

References

Abowd, J., B. Stephens, L. Vilhuber, F. Andersson, K. McKinney, M. Roemer, and S. Woodcock (2009). 'The LEHD Infrastructure Files and the Creation of the Quarterly Workforce Indicators.' In T. Dunne, J. Bradford, and M. Roberts, eds., *Producer Dynamics: New Evidence from Micro Data*, 68, Studies in Income and Wealth. Chicago: University of Chicago Press, pp. 149–230.

Coile, C. and P. Levine (2009). 'The Market Crash and Mass Layoffs: How the Current Crisis May Affect Retirement.' NBER Working Paper No. 15395. Cambridge, MA: National Bureau of Economic Research.

Coile, C. and P. Levine (2011). 'Recessions, Retirement, and Social Security.' *American Economic Review: Papers and Proceedings*, 101(3): 23–28.

Coile, C. and H. Zhang (2024). 'Recessions and Retirement: New Evidence from the COVID-19 Pandemic.' In O. S. Mitchell, J. Sabelhaus, and S. Utkus, eds., *Real-World Shocks and Retirement System Resiliency*. Oxford, UK: Oxford University Press, pp. 52–70.

Crane, L., H. Hyatt, and S. Murray (2023). 'Cyclical Labor Market Sorting.' *Journal of Econometrics*, 233 (2): 524–543.

Deshpande, M., I. Fadlon, and C. Gray (2020). 'How Sticky is Retirement Behavior in the US? Responses to Changes in the Full Retirement Age.' NBER Working Paper No. 27190. Cambridge, MA: National Bureau of Economic Research.

Gorodnichenko, Y., J. Song, and D. Stolyarov (2013). 'Macroeconomic Determinates of Retirement Timing.' NBER Working Paper No. 19638. Cambridge, MA: National Bureau of Economic Research.

Haltiwanger, J., H. Hyatt, L. Kahn, E. McEntarfer, E. (2018). 'Cyclical Job Ladders by Firm Size and Firm Wage.' *American Economic Journal: Macroeconomics*, 10(2): 52–85.

Nie, J. and S. Yang (2021). 'What Has Driven the Recent Increase in Retirements?' *Federal Reserve Bank of Kansas City Economic Bulletin*, August 11, 2021.

Ruhm, C. (1990). 'Bridge Jobs and Partial Retirement.' *Journal of Labor Economics*, 8(4): 482–501.

US Census Bureau (2017). *2017 National Population Projections*. https://www.census. gov/data/tables/2017/demo/popproj/2017-summary-tables.html.

Chapter 4

Recessions and Retirement

New Evidence from the COVID-19 Pandemic

Courtney Coile and Haiyi Zhang

The COVID-19 pandemic is a public health crisis resulting in one million deaths in the US and over six million deaths globally during its first two years. The pandemic impacted life in myriad ways, interrupting education, health care access, travel, social activities, and more. The economic and labor market disruptions have been particularly severe. In March and April 2020, US employment fell by over 22 million jobs, abruptly ending the longest period of employment expansion in US history. This 15 percent decline in employment dwarfs job losses in other recent economic downturns, including the 6 percent decline that occurred during the Great Recession of 2007–2009 (Bureau of Labor Statistics 2021a).

Older workers are unlikely to be immune from the pandemic's labor market effects, for reasons related to both labor demand and supply. Over the past several decades, the rates of job loss for older and younger workers have converged, reducing the historical advantage of age (Farber 2017). Older workers are well represented in occupations that experienced heavy job losses during the pandemic, such as the service sector—in 2019, one in five service sector workers was age 55 or above, a figure only slightly below older workers' share of the overall workforce (Bureau of Labor Statistics 2019). Age discrimination tends to increase and the effectiveness of age discrimination protections diminish during recessions (Dahl and Knepper 2020; Neumark and Button 2014). On the supply side, older workers may be concerned about the health risks of work during the pandemic, given that COVID mortality is eight times higher for individuals 55–64 than for individuals under age 54, and far higher still for those age 65 plus (Yanez et al. 2020). Most workers age 62 and above also have access to social security benefits, an alternative source of income unavailable to younger workers.

Past research suggests that labor market conditions are a key factor in retirement decisions. The probability of retirement increases with the local

Courtney Coile and Haiyi Zhang, *Recessions and Retirement*. In: *Real-World Shocks and Retirement System Resiliency*.
Edited by: Olivia S. Mitchell, John Sabelhaus, and Stephen P. Utkus, Oxford University Press.
© Pension Research Council (2024). DOI: 10.1093/oso/9780198894131.003.0004

unemployment rate, particularly for workers who have reached the social security eligibility age (Coile and Levine 2007; Gorodnichenko et al. 2013; Marmora and Ritter 2015). A similar relationship between labor market conditions and retirement has been observed among workers in the UK and Sweden (Hallberg 2011; Disney et al. 2015). Earlier retirement induced by labor market downturns can have important long-term consequences for retiree wellbeing. Workers who experience a weak labor market as they near the traditional retirement age tend to claim social security benefits earlier and to have lower retirement income in their 70s (Coile and Levine 2011). Such workers also have lower survival rates at older ages, plausibly due to the lower levels of employment, health insurance coverage, and health care utilization that near-retirement-age workers experience in the wake of an economic downturn (Coile et al. 2014).

The Great Recession of 2007–2009 may offer lessons as to the eventual effects of the COVID-19 pandemic on retirement. This recession resulted in a loss of over eight million jobs, which would be expected to increase retirements. Nevertheless, concurrent sharp declines in stock and housing prices reduced median wealth by 15 percent for households age 55–64 between 2007 and 2009 (Bricker et al. 2011), which could have led some workers to delay retirement (Goda et al. 2011; Helppie McFall 2011; Ondrich and Falevich 2016). Based on workers' sensitivity to fluctuations in labor, equity, and housing markets, Coile and Levine (2011) predict a small net increase in retirements, of about 120,000, due to the Great Recession. Bosworth (2012) confirmed that the labor market effect was the more important determinant of retirement decisions during that period. The long-term trend of increasing labor force participation for older men and women continued unabated during this period, indicating that any net effect of the Great Recession on retirement was small relative to the trend (Burtless 2016).

There are reasons to believe that the COVID-19 pandemic will result in a substantial increase in retirements, even though this did not take place during the Great Recession. First, health concerns, which were unique to this recession, may lead some workers to retire early. Second, stock and housing market prices have risen sharply during the pandemic, working in tandem with the labor market downturn to raise retirements rather than lower them. Third, the federal government provided unprecedented support in response to the COVID-19 recession, providing stimulus payments and supplementing and expanding eligibility for unemployment insurance benefits.

Perhaps as a result of these factors, labor force participation at older ages has fallen since the pandemic began, reversing a decades-long trend. Between the last quarter of 2019 and the last quarter of 2021, the labor force participation rate for men and women age 55–64 fell by 1.3 and 0.4 percentage points, respectively. At older ages, the change was even more dramatic, as participation fell by 1.4 percentage points for men and 1.2 percentage points for women, or 5.4 and 7.0 percent relative to pre-pandemic levels.[1] According to one estimate based on pre-pandemic trends, by August 2021, roughly 2.4 million people had retired earlier that they otherwise would have (Faria-e-Castro 2021).

This chapter revisits the relationship between recessions and retirement in the COVID-19 era, using data from the Current Population Study (CPS) from January 2017 through November 2021. To capture the effect of economic conditions and other COVID-related factors, we supplement the CPS data with unemployment rate data from the Bureau of Labor Statistics, data on COVID cases from the New York Times, and data on local government responses to the pandemic from the Oxford COVID-19 Government Response Tracker, all measured at the state level. Making use of the fact that the CPS follows individuals over a 16-month period, we estimate regression models relating the probability of transitioning from being employed to being out of the labor force between one CPS interview and the next to the local unemployment rate, level of COVID cases per capita, and level of government response (an index encompassing containment and closure measures, economic responses, health system responses, and vaccination policies). Our models include a measure of whether the individual was in an occupation that lends itself to telework, following Dingel and Neiman (2020), as well as demographic characteristics and state and time fixed effects.

We have several key findings. First, we show that higher unemployment rates were associated with an increased probability of retirement prior to the pandemic, in line with earlier studies. Perhaps surprisingly, however, this effect essentially disappeared during the pandemic, indicating that retirement transitions since March 2020 were largely insensitive to local labor market conditions. We find no effect of local COVID cases on retirement transitions, yet we do provide evidence that a stronger government response to the pandemic was associated with a reduced probability of retirement. We observe that workers able to telework retire later than other workers, and this effect intensified during the pandemic. All these findings are stronger for workers age 62 and above. Overall, our conclusion that the probability of retirement increased during the pandemic, while retirements were largely unrelated to local economic conditions or local COVID-related factors, points to a potential role for common national factors. These include generalized fear of COVID (unrelated to recent local COVID conditions), the impact of common policies like federal pandemic relief, or higher equity and housing market returns, though we offer no direct tests of these hypotheses.

In what follows, we provide a review of relevant literature and describe our data and empirical methods. Following a presentation of the results, we conclude with thoughts about the implications of our findings.

Previous Literature

A number of recent studies have explored the effect of the pandemic on older workers. Several analyses compare the pandemic's impact on older vs. younger workers, and these studies have tended to find larger declines in employment for older workers in relative (percent) terms, but not necessarily in absolute (percentage point) terms, given that employment rates at older ages are low. Bui et al. (2020) found employment declines of 19 percent for women age 65+ and of 17 percent for men of this age in April 2020, compared to declines of 10–14 percent for younger groups. Lee et al. (2021) reported that, while absolute changes in employment were initially larger for younger workers (age 20–49) than for older workers (age 50–65), changes were largely similar across age groups by November 2020. Davis (2021) showed that the larger relative decline in employment for older workers during the pandemic was the reverse of the pattern seen during the Great Recession, and it was not explained by differences in industry or occupation.

Other analyses examined how work and retirement decisions of older individuals changed due to the pandemic. Using the CPS, Goda et al. (2021) found that employment during the first year of the pandemic was 5.7 percentage points (8.3%) lower for 50–61-year-olds, and 3.9 percentage points (10.7%) lower for 62–70-year-olds, relative to what would have been predicted pre-pandemic. For the older group, the decrease in employment was largely accounted for by more unemployment (50%) and more labor force exits to retirement (30%); for the younger group, unemployment and labor force exits for reasons other than retirement or disability accounted for similar shares (63% and 30%, respectively) of the decline. Perhaps surprisingly, the authors did not find a rise in those claiming social security retired worker benefit, suggesting that many older workers leaving employment were not accessing this alternative source of income right away. Davis (2021) reported that part-time workers were responsible for nearly 70 percent of the increase in retirements, well above their share of the older workforce.

Several studies have compared the pandemic's effect on retirement by demographic group. Sanzenbacher (2021) reported that the tendency of lower-income workers to transition to retirement at higher rates than higher-income workers increased during both the Great Recession and the COVID-19 pandemic. Interestingly, among workers age 62–70 (but not those age 50–61), higher-income workers retired at a much higher rate during the pandemic than they had during the Great Recession, suggesting a possible role for wealth shocks or health concerns. Davis et al. (2021) similarly found that there was a larger increase in the retirement rate for college-educated individuals age 65–79, relative to pre-pandemic predictions, than in the retirement rate for non-college-educated individuals in this age group. By contrast, for individuals age 55–64, the retirement rate fell for the college-educated but rose for the non-college-educated. Among older workers (age 65–79), employment was slower to rebound for women than men and (after an initially smaller drop) for white than for Black or Hispanic workers (Davis 2021).

Relatively few analyses explore the reasons for the increase in retirements during the pandemic. In a paper with similarities to our analysis, Quinby et al. (2021) used CPS data to explore how retirement transitions were affected by local economic and COVID conditions. Both studies explore transitions out of employment, though Quinby et al. (2021) focused on a single transition per worker over a one-year period, while our analysis (described below) examines monthly transitions. Our study uses data through November 2021, while Quinby et al. (2021) used data through December 2020. A final difference is that we include a measure of state governments' response to the pandemic. A second relevant study is McEntarfer (2024), who used the US Census Bureau's Longitudinal Employer-Household Dynamics data to examine quarterly flows between full-time work, partial retirement, and full retirement (defined based on earnings) between 2000 and 2021. We compare our results to those of these two studies below.

While we do not examine the effects of pandemic-induced early retirement on wellbeing, this is a high priority for future research. Abrams et al. (2022) showed that COVID-related employment transitions were associated with decreases in mental health in the short term. Several other essays have argued that the pandemic highlighted the need for a retirement system more resilient to labor market and other shocks (Freeman 2022; Mitchell 2020).

Data and Methods

The primary data source for the analysis is the monthly CPS, the leading source of labor statistics in the US. In a typical month, about 50,000 households, or 110,000–120,000 respondents, are surveyed.[2] Households are interviewed for four consecutive months, then not interviewed for eight months, then interviewed for an additional four months, for a total of eight interviews over 16 months. Interviews are conducted during a 'reference week' that contains the 12th of each month, and a new group of households ('rotation group') enters the survey each month.

We use the panel nature of the CPS to study monthly employment transitions.[3] We focus on individuals between age 55–74. We condition the sample on being employed at the first interview month and define retirement as occurring when we first observe the worker transition from being employed to being out of the labor force (if such a transition occurs during the sample period). Individuals contribute one person-month observation to the sample for each interview month (second–eighth interview) until they either exit the survey or report being out of the labor force, for a maximum of seven observations. In the analysis below, we cluster standard errors by individual. We use data from January 2017 through November 2021 in the analysis. As the pandemic's effects on the labor market were first observed in April 2020, this period includes employment transitions that occurred both before and during the pandemic.

We focus on exits from the labor force rather than exits from employment, so as to focus on the worker's decision to stop working or looking for work rather than on transitions from employment to unemployment that may reflect a job loss.[4] Our approach captures retirements that include a spell of unemployment if the worker ultimately exits the labor force during the sample period. One limitation of our definition is that some of the retirement transitions we observe may not be permanent. We do not impose the requirement that a worker be out of the labor force for some specified amount of time to be considered retired, since doing so would limit the sample to retirements that occur early enough to allow for a follow-up period. Similarly, we do not explicitly analyze labor force re-entry, due to the short nature of the CPS panel. Other retirement definitions that are sometimes used in the literature rely on earnings falling below a threshold, the receipt of social security benefits or other retirement income, or the worker indicating that she considers herself to be retired. These definitions are not well suited to an analysis of the CPS because the necessary information either is not available or is collected only annually.

We supplement the CPS data with information from several other sources. Seasonally-adjusted state-level monthly unemployment data were obtained from the Bureau of Labor Statistics (BLS),[5] and state-level COVID-19 cases are from the New York Times (NYT), collected from state and local health agencies. State government responses to the pandemic are from the Oxford COVID-19 Government Response Tracker (Hale et al. 2021). The composite index variable we use (measured on a 100-point scale, where higher values correspond to more stringent actions) reflects government action along four dimensions: (1) containment and closure (e.g., stay at home requirements, school closings); (2) economic response (e.g., debt relief, income support); (3) health systems (e.g., public information campaign, face coverings); and (4) vaccine policies (e.g., eligibility, availability).

Our analysis lags the economic, COVID, and government response variables by one month. For unemployment, for example, we match the June 2020 unemployment rate, measured by the BLS using June 2020 CPS survey data, to observations reflecting employment transitions made between the June and July 2020 surveys. For COVID-19 cases, we calculate the total number of new cases per 100 population between May 12 and June 11 (reference dates for the CPS surveys) and match this to June–July employment transitions. We similarly lag the government response tracker by one month. To address the eight-month gap between the fourth and fifth interview month, we use the averages of the monthly unemployment rates, COVID cases, and tracker values in the eight months between the interviews (lagged one month as described above).[6]

To address the possibility that people's ability to work remotely could have affected employment transitions during the pandemic,[7] we make use of occupation-level data from Dingel and Neiman (2020). These authors use the Occupation Information Network (O*NET), a survey of the requirements and characteristics of nearly 1,000 occupations in the US economy, to classify occupations as teleworkable or not teleworkable based on answers to questions about job characteristics, such as whether the job involves the use of email, entails working outside or significant walking, or requires the wearing of protective equipment, among others. We merge their measure with the CPS data, using the worker's occupation at the first interview.[8]

The empirical analysis conditions on employment at the first CPS interview so that we examine monthly transitions from employment to being out of the labor force. We estimate models of the following form:

$$Retire_{iast} = \beta_0 + \beta_1 UnemploymentRate_{st-1} + \beta_2 After_t \times UnemploymentRate_{st-1}$$
$$+ \beta_3 COVIDper100_{st-1} + \beta_4 GovernmentIndex_{st-1} + \beta_5 Teleworkable_i$$
$$+ \beta_3 After_t \times Teleworkable_i + \beta_7 X_i + Interview4\_5_i + \gamma_a + \gamma_t \varepsilon_{iast}$$

where $Retire_{iast}$ is a dummy variable equal to one if individual i of age a living in state s at time t transitions from employment to being out of the labor force, $UnemploymentRate$ is the unemployment rate (lagged), $After$ is a dummy variable equal to one for April 2020 and later months, $COVIDPer100$ is the total number of COVID-19 cases per 100 population (lagged), $GovernmentIndex$ is the value of the government response index (on a 0–100 scale, lagged), $Teleworkable$ is a value between zero and one that corresponds to the probability that the individual can work remotely based on his or her occupation, and X is a vector of characteristics including race, Hispanic ethnicity,

gender, and education. *UnemploymentRate* and *Teleworkable* are each interact-
ed with *After* to allow the effect of these factors to differ during the pandemic
versus pre-pandemic. *Interview4_5* is a dummy variable equal to one if the
transition is between the fourth and fifth CPS interviews; it is included to
account for the higher probability of retirement during the eight-month
gap between the fourth and fifth interview, as opposed to the one-month
gap between other interviews. Age, state, and year-month fixed effects are
included as γ_a, γ_s, and γ_t, respectively. State fixed effects capture time-
invariant differences across states in retirement behavior and year-month
fixed effects capture time effects that are common across states, leaving the
UnemploymentRate coefficient to measure the effect of bigger or smaller than
average changes in the unemployment rate over time in particular states, a
standard approach in the literature.

Summary statistics for the data are reported in Table 4.1. The average
probability of retirement between one CPS interview and the next is 3.6
percent during the pre-pandemic period, and 4.0 percent during the pandemic, or about 10 percent higher than the pre-pandemic value.[9] The
average unemployment rate is 3.8 percent pre-pandemic and 6.9 percent
during the pandemic. Average total monthly COVID-19 cases are 0.7 per
100 and the average value of the government index during the pandemic is
46 out of 100.

TABLE 4.1 Summary statistics

	(1) Pre-Pandemic		(2) Pandemic	
	Mean	Std. Deviation	Mean	Std. Deviation
Retire	0.036	0.185	0.040	0.196
Unemployment rate	3.798	0.794	6.872	3.142
COVID-19 cases per 100	0.000	0.000	0.685	0.732
Government response index	0.049	0.398	46.180	15.195
Teleworkable	0.433	0.466	0.450	0.467
Female	0.469	0.499	0.467	0.499
White	0.860	0.347	0.858	0.349
Hispanic	0.078	0.268	0.077	0.266
High school graduate	0.279	0.449	0.269	0.444
Some college but no degree	0.277	0.448	0.278	0.448
College degree or more	0.384	0.486	0.402	0.490
Interview month 4-5	0.117	0.322	0.140	0.347
N		307,665		165,144

Notes: The table shows the summary statistics of the sample. The first two columns are the
means and standard deviations of variables before the pandemic began in April 2020. The last
two columns are the means and the standard deviations of variables after the pandemic began.
The sample starts in February 2017 and ends in November 2021.
Source: Authors' calculations.

Results

Our primary regression results are presented in Table 4.2. The coefficient on the unemployment rate reflects the baseline effect of state-level economic conditions on individuals' transitions out of employment in the pre-pandemic period. The coefficient is positive and statistically significant, consistent with previous studies that have found that the probability of retirement is cyclical, increasing with local unemployment. The magnitude of the coefficient suggests that a 1 percentage point increase in the unemployment rate is associated with a 0.0018 percentage point increase in the probability of retirement, or a roughly 5 percent increase relative to the mean retirement rate (of 0.036%).

The coefficient on *After* X *UnemploymentRate* reflects the additional effect of unemployment on employment transitions during the pandemic. Surprisingly, this coefficient is negative, statistically significant, and nearly equal in magnitude to the main unemployment rate effect. This implies that the net effect of the local unemployment rate on people's employment transitions during the pandemic was near zero, indicating that state-level labor market conditions were not an important determinant of pandemic-era retirement decisions.

The second specification on Table 4.2 adds the number of monthly COVID cases per 100 population (lagged). Its effect is negative but statistically insignificant, which is the opposite of what would be expected if people retired in response to health concerns. In the third column, we add the government response index. The inclusion of this variable reduces the magnitude of the *After* X *Unemployment Rate* coefficient by about one third and renders it statistically insignificant, as a result of the collinearity between the two variables. The government response index coefficient itself is negative and statistically significant. Taken at face value, this coefficient suggests that people were less likely to retire if the state government had a more assertive response to the pandemic, potentially because workers felt safer if the state took actions such as imposing mask mandates or school closures. The magnitude of the coefficient implies that a 10-point increase in the index increased the probability of making an employment transition by 0.0018 percentage points, about the same size effect as a one percentage point increase in unemployment in the pre-pandemic period. The model includes state and year-month fixed effects, so the effect of the index is identified from the large differences across states in how many actions were taken, how quickly actions were discontinued, and whether actions were reinstituted later in the pandemic.

The fourth specification in Table 4.2 adds a measure of whether the worker's job was teleworkable. Unlike the unemployment rate, COVID cases, and government response index variables, which varied only by state and month,

TABLE 4.2 Retirement regressions

	(1)	(2)	(3)	(4)
Unemployment rate (x10)	0.018**	0.018**	0.018**	0.018**
	(0.008)	(0.008)	(0.008)	(0.008)
After × Unemployment rate (x10)	−0.015**	−0.014**	−0.010	−0.010
	(0.007)	(0.007)	(0.008)	(0.008)
COVID cases (x100)		−0.094	−0.099	−0.100
		(0.112)	(0.112)	(0.112)
Government index (x100)			−0.018***	−0.017***
			(0.006)	(0.006)
Teleworkable				−0.005***
				(0.001)
After × Teleworkable				−0.004***
				(0.001)
Female	0.008***	0.008***	0.008***	0.009***
	(0.001)	(0.001)	(0.001)	(0.001)
White	−0.007***	−0.007***	−0.007***	−0.006***
	(0.001)	(0.001)	(0.001)	(0.001)
Hispanic	0.004***	0.004***	0.004***	0.004***
	(0.001)	(0.001)	(0.001)	(0.001)
High school graduate	−0.013***	−0.013***	−0.013***	−0.012***
	(0.002)	(0.002)	(0.002)	(0.002)
Some college but no degree	−0.018***	−0.018***	−0.018***	−0.016***
	(0.002)	(0.002)	(0.002)	(0.002)
College degree or more	−0.020***	−0.020***	−0.020***	−0.017***
	(0.002)	(0.002)	(0.002)	(0.002)
Interview month 4-5	0.055***	0.055***	0.055***	0.055***
	(0.001)	(0.001)	(0.001)	(0.001)
Age fixed effects	Yes	Yes	Yes	Yes
State fixed effects	Yes	Yes	Yes	Yes
Year-month fixed effects	Yes	Yes	Yes	Yes
Mean of dep. variable	0.037	0.037	0.037	0.037
Observations	472,809	472,809	472,809	472,809

Notes: The table uses a linear probability model with full sample data. For each column, the dependent variable is a retirement dummy, defined as conditional on being employed when first entering the survey, the first time an older worker exits the labor force. The Unemployment Rate coefficient shows the effect of a 10-point change; the COVID cases coefficient shows the effect of an increase of 100 cases (per 100 population); the Government Index coefficient shows the effect of a 100-point change. Standard errors are in parentheses. Significance levels are $^*p < 0.10$, $^{**}p < 0.05$, $^{***}p < 0.01$.
Source: Authors' calculations.

this factor varied across individuals. The main *Teleworkable* coefficient measures the effect of having a job with this attribute in the pre-pandemic period. The coefficient is negative and statistically significant, indicating that workers with teleworkable jobs tended to retire later than other workers. This is the expected sign, given that jobs that allow individuals to work from home tend to require less physical activity and may have other desirable characteristics that encourage workers to work longer. The coefficient of –0.005 indicates that having a teleworkable job reduces the probability of retirement by about 15 percent relative to the mean retirement rate (0.036). The *After* X *Teleworkable* coefficient also has a negative and significant effect, of nearly the same size as the main teleworkable coefficient. This indicates that the tendency of those with teleworkable jobs to retire later was nearly twice as strong during the pandemic as it was pre-pandemic.

Other coefficients in the table are consistent with expectations and previous research: the probability of retirement is higher for female, non-white, and Hispanic workers, and it decreases with education. The *Interview4_5* coefficient is large and highly significant, reflecting the higher probability of transitioning out of employment during the eight months between these two surveys as compared to the transition probability between surveys in adjacent months.

To better illustrate the increase in the monthly probability of transitioning from being employed to being out of the labor force that occurred during the pandemic, we plot the year-month fixed effects in Figure 4.1. These coefficients show the estimated difference in the probability of retiring in a given month (relative to the probability in the omitted month) after accounting for other factors that may vary over time, like the unemployment rate. Values during the pandemic period are on the order of 0.010–0.015 higher than values in the pre-pandemic period, indicating that the probability of a monthly transition—if other factors are held constant—would be about one-third higher during the pandemic, relative to the pre-pandemic transition probability (0.036).

Overall, our results are broadly consistent with the previous literature. For instance, our estimates of the effect of unemployment on retirement in the pre-pandemic period is roughly three times the size of Coile and Levine (2007)'s estimate, evaluated relative to the mean, though their analysis used data from an earlier period and focused on retirement transitions over a one-year period. Quinby et al. (2021) estimated the effect of the minimum employment rate over the past 12 months on retirement transitions and found that a higher employment rate was associated with a decreased probability of retirement pre-pandemic, consistent with our findings; due to a lack of statistical precision, their study was not able to determine whether this effect reversed during the pandemic period, as we found. McEntarfer (2024) found that transitions from full-time work to partial or full

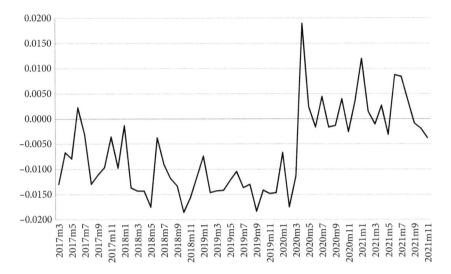

Figure 4.1 Monthly retirement probability, relative to reference month

Note: Coefficients are year-month fixed effects from the estimated retirement regression shown in Table 4.2, specification 4.
Source: Authors' calculations.

retirement increase with the unemployment rate, and used these results to estimate that almost 5 percent of workers over age 55 may have initiated retirement sooner than planned during the pandemic period. Her approach differed from ours in several respects. First, she did not explore whether the relationship between unemployment and retirement weakened during the pandemic, but rather used estimates from the full sample period (2000–2021) for her projections. Second, some unemployed individuals whom we treated as being in the labor force (and not retired) would be classified as retired in her analysis, based on a decline in their quarterly earnings. As already noted, we observe an increase in the mean retirement rate during the pandemic and an even larger increase in the year-month fixed effects (Figure 4.1), consistent with a substantial increase in retirements during the pandemic. A finding that is unique to our analysis and not contradicted by any other study is that retirement transitions were less responsive to local economic conditions during the pandemic than they had been prior to the pandemic.

Table 4.3 repeats the main regression analysis, now estimating models separately for those below and above age 62, the age of social security eligibility, and separately for females and males. For brevity, we only report results from the full model (the final specification in Table 4.2). Looking first at the main (pre-pandemic) unemployment coefficient, we see that the coefficient is six times as large for the age 62 and above group as for the

TABLE 4.3 Retirement regressions, by age and gender

	(1) Above Age 62	(2) Below Age 62	(3) Female	(4) Male
Unemployment rate (x10)	0.033**	0.006	0.031***	0.006
	(0.014)	(0.009)	(0.012)	(0.011)
After × Unemployment rate (x10)	−0.028**	0.005	−0.019	−0.002
	(0.014)	(0.008)	(0.011)	(0.010)
COVID-19 cases (x100)	−0.071	−0.128	−0.231	0.022
	(0.200)	(0.119)	(0.171)	(0.148)
Government response index (x100)	−0.017	−0.017**	−0.018*	−0.016*
	(0.011)	(0.007)	(0.010)	(0.008)
Teleworkable	−0.007***	−0.004***	−0.004***	−0.007***
	(0.001)	(0.001)	(0.001)	(0.001)
After × Teleworkable	−0.006**	−0.003**	−0.005**	−0.004**
	(0.002)	(0.001)	(0.002)	(0.002)
Female	0.010***	0.008***		
	(0.001)	(0.001)		
White	−0.006***	−0.006***	−0.003***	−0.009***
	(0.002)	(0.001)	(0.001)	(0.001)
Hispanic	0.002	0.004***	0.009***	−0.001
	(0.002)	(0.001)	(0.002)	(0.001)
High school graduate	−0.015***	−0.010***	−0.015***	−0.011***
	(0.003)	(0.002)	(0.003)	(0.002)
Some college but no degree	−0.021***	−0.012***	−0.019***	−0.014***
	(0.003)	(0.002)	(0.003)	(0.002)
College degree or more	−0.022***	−0.014***	−0.019***	−0.017***
	(0.003)	(0.002)	(0.003)	(0.002)
Interview month 4-5	0.080***	0.033***	0.061***	0.050***
	(0.002)	(0.001)	(0.002)	(0.002)
Age fixed effects	Yes	Yes	Yes	Yes
State fixed effects	Yes	Yes	Yes	Yes
Year-month fixed effects	Yes	Yes	Yes	Yes
Mean of dep. variable	0.055	0.023	0.041	0.034
Observations	205,825	266,984	221,463	251,346

Notes: The table uses a linear probability model. The dependent variable is a retirement dummy, defined as conditional on being employed when first entering the survey, the first time an older worker exits the labor force. The Unemployment Rate coefficient shows the effect of a 10-point change; the COVID cases coefficient shows the effect of an increase of 100 cases (per 100 population); the Government Index coefficient shows the effect of a 100-point change. Column (1) restricts the regression to only older workers above age 62. Column (2) only includes observations below age 62. Column (3) and column (4) are regression results separately on female older workers and male older workers. Standard errors are in parentheses. Significance levels are * $p < 0.10$, ** $p < 0.05$, *** $p < 0.01$.
Source: Authors' calculations.

below age 62 group: a 1 percentage point increase in the unemployment rate raised the probability of retirement by 0.0033 percentage points for the older group, vs. by 0.0006 points for the younger group. The effect is statistically significant only for the older group. While the older group has a higher probability of retirement, the effect of unemployment remains larger for this group, even when measured relative to the group-specific mean retirement rate. This is consistent with past findings that the sensitivity of retirement transitions to labor market conditions begins as workers near age 62 (Coile and Levine 2007; Gorodnichenko et al. 2013). The *After* X *Unemployment* coefficient is similarly much larger in the older group, so that the net effect of unemployment during the pandemic on employment transitions was near zero for this group. For the younger group, the interaction coefficient is not statistically significant. The coefficient on the government response index is essentially identical for the two groups. In the case of the *Teleworkable* variable and its interaction with the *After* variable, all coefficients are statistically significant for both age groups. The magnitude of the telework effect is larger for the older group in absolute terms, but not relative to their higher mean probability of retirement—during the pandemic, workers age 62+ who could telework were 1.2 percentage points (or 22%) less likely to retire than those who could not, versus 0.7 percentage points (or 31%) for workers age 55–61.

The final two columns in Table 4.3 compare results by gender. Employment transitions in the pre-pandemic period were more strongly influenced by labor market conditions for women as compared to men, while the effects of the government tracker were similar for both genders. The *Teleworkable* variable was more important for men in the pre-pandemic period, but the additional effect of this factor during the pandemic was similar for both genders and highly statistically significant. The year-month fixed effects from the analyses by age and gender (not shown) reflect a bigger increase in retirement during the pandemic for the older group and for women, the groups more responsive to labor market conditions in the pre-pandemic. Since these coefficients capture residual time trends in retirement behavior, they imply that retirement increased more during the pandemic for older workers and women for reasons other than changes in labor market or COVID conditions.

Finally, in Table 4.4, we explore whether the effect of labor market conditions, COVID cases, and the government response index varied with education. These results are less precise due to smaller sample sizes, but the pattern of coefficients is consistent with a larger effect of labor market conditions on transitions into retirement for less educated workers in the pre-pandemic period, and with a roughly zero effect of labor market conditions on retirement during the pandemic for all education groups. There is no clear pattern by education in the COVID or government response

TABLE 4.4 Retirement regressions, by education

	(1) HS Less	(2) HS Grad	(3) Some College	(4) Above College
Unemployment rate (x10)	0.044 (0.043)	0.021 (0.016)	0.023 (0.015)	0.008 (0.012)
After × Unemployment rate (x10)	−0.029 (0.042)	−0.011 (0.015)	−0.018 (0.014)	0.001 (0.011)
COVID-19 cases (x100)	0.598 (0.583)	−0.460** (0.234)	−0.184 (0.204)	0.127 (0.168)
Government response index (x100)	0.018 (0.035)	−0.018 (0.013)	−0.031*** (0.012)	−0.013 (0.010)
Teleworkable	0.005 (0.006)	−0.006*** (0.002)	−0.007*** (0.001)	−0.003*** (0.001)
After × Teleworkable	−0.022** (0.011)	−0.005* (0.003)	−0.004* (0.002)	−0.003 (0.002)
Female	0.014*** (0.003)	0.008*** (0.001)	0.007*** (0.001)	0.011*** (0.001)
White	−0.006 (0.004)	−0.009*** (0.002)	−0.008*** (0.002)	−0.002 (0.001)
Hispanic	0.001 (0.004)	0.004* (0.002)	0.003 (0.002)	0.002 (0.002)
Interview month 4-5	0.061*** (0.006)	0.060*** (0.002)	0.056*** (0.002)	0.050*** (0.002)
Age fixed effects	Yes	Yes	Yes	Yes
State fixed effects	Yes	Yes	Yes	Yes
Year-month fixed effects	Yes	Yes	Yes	Yes
Mean of dep. variable	0.054	0.039	0.036	0.034
Observations	26,591	130,388	131,171	184,659

Notes: The table uses a linear probability model. The dependent variable is a retirement dummy, defined as conditional on being employed when first entering the survey, the first time an older worker exits the labor force. The Unemployment Rate coefficient shows the effect of a 10-point change; the COVID cases coefficient shows the effect of an increase of 100 cases (per 100 population); the Government Index coefficient shows the effect of a 100-point change. Column (1) restricts the regression to only older workers who are high school dropouts. Column (2) only includes older workers who are high school graduates. Column (3) has estimated coefficients for older workers who have some college experience but no degree. Column (4) has older workers who have college degrees or above. Standard errors are in parentheses. Significance levels are * $p < 0.10$, ** $p < 0.05$, *** $p < 0.01$.
Source: Authors' calculations.

coefficients. With respect to jobs being teleworkable, this factor is an important determinant of retirement pre-pandemic for all education groups, with statistically significant coefficients for all but the high school dropout group. The *After* X *Teleworkable* coefficient is also sizeable for all groups and statistically significant for all but the college group, indicating the importance of this factor for all workers. Overall, while the estimates are not sufficiently precise to draw firm conclusions about differences by education, they are suggestive of stronger effects of labor market conditions for less educated groups in the pre-pandemic period, and similar results across education groups for the other factors.

Conclusions

Our results present something of a puzzle. On the one hand, we find that the probability of making a transition from being employed to being out of the labor force rose during the pandemic, consistent with evidence from other studies that retirement rates increased during the pandemic. On the other hand, we fail to find the expected positive relationship between the unemployment rate and the probability of retirement during the pandemic, although we do observe a positive relationship in the pre-pandemic period, as had been found in previous studies.

In other words, while unemployment rates for older workers reached unprecedented levels during the pandemic, there is no evidence that older workers were more likely to retire in states where the rise in unemployment was sharpest. Nor can these results be explained by a few months of exceptionally high unemployment, as dropping the peak unemployment months just after the start of the pandemic from our analysis does not change results substantively.

Taken together, we conclude that retirements did increase during the pandemic, but this happened for reasons other than local economic or local COVID conditions. This points to a potential role for common national factors, such as generalized fear of COVID (unrelated to recent local COVID conditions), or the impact of policies affecting workers everywhere, like federal pandemic relief or expanded eligibility for unemployment insurance benefits. Alternatively, the increase in retirement could reflect wealth effects of the booming stock and housing markets. Additional research will be needed to better determine why retirements increased during the pandemic, and whether the early retirements that did occur will have negative long-term consequences for retiree wellbeing, as has been the case with past recessions.

Acknowledgments

Zhang acknowledges funding from the Jerome A. Schiff Fellowship. The authors acknowledge helpful comments from the Wellesley College Economics Research Seminar.

Notes

1. Authors' calculations from Bureau of Labor Statistics data, series LNU01300190, LNU01300199, LNU01300347, and LNU01300354.
2. From May–August 2020, the sample size was about 90,000–100,000 respondents per month. Many interviews were conducted via phone during the pandemic; as a result, it was more difficult to reach respondents and thus the response rate was lower (Heffetz and Reeves 2021).
3. We track individuals using CPSIDP, a numeric variable that identifies a person across different CPS survey months. To verify that CPSIPD uniquely identifies individuals, we check linkages to ensure that sex, race, and age are consistent over time. We find that approximately 1.5 percent of the sample has erroneous links and drop these observations.
4. There was some misclassification of workers' employment status in the CPS early in the pandemic, as some workers who should have been classified as being in 'unemployment on temporary layoff' were classified as being in 'employment but not at work' (Bureau of Labor Statistics 2021b). As we focus on transitions from employment to being out of the labor force, this misclassification issue is not a major concern for this analysis.
5. We focus on state-level unemployment rather than county-level because county-level geographic identifiers are available for only approximately 45 percent of CPS households.
6. We also test the robustness of our results to dropping the fifth interview month and find qualitatively similar results.
7. Interestingly, older individuals were about 5 percentage points more likely to be continuing to commute to work during the pandemic, compared to younger workers. Older workers were less likely to switch to remote working during the pandemic, in part because they were more likely to work remotely pre-pandemic (Brynjolfsson et al. 2020).
8. We are able to match more than 98 percent of workers in the CPS to the Dingel and Neiman (2020) data.
9. The mean monthly retirement rate excluding retirements in the 5th interview month (which occur over an eight-month period) during the pandemic period is 3.2 percent rather than 4.0 percent.

References

Abrams, L. R., J. M. Finlay, and L. C. Kobayashi (2022). 'Job Transitions and Mental Health Outcomes among US adults Aged 55 and Older during the COVID-19 Pandemic.' *The Journals of Gerontology, Series B, Psychological Sciences and Social Sciences*, 77(7): e106–e116.

Bosworth, B. (2012). 'Economic Consequences of the Great Recession: Evidence from the Panel Study of Income Dynamics.' CRR Working Paper 2012-4. Boston, MA: Center for Retirement Research at Boston College.

Bricker, J., B. Bucks, A. B. Kennickell, T. Mach, and K. B. Moore (2011). 'Surveying the Aftermath of the Storm: Changes in Family Finances from 2007 to 2009.' Finance and Economics Discussion Series Paper 2011-17. Washington, DC: Board of Governors of the Federal Reserve.

Brynjolfsson, E., J. J. Horton, A. Ozimek, D. Rock, G. Sharma, and H. Y. TuYe (2020). 'COVID-19 and Remote Work: An Early Look at US Data.' NBER Working Paper No. 27344. Cambridge, MA: National Bureau of Economic Research.

Bui, T. T. M., P. Button, and E. G. Picciotti (2020). 'Early Evidence on the Impact of Coronavirus Disease 2019 (COVID-19) and the Recession on Older Workers,' *Public Policy & Aging Report*, 30(4): 154–159.

Bureau of Labor Statistics (2019). '2019 Annual Averages—Household Data—Tables from Employment and Earnings, Table 11b.' https://www.bls.gov/cps/cps_aa2019.htm.

Bureau of Labor Statistics (2021a). 'COVID-19 Ends Longest Employment Recovery and Expansion in CES History, Causing Unprecedented Job Losses.' https://www.bls.gov/opub/mlr/2021/article/covid-19-ends-longest-employment-expansion-in-ces-history.htm.

Bureau of Labor Statistics (2021b). 'Effects of COVID-19 Pandemic on the Employment Situation New Release and Data.' https://www.bls.gov/covid19/effects-of-covid-19-pandemic-and-response-on-the-employment-situation-news-release.htm#ques12

Burtless, G. (2016). 'Labor Force Dynamics in the Great Recession and its Aftermath: Implications for Older Workers.' CRR Working Paper 2016-1. Boston, MA: Center for Retirement Research at Boston College.

Coile, C. C. and P. B. Levine (2007). 'Labor Market Shocks and Retirement: Do Government Programs Matter?' *Journal of Public Economics*, 91(10): 1902–1919.

Coile, C. C. and P. B. Levine (2011). 'Recessions, Retirement, and Social Security.' *American Economic Review: Papers & Proceedings*, 101(3): 23–28.

Coile, C. C., P. B. Levine, and R. McKnight (2014). 'Recessions, Older Workers, and Longevity: How Long Are Recessions Good for Your Health?' *American Economic Journal: Economic Policy*, 6(3): 92–119.

Dahl, G. B. and M. M. Knepper (2020). 'Age Discrimination across the Business Cycle.' NBER Working Paper No. 27581. Cambridge, MA: National Bureau of Economic Research.

Davis, O. (2021). 'Employment and Retirement Among Older Workers During the COVID-19 Pandemic.,' Working Paper 2021-6. New York, NY: Schwartz Center for Economic Policy Analysis at The New School for Social Research.

Davis, O., B. Fisher, T. Ghilarducci, and S. Radpour (2021). 'The Pandemic Retirement Surge Increased Retirement Inequality.' Status of Older Workers Report Series. New York, NY: Schwartz Center for Economic Policy Analysis at The New School for Social Research.

Dingel, J. I. and B. Neiman (2020). 'How Many Jobs Can Be Done at Home?' *Journal of Public Economics*, 189: 104235.

Disney, R., A. Ratcliffe, and S. Smith (2015). 'Booms, Busts and Retirement Timing.' *Economica*, 82(327): 399–419.

Farber, H. S. (2017). 'Employment, Hours, and Earnings Consequences of Job Loss: US Evidence from the Displaced Workers Survey.' *Journal of Labor Economics*, 35(S1): S235–S272.

Faria-e-Castro, M. (2021). 'The COVID Retirement Boom.' Economic *Synopses*, 25: 1–2.

Freeman, R. B. (2022). 'Planning for the "Expected Unexpected": Work and Retirement in the US After the COVID-19 Pandemic Shock.' NBER

Working Paper No. 29653. Cambridge, MA: National Bureau of Economic Research.

Goda, G. S., E. Jackson, L. H. Nicholas, and S. S. Stith (2021). 'The Impact of Covid-19 on Older Workers' Employment and Social Security Spillovers.' NBER Working Paper No. 29083. Cambridge, MA: National Bureau of Economic Research.

Goda, G. S., J. B. Shoven, and S. N. Slavov (2011). 'What Explains Changes in Retirement Plans during the Great Recession?' *American Economic Review*, 101(3): 29–34.

Gorodnichenko, Y., J. Song, and D. Stolyarov (2013). 'Macroeconomic Determinants of Retirement Timing.' NBER Working Paper No. 19638. Cambridge, MA: National Bureau of Economic Research.

Hale, T., N. Angrist, R. Goldszmidt, B. Kira, A. Petherick, T. Phillips, S. Webster, E. Cameron-Blake, L. Hallas, S. Majumdar, and H. Tatlow (2021). 'A Global Panel Database of Pandemic Policies (Oxford COVID-19 Government Response Tracker).' *Nature Human Behavior*, 5: 529–538.

Hallberg, D. (2011). 'Economic Fluctuations and Retirement of Older Employees.' *Labour*, 25(3), 287–307.

Heffetz, O. and D. Reeves (2021). 'Measuring Unemployment in Crisis: Effects of COVID-19 on Potential Biases in the CPS.' NBER Working Paper No. 28310. Cambridge, MA: National Bureau of Economic Research.

Helppie McFall, B. (2011). 'Crash and Wait? The Impact of the Great Recession on the Retirement Plans of Older Americans.' *American Economic Review*, 101(3): 40–44.

Lee, S. Y. T., M. Park, and Y. Shin (2021). 'Hit Harder, Recover Slower? Unequal Employment Effects of the Covid-19 Shock.' *Federal Reserve Bank of St. Louis Review*, 103(4): 1–17.

Marmora, P and M. Ritter (2015). 'Unemployment and the Retirement Decisions of Older Workers.' *Journal of Labor Research*, 36(3): 274–290.

McEntarfer, E. (2024). 'Older Workers, Retirement, and Macroeconomic Shocks.' In O. S. Mitchell, J. Sabelhaus, and S. Utkus, eds., *Real-World Shocks and Retirement System Resiliency*. Oxford, UK: Oxford University Press, pp. 36–51.

Mitchell, O. S. (2020). 'Building Better Retirement Systems in the Wake of the Global Pandemic.' NBER Working Paper No. 27261. Cambridge, MA: National Bureau of Economic Research.

Neumark, D. and P. Button (2014). 'Did Age Discrimination Protections Help Older Workers Weather the Great Recession?' *Journal of Policy Analysis and Management*, 33(3): 566–601.

Ondrich, J. and A. Falevich (2016). 'The Great Recession, Housing Wealth, and the Retirement Decisions of Older Workers.' *Public Finance Review*, 44(1): 109–131.

Quinby, L., M. S. Rutledge, and G. Wettstein (2021). 'How Has COVID-19 Affected the Labor Force Participation of Older Workers?' CRR Working Paper 2021-13. Boston, MA: Center for Retirement Research at Boston College.

Sanzenbacher, G. (2021). 'How Have Older Workers Fared during the COVID-19 Recession?' *Issue Brief 21-7*. Boston, MA: Center for Retirement Research at Boston College.

Yanez, N. D., N. S. Weiss, J. A. Romand, and M. M. Treggiari (2020). 'COVID-19 Mortality Risk for Older Men and Women.' *BMC Public Health*, 20(1): 1–7.

Part II

The Changing Financial Environment and Retirement Security

Chapter 5

Wealth Inequality and Retirement Preparedness

A Cross-Cohort Perspective

John Sabelhaus and Alice Henriques Volz

Much of the empirical research on the distribution of household wealth is focused on wealth inequality. A common question in many of those studies involves 'top shares' of household wealth (Saez and Zucman 2016; Bricker et al. 2016; Smith et al. 2021). Although there is still substantial debate about exactly how much wealth is owned by the top 1 percent, top 0.1 percent, or the top 0.01 percent of the population, there is general agreement that household wealth is highly skewed and has become more unequal over time. Our recent paper shows that those conclusions about trends in top wealth shares hold even after broadening the concept of the wealth to include the present value of private and public retirement benefits (Sabelhaus and Volz 2022).

Another important reason to conduct empirical research with household wealth data is to study lifecycle wealth accumulation, with a focus on the state of retirement preparedness or 'adequacy.' Some retirement adequacy studies compare accumulated wealth to the predictions of a lifecycle consumption smoothing model; other studies involve more straightforward questions and calculations, such as whether the annuitized value of accumulated wealth is sufficient to maintain preretirement income or consumption levels. The literature on retirement adequacy is in many ways much less settled than the top wealth shares literature, with conclusions ranging from 'more than half' to 'fewer than 20 percent' of US families are inadequately prepared for retirement.

One common element in both wealth distribution literatures is the need for a comprehensive measure of household wealth. The starting point for wealth is marketable assets less liabilities, which is the concept captured in the Survey of Consumer Finances (SCF) and estimated by the Federal

John Sabelhaus and Alice Henriques Volz, *Wealth Inequality and Retirement Preparedness*. In: *Real-World Shocks and Retirement System Resiliency*. Edited by: Olivia S. Mitchell, John Sabelhaus, and Stephen P. Utkus, Oxford University Press. © Pension Research Council (2024). DOI: 10.1093/oso/9780198894131.003.0005

Reserve Board at $96.1 trillion in the 2019 survey (Bhutta et al. 2020). Nevertheless, comprehensive household wealth should also include the present value of defined benefit (DB) pension claims, which adds another $19.1 trillion to household wealth in 2019. DB wealth is not measured directly at the household level, but the aggregates can be allocated across the individuals in the SCF who have legal claims to those benefits (Sabelhaus and Volz 2019, 2022). Finally, the aggregate net present value of all future social security benefits less taxes (or social security wealth, SSW) for working age and retired individuals is substantial, adding another $23.9 trillion to household wealth in 2019 (Sabelhaus and Volz 2022).

Including DB pensions and SSW adds nearly 50 percent to marketable wealth overall, but the distributional effect of their inclusion is uneven. DB wealth and SSW, in particular, are more evenly distributed than the narrow concept ('base wealth')—marketable assets less liabilities—captured directly in the SCF. Adding DB wealth and SSW to the SCF base wealth concept lowers the top 1 percent and top 10 percent wealth shares substantially in the 1995–2019 survey waves, by 5 and 9 percentage points, respectively (Sabelhaus and Volz 2022). Including DB wealth and SSW does not change the trends in top shares, however, because the increasing wealth concentration of base wealth has not been offset by either faster growth or decreasing concentration of DB wealth and SSW.

The comprehensive wealth concept that includes DB wealth and SSW can be measured over the lifecycle and across cohorts using the SCF in a pseudo-panel framework. As noted, the comprehensive wealth measure does not reverse the trend in top wealth shares over time, but it does reveal stark differences in average wealth across age groups over time (Sabelhaus and Volz 2022). A large majority of the growth in average comprehensive wealth between 1995 and 2016 occurred at older ages. Adjusting the wealth measure for expected social security funding shortfalls makes the age differentials even larger, especially for the bottom half of the wealth distribution. In fact, average comprehensive wealth is estimated to be lower in 2019 than it was in 1995 for younger individuals in the bottom 50 percent of their wealth distribution. These findings motivate our approach to studying retirement adequacy.

In this chapter, we use the comprehensive wealth measures we developed for analyzing levels and trends in wealth concentration to study retirement adequacy. As noted, however, the issue of how to gauge the adequacy of retirement wealth is far from settled. One approach is to compare wealth to some target based on preretirement living standards, as measured by income or consumption. The simple financial advisor's rule that you should 'replace 70 percent of your preretirement income' is often put forth as a straw man, but researchers then go on to develop more complicated calculations built on that same principle. An alternate approach is to compare observed, individual wealth holdings against the predictions of a calibrated lifecycle model. Both approaches are sensitive to assumptions. What exactly does it mean to 'maintain' preretirement living standards? What is the appropriate utility function for a calibrated lifecycle model? What are the appropriate time preference and other parameters in such a model? How well does either approach capture environmental details like social insurance and income taxes?

We take an alternative approach to gauging retirement wealth adequacy to avoid these potential pitfalls. Our cross-cohort approach to studying retirement adequacy is based on *relative* wealth measures: how the wealth distribution of a cohort compares to the cohorts older than them at the same age. The relative wealth measures do not tell us anything directly about the fraction of a given population with or without adequate retirement wealth. Nevertheless, given a reference point—for instance, what fraction of current retirees are suffering hardship in retirement—we can draw conclusions about future retirees by looking at their *current* wealth distributions *relative* to the wealth distributions of current retirees when they were observed at younger ages.

To quantify differences across cohorts, we use two approaches to compare wealth distributions. The first approach is creating *relative rank distributions* that answer the question 'where would an individual of a given cohort be if their wealth were mapped into the distribution of an earlier cohort?' The second approach is *percentile point comparisons*, that answer the question 'how do the wealth holdings differ for an individual at a given percentile of the wealth distribution across cohorts and ages?'[1]

The relative rank charts tell us about people—how many individuals, in terms of comprehensive wealth, are ahead of or behind their counterparts in earlier cohorts at the same age. The key messages about inequality and retirement preparedness come from seeing the entire cohort arrayed along the relative wealth distribution. We use the term 'relative rank gap' to describe the distance, in percentile points, between the two cohorts' distributions. When a younger cohort is ahead of an earlier cohort, the relative rank gap will be positive (so that a negative gap suggests a shortfall).[2] Complementing that perspective, the percentile points comparison charts tell us about dollars—cross-cohort differences in wealth at a given age for a fixed percentile of the distribution. The focus on one percentile at a time allows us to drill down into the relevance of the various wealth components across the wealth distribution and how they change over the lifecycle and time.

As an example, consider comparing Early Baby Boomers (1940s cohort) to the 1930s cohort, their reference cohort, at age 60. We observe that Early Boomers' wealth is generally on par with or above the 1930s cohort across the full wealth distribution. That is, the relative ranks of the 1940s cohort are all greater than the 1930s cohort ranks. As a result, when we look at the percentile point comparisons, the 1940s cohort's comprehensive wealth value above the 1930s cohort's comprehensive wealth value at the 10th, 25th, 50th, 75th, and 90th percentiles. What the percentile point comparisons point to is the key contribution of social security to that result, that the 1940s are ahead of 1930s, especially at the bottom of the wealth distribution where base wealth values are lower for the 1940s cohort.

Our dataset spans 30 years, and thus we can also compare the 1950s cohort to the 1930s cohort, still the reference cohort, at age 60. The relative wealth holdings of the 1950s cohort (the 'Mid-Boomers') at age 60 gives us the first indications of deterioration at the bottom of the wealth distribution. The extent of the shortfall, though, depends on the wealth concept. For example, the base concept (i.e., excluding SSW) shows a relative rank gap of between –5 and –10 for individuals in the 1950s cohort relative to the 1930s cohort in the bottom half of the wealth distribution. However, the comprehensive wealth measure including SSW completely reverses those gaps to the point where the rank gap is at least two for nearly all of the bottom half of the distribution.

Looking at younger ages, there is more evidence of relative deterioration in the bottom and middle of the wealth distribution for 'Late Boomers' (born in the 1960s) and 'Gen Xers' (born in the 1970s). Base wealth at the 10th and 25th percentiles of the Late Boomer and Gen X distributions is well below the wealth of earlier cohorts observed at the same ages. In contrast, further up the wealth distribution, there are notable, positive relative rank gaps.

Social security is an important offset to base wealth declines at the bottom of the wealth distribution for younger cohorts. Adding SSW and estimating the comprehensive wealth distribution reverses many of the points about relative deterioration at low wealth levels across cohorts and ages. In that sense, social security has become *relatively* more important in terms of total wealth for the bottom half of the wealth distribution for younger cohorts, with the higher expected benefits based on lower (relative) earnings and higher (relative) life expectancy. However, the fact that those social security benefits are not expected to be fully payable for the youngest cohorts under current law overrides the relative improvements in retirement adequacy coming from social security.

The chapter proceeds as follows. In the next section, we discuss how we construct our comprehensive measure of wealth. In the third section, we review the literature on measuring retirement adequacy and discuss how the required (and debatable) assumptions motivate our relative wealth approach. The fourth section presents the relative rank distributions, and the fifth shows percentile point comparisons. Section six concludes.

Data and Methods

Our approach to studying retirement adequacy requires a comprehensive, individual-level wealth measure across birth cohorts and over the lifecycle. Achieving this goal involves starting with high-quality, household-level balance sheet data and adding in household-level estimates of SSW and DB wealth.[3] The micro data used here are the Survey of Consumer Finances (SCF) for 1989 through 2019. The SCF is focused on household balance sheets, and the survey also has extensive information about incomes, demographics, and labor force experiences.[4] The SCF alone is not ideal for calculating a comprehensive wealth measure; we bring in additional information on earnings and relative mortality to estimate DB and SSW more precisely than would be possible with the SCF alone. We estimate lifecycle earnings for individuals and their spouse/partners, required since the SCF is a series of cross-section snapshots, as inputs to calculating social security taxes and benefits over the lifecycle. Since individual mortality rates are necessary to estimate present discounted values for both SSW and DB pensions, we differentiate mortality by age, sex, income, and birth year.

Estimating the present discounted value of retirement benefits is complicated for several reasons. One conceptual issue is whether to use 'expected' versus 'termination' benefits (Sabelhaus and Volz 2022). The concept of termination value for SSW—what any given individual would receive if the system shut down today—is not well suited for the analysis here because the assumptions about who would receive benefits under a terminated system have less real-world relevance. In contrast, expected SSW is the present discounted value of total benefits less future taxes, conditioned on the individual working and paying taxes through a given expected retirement age (as captured in the survey) and receiving benefits as soon as possible (age 62 or the first year after labor force exit, whichever is later). The labor force and earnings history along with expectations data in the SCF are used in conjunction with typical lifecycle earnings patterns derived from linked longitudinal survey and administrative data in the Health and Retirement Study (HRS). The detailed assumptions needed to create the required inputs for computing expected SSW in the SCF are discussed in earlier papers (Sabelhaus 2019; Sabelhaus and Volz 2022).

The measure of DB wealth consistent with the household balance sheet is the present value of future DB benefits, which is equivalent to the value of the financial assets held now that will be liquidated over time to pay the promised stream of DB benefits when those liabilities come due. The SCF collects details about DB pension benefits in three different survey modules. The three categories cover: (1) DB benefits already being received; (2) DB benefits associated with a past job where the known benefit amount will be received at a specific future date; and (3) DB benefits associated with a current job, where the ultimate benefit will depend on how much longer the worker is covered by the plan and their final salary.

For currently received benefits and reported expected benefits from past job pensions, the respondent is asked how much is currently being received or how much will be received when the benefit begins. These benefit payments are the primary input to a present discounted value calculation that also involves an assumed interest rate and demographically differentiated mortality rates (described below). This present discounted value calculation is equivalent to the level of financial assets that the retirement plan sponsor must hold to pay those promised benefits, and thus corresponds directly to the base household wealth measure captured in the survey.

Calculating DB pension wealth for workers covered by a plan on their current job is more complicated, because the benefit that will be received in the future is unknown as of the survey date. The aggregate measure of DB wealth that corresponds to our comprehensive household wealth is the financial liability of retirement plan sponsors; it corresponds only to the DB wealth that the worker has accumulated to date. Plan sponsors are required to hold only the present value of benefits already earned by the worker, the termination value, or accrued benefit obligation. The termination value represents the worker's legal claim to DB wealth, because that level of assets is equivalent to the present value of benefits they will receive if their plan coverage ended today.

The core demographics in the SCF—age, sex, and income—are key inputs to the differential mortality adjustment, which is key for estimating present values for retirement income streams.[5] Constructing the present value of social security and DB pension incomes requires survival probabilities, which are computed for each SCF respondent and their spouse/partner, if present, through age 99. The starting point is Social Security Administration (SSA) cohort mortality by age and sex. These are modified by a differential mortality adjustment by income percentile within groups defined by age and sex based on Chetty et al. (2016). Chetty et al. (2016) map SSA death records onto income tax records to study mortality differences across the income distribution, which we transform into a differential adjustment (for methodological detail, see the appendix to Sabelhaus and Volz 2022).

How Do We Know If Retirement Wealth Is 'Adequate'?

Financial advisors have long advocated a 'replacement rate' approach to retirement planning. A standard rule of thumb is that individuals should be able to replace approximately 70 percent of their preretirement income through their retirement years. The 70 percent rule is an average, and good financial advisors are quick to note that differences in individual circumstances will move the target up or down. Heterogeneity in circumstances is also a recognized key in the academic literature on retirement adequacy.

The question of retirement adequacy is far from resolved. One evaluation of retirement adequacy creates an index based on the SCF to estimate what fraction of the population is predicted to have enough resources (both wealth and income) at age 65 to maintain their preretirement standard of living, as measured by consumption (Munnell et al. 2021). The authors find that about half of current US households will fall more than 10 percent short of reaching their target, up from about a third of households in the 1980s. The model underlying the index is very complex, with income replacement targets that vary by factors such as housing tenure and effective income tax rates. However, key assumptions on inputs, such as consumption levels during retirement, are not consistent with observed age-spending patterns, and that biases absolute adequacy measures toward shortfalls (Hurd and Rohwedder 2012).

Comparing actual wealth from a survey such as the SCF to predicted 'optimal' wealth from a calibrated lifecycle model is an alternative way to measure retirement adequacy (e.g., Engen et al. 1999). Rather than ask what level of wealth is needed to meet a given target replacement rate, this approach defines 'adequate' as enough wealth to smooth the predicted marginal utility of consumption over the lifecycle. Relatively simple lifecycle models can provide a wide range of predictions about optimal lifecycle wealth, depending on assumed inputs such as time discount factors, earnings paths, mortality, and even the arguments in the utility function. A lack of heterogeneity in structural model inputs leads to predictions that average across observations, and a larger fraction of the population will far short of those average targets.

Studies defining 'optimal' wealth using structural lifecycle models that capture more heterogeneity across the population generally seem to suggest that fewer US families have inadequate retirement savings. One such study, using the Health and Retirement Study (HRS), makes use of detailed earnings histories and demographic characteristics and, thus, is able to fine tune lifecycle model predictions to specific types of households (Love et al. 2008). They find that only 18 percent of households in 2006 would fall short of maintaining income at more than 150 percent of poverty over their remaining lifetimes.

Another, even more finely tuned, comparison of actual and optimal wealth solves a different lifecycle optimization problem for every household in the HRS based on their unique characteristics (Scholz et al. 2006). They find that fewer than 20 percent of households are saving below their optimal target, and the shortfalls of those who are undersaving are generally small.

The predicted wealth from any structural lifecycle model still depends on exactly which circumstances (or 'state' variables) are included in the model, and computational constraints limit which characteristics can be included. Furthermore, structural models are inherently static in nature and cannot capture how circumstances might be evolving for future populations.

Dynamic microsimulation is another approach to capturing heterogeneity and does not suffer from the computational limits nor the static nature of structural lifecycle models. A dynamic microsimulation uses stochastic transition equations to age a population forward through time, simulating the wide range of outcomes that will be experienced. One such study projected future earnings and retirement incomes for the Baby Boom generation and found that *typical* outcomes should continue to improve for the Baby Boom generation relative to their parents, but changing demographic and earnings patterns are leaving more individuals economically vulnerable (Butrica et al. 2007). The dynamic microsimulation draws attention to retirement wealth adequacy for specific groups whose circumstances are changing over time: divorced women, never-married men, Hispanics, high school dropouts, those with weak labor force attachment, and those with the lowest lifetime earnings.

Another recent paper looking at future retirement outcomes captures heterogeneity and many of the benefits of dynamic microsimulation with a reduced-form, empirical approach (Brown et al. 2020). Their approach avoids lots of assumptions, and their findings further motivate our approach to studying retirement adequacy. The authors use early waves of the HRS, for whom economic and demographic characteristics are observed just before and through retirement, to assess which characteristics of pre-retirees are useful for predicting economic hardship during retirement. They use those correlations to predict how the cohorts approaching retirement today will fare in their retirement years. They find that those approaching retirement, particularly men, are indeed more likely to experience economic hardship, on average. Comparing cohorts at younger ages to help predict future outcomes is similar in spirit to what we do here. That is, what can we say about the likely outcomes for a cohort of pre-retirees by looking at a currently retired group when the current retirees were younger?

In sum, the wide range of opinion in the literature about how to map observed wealth into measures of retirement adequacy leads to a wide range of conclusions about how well US households are prepared for retirement. One can look at the same individuals and arrive at very different conclusions about their retirement wealth adequacy. Indeed, the uncertainty about assumptions needed to create such 'absolute' measures of retirement wealth adequacy directly motivates the alternative approach we use in this chapter. Our investigation focuses on how the wealth of younger cohorts compare to current retirees (or near-retirees) when they were at the same age in some earlier year.

Thus, rather than ask whether a given family or individual has 'sufficient' wealth for a secure retirement, we create relative adequacy measures by looking across cohorts at various ages. We introduce two ways to characterize relative wealth distributions, which answer the following questions. First, 'where would the individuals at a specific rank in the wealth distribution of a given cohort be if their wealth is mapped into the distribution of an *earlier* cohort observed at the same age?' We call this the *relative rank* distribution. The interpretations are all about *counts* of individuals. For example, if the relative rank distribution for a comparison cohort lies always at or above the reference cohort, we can say the comparison cohort is just as well or better off than the reference cohort at every point in the wealth distribution.

The second measure answers the question 'what wealth do individuals hold at a given percentile of the wealth distribution across cohorts and ages?' We call these charts *percentile point comparisons*. The percentile points comparison charts focus on a single slice of the wealth distribution across cohort and age, instead of characterizing the entire distribution like the relative rank charts. Another way to think of this is that the relative rank charts show us counts of people at points in the wealth distribution, while the percentile point comparisons are about dollar gaps for the people at one of those points. Though we can only focus on one wealth percentile at a time in a percentile point comparison, the data disentangle the contributions of different wealth sources across the distribution.

Relative Rank Distributions

We refer to *relative rank distributions* as the first approach we use to look at relative wealth distributions. Our charts answer the question 'what wealth rank would individuals of one cohort represent, if their wealth were mapped into the distribution of an earlier cohort?' The comparisons presented are specific to an age group and a wealth concept, so there are several permutations of such relative rank calculations.

We limit the number of comparisons by working with two wealth concepts across three age groups. As our base wealth measure, we use SCF net worth plus DB benefits, while comprehensive wealth—the base wealth measure plus SSW—is the alternative. The three age groups are '40' (age 38–42), '50' (age 48–52), and '60' (age 58–62), with reference cohorts 1930s, 1940s, and 1950s, respectively, for these age groups. Given the SCF time span, the age 60 relative rank comparisons (for example) use the 1930s as the reference cohort, and the 1940s and 1950s cohorts as the two comparison groups.[6]

The age 50 and age 40 relative ranks shift the reference and comparison cohorts forward one and two decades, respectively.

The goal of the relative rank and percentile point comparisons is to avoid making absolute statements about what 'adequate' retirement wealth means, though the approach does require an assumption about what it means for wealth levels to be 'comparable' across cohorts. The reference and comparison cohorts are either 10 or 20 years apart in time, so comparing nominal wealth is misleading. To convert wealth to real dollars, the inflation adjustment uses the data series used to calculate and inflation-adjust social security benefits (the CPI).

The relative rank distributions plot the comparison cohort percentiles on the x-axis, and the reference cohort cumulative percentiles on the y-axis. The graphs all include a 45-degree line that plots the reference cohort cumulative wealth against their own wealth distribution. Thus, the 45-degree line (trivially) shows that 1 percent of the reference cohort population is in each percentile of the reference cohort wealth distribution. However, that 45-degree line is a useful benchmark for the comparison cohorts, because if the comparison cohort relative rank distribution falls along the 45-degree line, the comparison cohort can be said to have the same wealth distribution as the reference cohort. If the relative rank distribution were above the 45-degree line, the comparison cohort wealth is above reference cohort wealth at that percentile.

With those chart-reading principles in mind, the first relative rank distribution in Figure 5.1a uses the base wealth concept (i.e., SCF net worth plus DB wealth) at age 60. The reference cohort for age 60 is the 1930s. The grey lines show the relative rank distributions for the 1940s (loosely, Early Boomer) cohort, and the dashed lines show the relative rank distributions for the 1950s (loosely, Mid-Boomer). The relative rank distributions for the 1940s cohort are on or above the 45-degree line. That means everyone in the 1940s cohort had the same or more wealth than their counterpart at the same point in the wealth distribution in the 1930s cohort at the same percentile. The horizontal distance between the relative rank and 45-degree lines measures the relative rank gap. For example, an individual around the 55th percentile of the 1940s cohort had the same wealth as an individual at the 70th percentile of the reference cohort, for a relative rank gap of 15. In the bottom 30 percent of the distribution, the relative rank gap was never above five. But the rank gap grew to about 10 at the median, reaching the highest value at the 70th percentile. The relative rank distributions only show people, not dollars. Accordingly, one cannot compare differences in the dollar amounts that correspond to the relative rank gaps, which we discuss that in the next section.

Although the relative rank distributions show an unambiguous improvement between the age 60 1930s and 1940s wealth distributions, the story

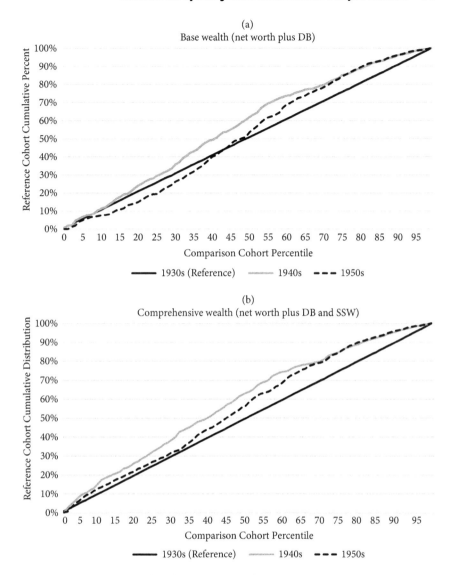

Figure 5.1 Relative rank distributions at age 60
Source: Authors' calculations.

is different for the 1950s cohort. The latter group tracks the first few percentiles of the 1930s cohort, but then it falls behind by a few rank points for much of the distribution. Around 45 percent of the 1950s cohort had less wealth than their counterparts in the 1930s group. The fact that the relative rank gap is positive for the 1950s cohort at higher percentiles is consistent with what we know about rising wealth inequality over time. Again, all we can say is that an individual in the 1950s cohort at (say) the 25th percentile of the wealth distribution had the same wealth as someone in the 1930s at the 20th percentile, which seems like a modest gap.

Adding expected SSW to the base wealth concept pushes the 1940s cohort even further above the 1930s, and it also improves the relative ranks for the 1950s cohort (Figure 5.1b).[7] The relative rank gap for the 1940s was above 10 for the 30th percentile of the reference cohort distribution, and the relative rank gaps were now all positive for the 1950s cohort. One way to interpret this shift in relative ranks is that social security was *relatively* more important for the 1940s and 1950s cohorts than it was for the 1930s reference cohort. Our approach to estimate SSW in the micro data captures the fact that changing demographics and lifetime wages produced differences in SSW for individuals at the same point in the wealth distribution across cohorts (Sabelhaus and Volz 2022). If average individuals in the comparison cohort at a given age and wealth percentile had a longer life expectancy, they would be allocated more SSW. Changes in social security replacement rates, marriage patterns, relative earnings between spouses (through spousal and survivor benefits), and labor force participation also matter, but the relative ranks show that, on net, SSW was relatively more important for the younger cohorts.

Shifting back to the base wealth concept and looking earlier in the life-cycle, the relative ranks at age 50 show that some of the 1950s cohort trailed the Early Boomer counterparts at low to modest wealth levels (Figure 5.2a). By contrast, the 1960s cohort trailed Early Boomers by a wide margin, approximately 10 rank points over much of the distribution. Individuals in the 20th –25th percentiles of the 1960s cohort had only as much wealth as those between the 12th and the 15th percentile of the 1940s wealth distribution. The highest wealth individuals in both the 1950s and 1960s cohorts caught up to and surpassed their counterparts in the reference cohort, again consistent with rising wealth inequality over time. Yet, more of the 1950s cohort was relatively higher than the reference cohort, than was the 1960s cohort.

Adding SSW to the base wealth concept notably changes the relative rank gaps at age 50 (Figure 5.2b). Since both the reference cohort and the comparison cohort wealth distribution included SSW, the relative rank lines shift if social security is *relatively* more important for the comparison cohorts at a given wealth percentile. In this case, the relative ranks for the 1950s and 1960s comparison cohorts using the comprehensive wealth concept implied relative improvement, compared to the base concept shown above (Figure 5.2a), as the 1950s now were ahead of the 1940s cohort and the relative rank gaps for the 1960s were notably smaller. For the 1960s cohort, there

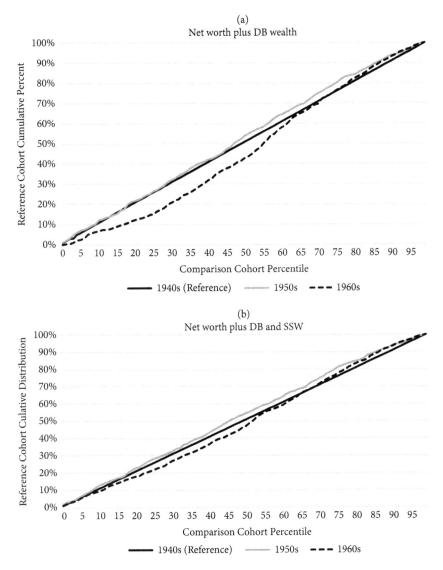

Figure 5.2 Relative rank distributions at age 50

Source: Authors' calculations.

was a modest deterioration in retirement preparation using this framework (a relative rank gap of a few points at most), though the wedge appears for most of the wealth distribution.

As noted in the introduction, our interest in relative wealth adequacy across cohorts at various ages is partly motivated by the observation that average wealth at younger ages has fallen over time, which is another way of saying that a disproportionate share of the wealth gains accumulated to older age groups (Sabelhaus and Volz 2022). Our approach allows us to consider these wealth declines at younger ages along two additional dimensions: where people fell in the wealth distribution, and for which cohorts wealth fell. The relative rank distributions for base wealth at age 40 confirm relative wealth declines at low wealth levels for the 1970s cohort, but there was little difference between the 1950s and 1960s cohort at low wealth levels (Figure 5.3a). It is worth noting here that a significant portion of the age 40 base wealth distribution was close to zero, with the 25th percentile of the reference cohort having around $25,000. This point becomes clearer when we focus on the low wealth percentiles in the percentile point comparison charts. Further up the distribution, the 1960s cohort did relatively better than the 1950s cohort, with a rank gap around 10 between the 60th and 80th percentiles of the reference cohort.

Social security was shown to be relatively important for relative rank distributions at age 50, which also held at age 40, such that the bottom quarter of the distribution for both the 1960s and 1970s cohorts had positive rank gaps (Figure 5.3b). It is particularly notable that including SSW closed the relative rank gaps across the whole wealth distribution for the 1970s cohort. Using a comprehensive wealth measure that includes scheduled SSW— payable or not—the 1960s and 1970s cohorts were slightly above the 1950s cohort.

Tying together the relative rank distributions at various ages using the most comprehensive wealth measure (Figures 5.1b, 5.2b, and 5.3b), one can assert that (1) the 1950s cohort tracked or was slightly behind the 1930s cohort at age 60; (2) the 1970s cohort tracked or was slightly behind the 1950s cohort at age 40; and thus, if the relative ranks are transitive across time, (3) the 1970s cohort was somewhere between tracking and slightly behind the 1930s cohort.

The optimistic conclusions from the relative ranks at age 40 are contingent on whether the increasing SSW offsets relative to declines in other types of wealth are in fact payable. Our assumption used to estimate payable benefits is simple: we adopt the SSA actuaries' projection that 78 percent of benefits are payable after 2033. Thus, payable SSW is the present value of scheduled benefits through 2033 plus 78 percent of scheduled benefits after. The timing is such that the youngest cohorts will face the largest lifetime cuts, and this result comes through in the relative rank distributions. When we compute relative ranks at age 40 using only payable SSW, there is more evidence of relative shortfalls for the 1960s and 1970s cohorts across much of the wealth distribution. The 1950s reference cohort will also face benefit cuts in the payable scenario, albeit proportionally less. The largest decrease in the rank gap for the 1960s cohort is around the 25th

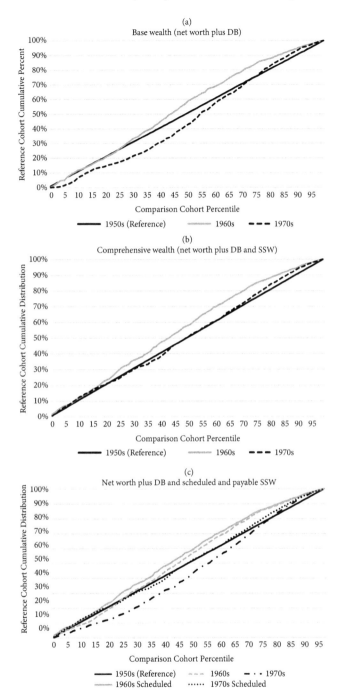

Figure 5.3 Relative rank distributions at age 40

Source: Authors' calculations.

percentile of the reference distribution, while the 1970s cohort now experiences notable rank gaps across the bottom two-thirds of the distribution (see Figure 5.3c). To evaluate how relative wealth declines under the payable benefits scenario, we examine this question next.

Percentile Point Comparisons

Cross-cohort shifts in relative rank positions are useful because they help us compare an entire cohort group relative to another. The shortcoming is that we cannot assess how large any shortfalls are because the charts are ordinal in nature. Accordingly, we next present *percentile point comparisons* to answer the question, 'what is the wealth level for the individual at a given percentile in wealth distributions across cohorts and ages?'

The percentile points comparison charts focus on a single slice of the wealth distribution across cohort and age groups. In addition to attaching dollars to the relative rank gaps, another advantage of this approach is being able to stack and disentangle the contribution of different wealth sources at various percentiles of the wealth distribution. Building on the relative rank charts in the previous section, we are particularly focused on three wealth components: SCF net worth plus DB, payable SSW, and scheduled but not payable SSW.

The percentile points comparison charts require a choice. Although it is obvious what it means to be at a given percentile for a given wealth concept, comparing multiple wealth components at a given percentile requires a decision about how to 'stack' wealth measures to show the dollar contribution of each wealth component. One could, in principle, identify individuals at a given percentile of the base wealth concept and then add average payable SSW and average scheduled but not payable SSW. The results are comparable across these two approaches but show slightly lower average base wealth compared to if one were to rank individuals by comprehensive wealth instead and calculate the components.

To build the percentile points charts, we start with comprehensive wealth (SCF net worth plus DB and scheduled SSW) for a given percentile-cohort-age combination and solve for the 10th percentile of that wealth measure. We then repeat the process for the other two measures: SCF net worth plus DB and payable SSW and the base wealth measure. The 10th percentile of SCF net worth plus DB and payable SSW is then solved for as the difference between the first two values, and the 10th percentile of SCF net worth plus DB is the difference between the second and third values.

We begin the percentile comparisons near the bottom of the wealth distribution, at the 10th percentile (Figure 5.4). The differences in overall bar heights within a given age and cohort comparison are dollar-valued

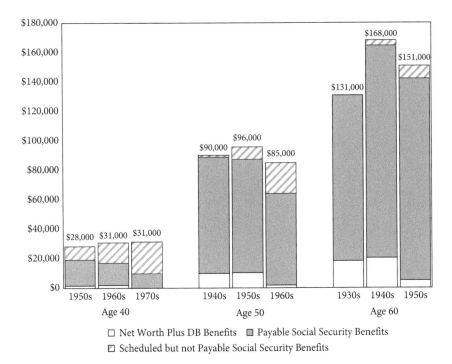

Figure 5.4 10th percentile of cross-cohort wealth distributions

Source: Authors' calculations.

analogous to the relative rank gaps at the 10th percentile using the comprehensive wealth measure. The fact that overall bar heights are generally similar is the parallel to the fact that the relative ranks were generally close to the 45-degree line; that is, the relative rank gaps were near zero, at the 10th percentile in the comprehensive wealth charts. One exception—the 1940s cohort at age 60 had more wealth at the 10th percentile than did the 1930s cohort—is analogous to the observation that the 1940s relative rank line was above the 45-degree line at low wealth levels (Figure 5.1b). The other standout feature of the 10th percentile point comparison is the role of SSW, first in overall dominance at every age, and second in terms of the importance of payable versus scheduled benefits at younger ages. The relative wealth of the 1970s cohort was dramatically lower than predecessor cohorts based on payable benefits alone.

At the 25th percentile of the wealth distribution, base wealth plays a slightly more important role in household resources, but social security still dominates (Figure 5.5). The relative deterioration in comparison cohorts' base wealth at the 25th percentile is notable for the 1970s cohort at age 40,

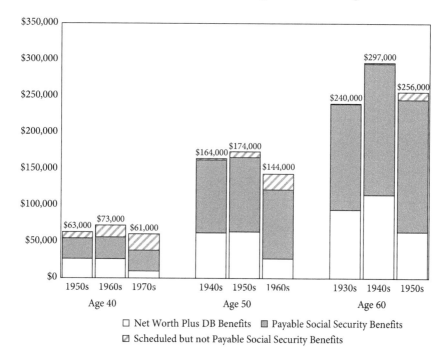

Figure 5.5 25th percentile of cross-cohort wealth distributions
Source: Authors' calculations.

the 1960s cohort at age 50, and the 1950s cohort at age 60. These shortfalls reflect the relative rank gaps of around −10 for the base wealth concept (Figures 5.1a, 5.2a, and 5.3a) at the 25th percentile. In contrast, the 1940s cohort at age 60 had higher base wealth. As with the 10th percentile, SSW reverses some of the relative wealth decline at the 25th percentile, but focusing on payable benefits alone, the prospects for low wealth individuals in the 1960s and 1970s cohorts are bleaker.

The contributions to total wealth from social security and non-social security sources are more balanced in the middle of the wealth distribution (Figure 5.6). Similar observations about relative declines in base wealth present at the 25th percentile also show up at the 50th percentile, but now only for the 1970s cohort at age 40 and the 1960s cohort at age 50, analogous to the negative relative rank gaps near the middle of the wealth distribution in those two instances. At the median, the 1950s cohort is comparable to the reference cohort at age 60. Nevertheless, the relative changes are more muted or are a relative improvement over the reference cohort using the comprehensive wealth measure, consistent with nearly all relative ranks

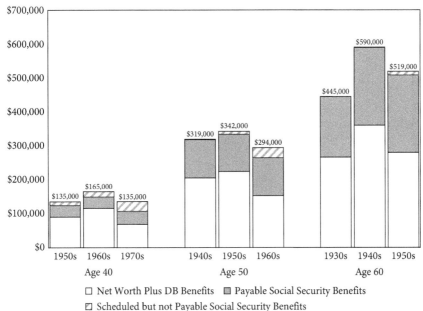

Figure 5.6 50th percentile of cross-cohort wealth distributions

Source: Authors' calculations.

above the 45-degree line at the 50th percentile (Figures 5.1b, 5.2b, and 5.3b). In general, the 50th percentile comprehensive wealth measures show less relative deterioration across cohorts when compared to lower wealth levels.

Retirement adequacy is about more than wealth levels, even in our relative wealth framework. Although it is possible that relative wealth would decline across cohorts at a given age in the top half of the wealth distribution, the data suggest that there is in fact less to worry about at the 75th percentile (Figure 5.7). In all cases, the data show gains in relative comprehensive wealth at the 75th percentile, although focusing on only payable SSW leads to some small relative shortfalls. Relative to the bottom half of the wealth distribution, social security is much less important for overall wealth in the top half of the wealth distribution. An important corollary to that statement, at least compared to the bottom half of the wealth distribution, is that social security solvency is a relatively less important determinant of the prospects for currently young, higher wealth individuals.

For a complete presentation of the wealth distribution, we also show wealth components at the 90th percentiles (Figure 5.8). Here there are few concerns for retirement adequacy: the impression is the mirror image of

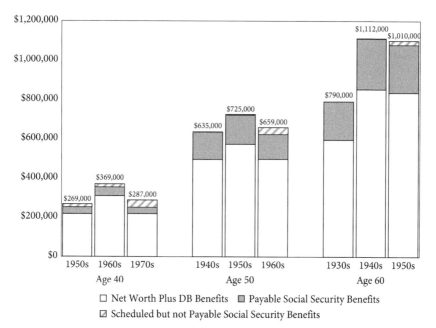

Figure 5.7 75th percentile of cross-cohort wealth distributions
Source: Authors' calculations.

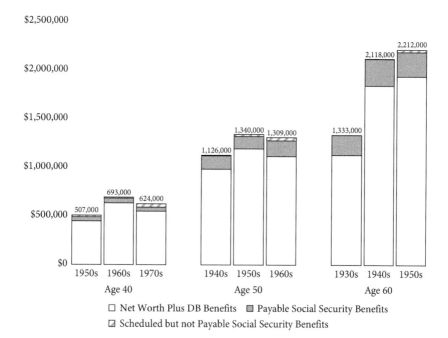

Figure 5.8 90th percentile of cross-cohort wealth distributions
Source: Authors' calculations.

the 10th percentile charts, in which SSW dominates. At the 90th percentile, social security is a relatively small component of comprehensive wealth, and the issue of whether social security is payable or not has very modest implications. At the 90th wealth percentile, slightly different than the takeaway from the 75th percentile—younger cohorts do look better off. The 90th percentile point comparisons are also consistent with the idea that rising wealth inequality is more about what's happening within the top 10 percent, and less about the 90th percentile relative to other groups per se, since there are only modest improvements of the comparison cohorts relative to the reference cohort.

Conclusions

Are the 60-year-olds who were born in 1960 well-prepared for retirement? Are the 50-year-olds born in 1970, and the 40-year-olds born in 1980, on a trajectory to be well prepared when they retire? Against a backdrop of rising wealth inequality, the concern about *some* future retirees seems justified. But *how many* future retirees will face economic hardships in their retirement years? How *large* are the expected shortfalls in terms of wealth needed for a secure retirement? Researchers with different retirement wealth adequacy yardsticks could look at the same wealth distributions and come to very different conclusions about the number of people facing retirement shortfalls, and how large those shortfalls might be.

In this chapter, we consider retirement wealth adequacy using *relative* yardsticks. The reference points are today's retirees, the cohort born in the 1930s, the Early Boomers born in the 1940s, and the Mid-Boomers born in the 1950s, all of whom are at different stages of retirement. We compare the wealth distributions of younger cohorts at the same ages, and we find support for the idea that rising wealth inequality in net worth and DB pensions is indeed driving relative wealth declines (and presumably retirement preparedness) in the bottom half of the distribution.

The *relative* wealth approach means we cannot say anything about absolute retirement preparedness for a given individual or a cohort. Yet if we believe that 20 percent of the 1930s cohort experienced financial hardship in retirement, which seems probable given Brown et al.'s (2020) analysis of the HRS, then some fraction below 20 percent of the 1940s cohort can be expected to experience financial hardship in retirement, based on their relative wealth distributions at age 60.[8] Depending on the wealth concept used, we conclude that somewhere between the 13th and 18th percentile of the 1940s cohort had as much wealth as the 20th percentile of the 1930s cohort at age 60, putting them moderately or significantly ahead of the 1930s cohort depending on whether social security is considered.

Also, and still depending on the specific wealth measure and the assumption about future social security benefit cuts, the inferences go in the other direction for younger cohorts, especially at low wealth levels. Under a payable social security scenario, the 30th percentile of the 1970s cohort had the same wealth as the 20th percentile of the 1950s cohort at age 40, meaning we could be looking at a 50 percent increase in the fraction of retirees facing hardship when the 20th percentile is our cutoff, presuming that the 1950s cohort have a similar rate of hardship in retirement as did the 1930s cohort. At the bottom of the wealth distribution, relative retirement preparedness depends on how policymakers address expected future social security shortfalls.

Disclosure

The analysis and conclusions set forth are those of the authors and do not necessarily reflect the views of the Brookings Institution or its funders, or indicate concurrence by other members of the research staff or the Board of Governors of the Federal Reserve System.

Notes

1. These are analogous to the 'rank gap' and 'level gap' concepts described in Bayer and Charles (2018) to discuss the evolution of the racial earnings gap. Our framework is slightly different in that we are comparing cohorts at different ages (instead of indexing to a calendar year), and we present the full distribution of relative ranks.
2. This is the opposite presentation of the rank gap as used by Bayer and Charles (2018).
3. A more detailed explanation of the methods used to construct comprehensive household wealth can be found in Sabelhaus and Volz (2019).
4. See Bhutta et al. (2020) for a discussion of the SCF and the most recent results, the 2019 survey.
5. The demographic variables are available for both the SCF respondent and the spouse/partner, which is important, because the SCF micro files always assign the male in a couple (person closest to age 40 in a same-sex couple) to be the respondent, and the other individual to be the spouse/partner, without regard to which is the primary earner.
6. Technically, because the SCF data spans 1989–2019, we use the last seven years of each decade to represent a birth cohort, so the '1930s' means 1930–1937 and '1970s' is 1970–1977. Birth years within a given cohort are systematically observed with different frequencies across survey waves at various ages, so we reweight by birth year within each cohort and age group to keep the cohort representation constant across the relative comparisons, i.e., each birth cohort gets equal weight.
7. There is only minor reranking of individuals when changing from the base wealth distribution to the comprehensive wealth distribution, as most households expect to receive social security benefits and the level of SSW is highly correlated with base wealth levels. Thus, an individual's rank is very similar across Figures 5.1a and 5.1b.

8. Brown et al. (2020) measure hardship of the 1932–1937 birth cohort in 2014, when they were age 77–82. They find that 6.5 percent of individuals were in poverty while 12.4 percent had annuitized wealth below 150 percent of the poverty line. Since this is a snapshot in time, it is likely that some fraction of those not *currently* in hardship experienced some difficulties earlier in retirement.

References

Bayer, P. and K. K. Charles (2018). 'Divergent Paths: A New Perspective on Earnings Differences between Black and White Men since 1940.' *Quarterly Journal of Economics*, 133(3): 1459–1501.

Bhutta, N., J. Bricker, A. C. Chang, L. J. Dettling, S. Goodman, J. W. Hsu, K. B. Moore, S. Reber, A. H. Volz, and R. A. Windle (2020). 'Changes in U.S. Family Finances from 2016 to 2019: Evidence from the Survey of Consumer Finances.' *Federal Reserve Bulletin*, 106(5): 1–42 (September).

Bricker, J., A. Henriques, J. Krimmel, and J. Sabelhaus (2016). 'Measuring Income and Wealth at the Top Using Administrative and Survey Data.' *Brookings Papers on Economic Activity*, 2016(1): 261–321.

Brown, J., K. Dynan, and T. Figinski (2020). 'The Risk of Financial Hardship in Retirement: A Cohort Analysis.' In O. S. Mitchell and A. Lusardi, eds., *Remaking Retirement: Debt in an Aging Economy*. Oxford, UK: Oxford University Press, pp. 60–85.

Butrica, B., H. M. Iams, and K. E. Smith (2007). 'Understanding Baby Boomers' Retirement Prospects.' In B. Madrian, O. S. Mitchell, and B. J. Soldo, eds., *Redefining Retirement: How Will Boomers Fare?* Oxford, UK: Oxford University Press, pp. 70–91.

Chetty, R., M. Stepner, S. Abraham, S. Lin, B. Scuderi, N. Turner, A. Bergeron, and D. Cutler (2016). 'The Association Between Income and Life Expectancy in the United States, 2001–2014.' *JAMA*, 315(16): 1750–1766.

Engen, E. M., W. G. Gale, and C. E. Uccello (1999). 'The Adequacy of Household Saving.' *Brookings Papers on Economic Activity*, 1999(1): 65–187.

Hurd, M. J. and S. Rohwedder (2012). 'Economic Preparation for Retirement.' In D. Wise, ed., *Investigations in the Economics of Aging*. Chicago, IL: University of Chicago Press, pp. 77–117.

Love, D. A., P. A. Smith, and L. C. McNair (2008). 'A New Look at the Wealth Adequacy of Older U.S. Households.' *Review of Income and Wealth*, 54(4): 616–642.

Munnell, A. H., A. Chen, and R. Siliciano (2021). 'The National Retirement Risk Index: An Update from the 2019 SCF.' Center for Retirement Research at Boston College No. 21–22. Boston, MA: Center for Retirement Research at Boston College.

Sabelhaus, J. (2019). 'Household Portfolios and Retirement Behavior.' Paper presented at the Stanford Institute for Economic and Policy Research (SIEPR) 2019 *Working Longer and Retirement* Conference, October 10–11, 2019.

Sabelhaus, J. and A. H. Volz (2019). 'Are Disappearing Employer Pensions Contributing to Rising Wealth Inequality?' *FEDS Notes*. February 1: https://doi.org/10.17016/2380-7172.2308.

Sabelhaus, J. and A. H. Volz (2022). 'Social Security Wealth, Inequality, and Life-cycle Saving.' In R. Chetty, J. N. Friedman, J. C. Gornick, B. Johnson, and A. Kennickell, eds., *Measuring Distribution and Mobility of Income and Wealth.* Chicago, IL: University of Chicago Press.

Saez, E., and G. Zucman (2016). 'Wealth Inequality in the United States since 1913: Evidence from Capitalized Income Tax Data.' *Quarterly Journal of Economics,* 131(2): 519–578.

Scholz, J. K., A. Seshadri, and S. Khitatrakun (2006). 'Are Americans Saving "Optimally" for Retirement?' *Journal of Political Economy,* 114(4): 607–643.

Smith, M., O. Zidar, and E. Zwick (2021). 'Top Wealth in America: New Estimates and Implications for Taxing the Rich.' NBER Working Paper No. 29374. Cambridge, MA: National Bureau of Economic Research.

Chapter 6

Changes in Retirement Savings during the COVID Pandemic

Elena Derby, Lucas Goodman, Kathleen Mackie, and Jacob Mortenson

The COVID-19 pandemic brought about a fast and severe global economic decline. By the end of March 2020, the US economy had lost over 13 million jobs, compared to 9 million jobs lost during the Great Recession (Cajner et al. 2020). Although some of the effects were mitigated by government interventions—increased unemployment insurance (UI), stimulus checks, government assistance to private entities, and other public assistance—changes in asset prices, employment, and consumption were substantial.

In this chapter, we use tax data to document how retirement savings—specifically, contributions to and withdrawals from tax-preferred savings accounts—changed during the COVID-19 pandemic in comparison to the Great Recession (from 2008 to 2010). Retirement savings behavior might plausibly have been affected both by the pandemic (and related recession) itself, as well as by the policy actions that Congress took in response to the pandemic.

We find little change in individuals' contributions to retirement plans in 2020, which increased from the previous year at a rate in line with recent trends, a stark difference from the drop in contributions that occurred during the 2007–2009 Great Recession (Argento et al. 2015; Goodman et al. 2021). This may have occurred because the effects of the COVID-19 pandemic were disproportionately worse for workers at the bottom of the income distribution, who save at much lower rates than middle- and high-income earners, while the earnings shocks during the Great Recession affected middle- and high-income workers to a greater degree than during COVID-19 (Larrimore et al. 2022). At the same time, we observe in publicly available Form 5500 data that employers reduced contributions to defined contribution (DC) plans.

Elena Derby et al., *Changes in Retirement Savings during the COVID Pandemic.* In: *Real-World Shocks and Retirement System Resiliency.* Edited by: Olivia S. Mitchell, John Sabelhaus, and Stephen P. Utkus, Oxford University Press.
© Pension Research Council (2024). DOI: 10.1093/oso/9780198894131.003.0006

Conversely, retirement plan withdrawal patterns in 2020 were meaningfully different from prior years, falling for older individuals and increasing for younger people. Both patterns were influenced by policy changes that Congress made in response to the pandemic. First, the requirement for older individuals to take certain withdrawals (known as required minimum distributions, or RMDs) was suspended in 2020. We find that people responded to this policy by sharply reducing their withdrawals, much as they did in response to the suspension of those same requirements in 2009. Second, Congress granted broad (but not complete) relief from the 10 percent penalty that applies to most early withdrawals made by individuals under age 59½. Using bunching methods, we find clear evidence that some individuals responded to this policy by taking large withdrawals near the exemption limit (approximately $100,000). Individuals who took such withdrawals were more likely to have experienced business losses and to have unemployment insurance income in 2020. At the same time, we also find that many people (at least, those near age 59½) took withdrawals consistent with the penalty remaining in place.

Our analysis builds on prior research examining the effects of the COVID-19 pandemic—and subsequent federal policy changes—on economic activity. Prior work has examined changes in unemployment and inequality (Bartik et al. 2020; Cajner et al. 2020; Clark et al. 2021; Coibion et al. 2020; Guerrieri et al. 2020), consumer spending (Chetty et al. 2020), and early retirement (Goda et al. 2021; Bui et al. 2020; Davis 2021) during the pandemic. Others have studied the effects of both federal and state government interventions during the pandemic including stay-at-home orders (Forsythe et al. 2020), and federal assistance programs like unemployment insurance and stimulus payments (Baker et al. 2020; Chetty et al. 2020; Larrimore et al. 2022).

We also contribute to the body of work exploring the effect of economic shocks and policy changes on retirement savings. Hurwitz et al. (2021) found that economically-vulnerable individuals are more likely to recommend savings reductions in the response to the onset of COVID. On the topic of RMDs, Brown et al. (2017) showed that the suspension of RMDs in 2009 resulted in a large decrease in withdrawals for TIAA-CREF retirement savings participants, particularly among relatively wealthier individuals with large balances, and those with longer retirement horizons (people closer to the starting age for RMDs). Mortenson et al. (2019) found that 32–52 percent of individuals subject to RMDs would prefer to take a withdrawal below the required minimum, but that even when the RMD is suspended, some individuals take withdrawals at the 'phantom' (i.e., not in effect for that year) RMD threshold. Bershadker and Smith (2005) also estimated, using Current Population Survey (CPS) data, that about 45 percent of individuals with positive account balances did not take withdrawals until they were required to do so by law.

Research exploring the effect of the early withdrawal penalty is sparser than the RMD literature. Goda et al. (2016) measured individuals' responsiveness to the penalty by estimating the increase in withdrawals at the threshold age of 59½, finding that the probability of a withdrawal increased by 93 percent at this age. Stuart and Bryant (2021) similarly documented that early withdrawal penalties (and RMDs) substantially influence timing or withdrawals from retirement accounts. Several studies found that the likelihood of taking early withdrawals increased significantly with negative shocks, including divorce and job loss or wage reduction, the latter of which applies directly to the COVID-19 employment shocks (Argento et al. 2015; Amromin and Smith 2003; Goodman et al. 2021; Brady and Bass 2019). Focusing on the Great Recession, Argento et al. (2015) also reported that contributions to DC plans declined significantly, and Goodman et al. (2021) found that net contributions did not recover their inflation-adjusted 2007 levels until 2014. Both papers also found that early withdrawals increased during the Great Recession, although to a smaller extent than the change in contributions. Goodman et al. (2021) reported that the share of contributions made by working-age Americans who exited the retirement saving system increased modestly during the Great Recession, from a base rate of around 22 percent to 26 percent in 2009.

There has also been a focus on the effects of economic downturns on early retirement. Coile and Levine (2007) reported that economic downturns caused an increase in the percentage of people who decided to retire, equivalent to the effect of a negative health shock or retirement incentives. Neumark and Button (2014) noted that age discrimination was a problem for workers nearing retirement during the Great Recession. However, Goda et al. (2011) found that, during the Great Recession, the probability of retiring early actually went down, which may have been a reaction to stock market conditions at that time. More recently, Coile and Zhang (2024) found that retirements increased during the COVID-19 pandemic, but that this trend was unrelated to economic circumstances and was more likely due to general concerns about health, changes in government policies, or stock market and real estate gains.

However, as Goda et al. (2021) found, despite evidence suggesting that the COVID-19 pandemic caused an increase in early retirements, there was no significant increase in applications for social security benefits. Similarly, Maestas and Mullen (2024) found that the number of Social Security Disability Insurance (SSDI) applicants fell continuously between March 2020 and January 2021, although they also observed that the number of SSDI applications received at field offices began to increase again in 2021. Both papers speculated that the drop in applications may be partially explained by increases in unemployment insurance and the issuance of stimulus checks in 2020, possibly giving individuals some financial flexibility to hold off on claiming SSDI benefits. These studies are in line with our findings, as we do not see an increase in retirement withdrawals for individuals between the ages of 60 and 70.

Background and Policy Changes

Under the Coronavirus Aid, Relief, and Economic Security (CARES) Act of 2020, the rules for distributions and withdrawals from retirement accounts changed in two ways: required minimum distributions were temporarily suspended, and 'coronavirus-related' early withdrawals were exempted from early distribution penalties. There were also changes to rules regarding rollovers, loan limits and repayments, and partial plan terminations, but we omit these from our discussion as they are beyond the scope of our analysis.[1]

In general, owners of IRAs and DC accounts must begin taking withdrawals known as RMDs from their accounts in the year in which they reach age 72. These withdrawals are equal to a specified fraction of their prior-year balance. In the CARES Act, Congress suspended RMDs for calendar year 2020, meaning that no such withdrawals were required during that year.[2] Congress granted similar relief during the Great Recession, suspending RMDs in 2009 (JCT 2020; Topoleski and Myers 2020).

Non-rollover withdrawals from IRAs and DC accounts made prior to age 59½ are generally subject to a 10 percent penalty, in addition to (for traditional, non-Roth accounts) being subject to ordinary income tax at the time of withdrawal. In the CARES Act, Congress created an exception from the early withdrawal penalty for 'coronavirus-related' withdrawals from IRAs or eligible retirement plans (such as employer-provided 401(k) and 403(b) plans). This exception was quite broad: it applied to withdrawals up to $100,000 received by any individual who experienced self-attested economic or health hardships during 2020.[3] The law also permitted the recognition of coronavirus-related withdrawals over three years, rather than at the time of this withdrawal, which provided taxpayers with greater liquidity, allowed them to take advantage of the time value of money, and provided an opportunity to smooth their income and minimize tax payments under a progressive tax schedule. The law additionally permitted individuals to 'recontribute' coronavirus-related withdrawals at any point in 2020, 2021, or 2022, by making contributions back into the distributing account. All such repayments were to be treated as if they were never withdrawn (i.e., there would be no income inclusion).

Data

The data we use to generate the estimates, figures, and tables in this chapter are drawn from administrative tax records in the US. These include data compiled from Form 1040, filed by individual taxpayers, and many information returns filed by third parties including Forms W-2, 1099-R, 1099-SSA, and 5498. The base data are in the form of an unbalanced individual-level panel including 5 percent of all individuals in the US tax population.[4] While the panel is unbalanced, it is representative of the population of taxpayers within each year from 2003–2020. Individuals can enter the panel by immigration, birth, or receiving a tax form, and they can exit the panel by emigration, death, or failing to receive a tax form.[5]

Here we rely most heavily on several pieces of information retrieved from administrative data: date of birth and death from the Social Security Administration's (SSA) DM-1 file, IRA contributions from Form 5498, wages and deferred contributions from Form W-2 (wages), social security benefits from Form 1099-SSA, and retirement distributions from Form 1099-R. All dollar amounts are adjusted to 2020 price levels using chained consumer price index (CPI).

Form 1099-R allows us to distinguish between distributions made from IRAs, Roth IRAs, and workplace pension plans. Yet within the category of workplace pension plans, we are unable to distinguish between distributions made from DC plans and those made from DB plans. Goodman et al. (2021) previously applied an algorithm to classify distributions reported on Form 1099-R as DB or DC based on various factors, but it is unable to classify data from 2020 because it requires several years of 'burn-out' (i.e., the last several years of data are used to classify earlier distributions but cannot be classified themselves). Therefore, when analyzing distributions from workplace pension plans, we combine both types of distributions.

Additionally, for the purpose of calculating contributions made by employers to retirement plans, we make use of publicly available data from Form 5500. All retirement plans covered by ERISA must file Form 5500. The form contains a variety of information including total participants, participants contributions, and employer contributions.[6]

Unless stated otherwise, all dollar values in this chapter are indexed to inflation using the Chained CPI series; we express our findings in 2020 dollars.

Retirement Savings Changes

Contributions. We begin by examining the aggregate amount of contributions made by individuals and employers to employer-sponsored DC accounts and IRAs. The upper panel (Figure 6.1a) displays total contributions, while the bottom panel (Figure 6.1b) indexes each series to one in 2019. The figure shows that, during the Great Recession, contributions of all types fell. For example, employee contributions to DC plans fell

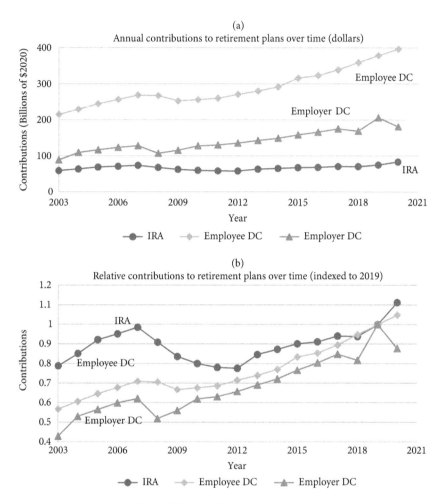

Figure 6.1 Aggregate DC and IRA contributions by year

Notes: This figure plots three series of total contributions to retirement plans. The three series are employee contributions to DC plans, employer contributions to DC plans, and individual contributions to IRAs (excluding rollovers and similar transfers). Panel (a) plots the dollar amounts in billions; Panel (b) plots the same series indexed to one in 2019.

Source: Authors' calculations based on a 5 percent random sample of IRS records derived from tax returns and information returns. All dollar amounts are adjusted to inflation using the chained CPI and expressed in 2020 dollars.

from $269 billion in 2007 to $253 billion in 2009, a 6 percent reduction. Employer contributions fell even more sharply from 2007 to 2008, falling 18 percent from $235 billion to $193 billion. Direct IRA contributions fell from a peak of $73 billion in 2007 to a low of $58 billion in 2012, a 21 percent reduction.[7]

We find significantly different patterns for individual contributions at the onset of the COVID-19 pandemic. Employee contributions to DC plans remained on a steady growth path, growing 5 percent from 2019 to 2020—similar to the yearly growth rates experienced from 2017 onward. In fact, direct IRA contributions by individuals accelerated somewhat, growing 10 percent from 2019 to 2020. Employer contributions, however, fell noticeably, declining by 12 percent from 2019 to 2020.

There are several explanations for the disparate pattern we see during the COVID-19 pandemic in comparison to the Great Recession. First, retirement savings are concentrated in the upper half of the wage income distribution: in 2019, approximately 90 percent of contributions to employer-sponsored DC plans were made by workers in the top two quintiles of the wage distribution. As shown in Larrimore et al. (2022), the labor income shocks of the COVID-19 recession were concentrated in the lower half of the wage earnings distribution relative to the Great Recession, reducing the scope for negative income shocks to affect retirement contributions in the aggregate. At the same time, large firms responsible for the bulk of employer DC contributions received comparatively less direct fiscal support, as they were mostly ineligible for programs such as the Paycheck Protection Program; this may partially explain why employers reduced contributions.[8]

Second, the pandemic and associated closures reduced the marginal utility of consumption, especially in the upper half of the income distribution. As Chetty et. al. (2020) found, consumer spending among those in the bottom quartile of the US income distribution remained about the same after June 2020; however, consumption among those in the top quartile of income dropped by about 13 percent. This reduction in the opportunity cost of contributing to a retirement account made retirement saving relatively more attractive, pushing against any reductions in saving caused by negative labor income shocks. There is no direct analogue of this part of the pandemic experience for employers; thus, this may be a further explanation for the divergence between employee and employer contributions during the pandemic.

To further explore contribution changes, Figure 6.2 displays the time series of employee contributions to DC accounts according to earnings groups (which we define as wage earnings plus unemployment insurance).[9] Specifically, the groups are: (1) the bottom half of the wage distribution; (2) percentiles 51–80; (3) percentiles 81–95; and (4) the top five percentiles. The top panel (Figure 6.2a) plots the dollar amounts, in billions.

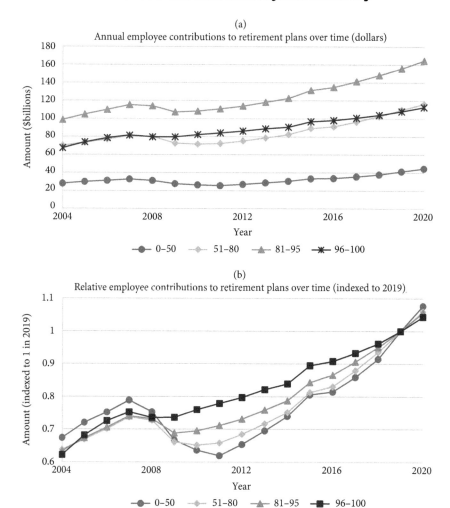

Figure 6.2 Employee DC contributions by income groups

Notes: This figure plots total employee contributions to DC plans in four earnings groups, defined by the sum of current-year wage income and unemployment insurance income. Panel (a) plots the dollar amounts in billions; Panel (b) plots the same series indexed to one in 2019. *Source:* Authors' calculations based on a 5 percent random sample of IRS records derived from tax returns and information returns. All dollar amounts are adjusted to inflation using the chained CPI and expressed in 2020 dollars.

There are large differences in levels between the groups. In 2019, the bottom 50 percentiles were responsible for only 10 percent of total contributions, percentiles 51–80 were responsible for 26 percent, percentiles 81–95 were responsible for 38 percent, and the top 5 percentiles were responsible for 26 percent.

The bottom panel (Figure 6.2b) plots each of these series indexed to the base in 2019. This figure reveals that, during the Great Recession, contributions fell relatively more in lower income groups. In the bottom 50 percentiles, contributions fell by 21 percent from 2007 and 2011; in the top 5 percentiles, contributions fell by only 2 percent from 2007 to 2008 before growing again. The two intermediate income groups had contributions decreases between these two extremes. By contrast, contributions in all incomes groups grew from 2019 to 2020, each at a growth rate broadly in line with growth rates in previous years. It is possible that the substantial fiscal support to low- and middle-income individuals prevented the large decreases in retirement contributions among this group that occurred during the Great Recession.

Of course, stock market conditions differed dramatically between the Great Recession and the COVID-19 pandemic. In October of 2007, the S&P 500 attained a high of 1,565, after which it tumbled over the course of 17 months to achieve a nadir of 677 in March of 2009, before embarking on a steady recovery. It did not revert to its October 2007 value until April 2013. By contrast, the COVID-19 pandemic saw only a very brief downturn. On January 31, 2020, the S&P 500 closed at 3,226, then fell to a low of 2,237 on March 23, 2020, then proceeded to recover rapidly. The market re-attained its January 31, 2020, value by June 8, 2020. Given the well-known recency bias in investment decision-making (Tversky and Kahneman 1973)—especially by retail investors who are responsible for the bulk of retirement savings (Nofsinger and Varma 2013)—the longer bear market during the Great Recession may have had a larger effect on contributions than the V-shaped market during the COVID pandemic.

Withdrawals. Figure 6.3 plots aggregate withdrawals (non-rollover or conversion distributions) from IRAs and employer plans over time. As with Figures 6.1 and 6.2, the top panel (Figure 6.3a) plots the aggregate dollar amounts while the bottom panel (Figure 6.3b) indexes each series to one in 2019. Roughly speaking, both IRA and employer account withdrawals follow a smooth upward trend over time, with IRA distributions generally growing faster. In both 2009 and 2020—years in which RMDs were suspended—there are noticeable reductions in IRA withdrawals. By contrast, in 2020, employer plan withdrawals grew by 10 percent, considerably faster than the 2–4 percent annual growth rates in prior years.

In Figure 6.4, we disaggregate the withdrawal trends in Figure 6.3 for specific time periods, plotting mean withdrawals by age, from 2008 to 2010 (Figures 6.4a and 6.4b), and from 2018 to 2020 (Figures 6.4c and 6.4d). Figure 6.4a shows the change in mean withdrawals from IRAs by age during the Great Recession, from 2008 to 2010. Figure 6.4b does the same for non-IRA

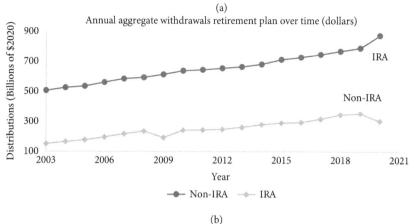

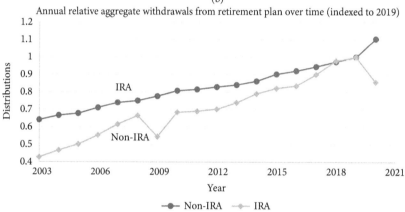

Figure 6.3 IRAs and other retirement withdrawals, by year

Notes: This figure plots a time series of withdrawals from retirement plans. Panel (a) plots the total dollar amount of withdrawals from IRAs and non-IRAs, the latter of which primarily represents employer DC and DB plans. Panel (b) plots the same two series but indexed to a value of one in 2019.

Source: Authors' calculations based on a 5 percent random sample of IRS records derived from tax returns and information returns. All dollar amounts are adjusted to inflation using the chained CPI and expressed in 2020 dollars.

accounts—primarily employer-sponsored DC and DB plans—from 2008 to 2010. Figures 6.4c and 6.4d are analogous figures for the COVID recession, comparing 2018–2019 with 2020.

Several facts emerge. First, withdrawals from IRAs fell substantially in 2009 and 2020 for ages that would otherwise be subject to RMD. Second, we see no large changes in withdrawals in those same years for individuals age 60–70, people relatively unaffected by the major policy changes. Third,

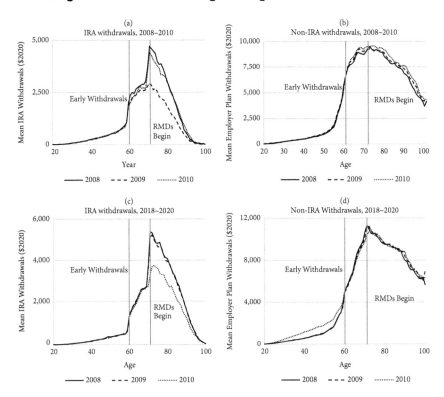

Figure 6.4 Mean withdrawals from IRAs and other retirement accounts, by age

Notes: This figure plots mean withdrawals from IRAs (Panels (a) and (b)) and workplace DC and DB plans (Panels (b) and (d)) as a function of age, separately by year. Withdrawals are derived from Form 1099-R and exclude rollovers and Roth conversions. All dollar amounts are adjusted to 2020 price levels. The sample is representative of all individuals of a given age that appear on a tax return or an information return, including those who do not take a withdrawal.
Source: Authors' calculations based on a 5 percent random sample of IRS records derived from tax returns and information returns. All dollar amounts are adjusted to inflation using the chained CPI and expressed in 2020 dollars.

while withdrawals from workplace DB and DC pension plans remained similar across years during the Great Recession, there is a noticeable increase in early withdrawals for preretirement-age cohorts in 2020 relative to the previous two years.

The effects of the 2020 RMD suspension are consistent with the same 2009 policy change. In Figure 6.5, we graph the mass of withdrawals from IRAs taken by 75-year-olds scaled by their prior year balance, with reference to their RMD (or what the RMD would have been in the absence of the rule suspension).[10] The top panel (Figure 6.5a) plots withdrawal levels in

2009 (line) along with the same withdrawal levels in 2008 (dots), and the bottom panel (Figure 6.5b) plots withdrawal levels in 2020 (line) and 2019 (dots) for comparison. In both cases, there is a substantial shifting of mass from exactly the RMD to zero. Furthermore, there remains some mass at the RMD in 2009 and 2020, potentially reflecting a mix of inertia, a perception of the RMD as 'guidance,' or withdrawals taken during the year prior to the policy change (Brown et al. 2017; Mortenson et al. 2019).

The population near retirement age is also of interest, as there has been concern that the pandemic and related recession induced people to retire earlier than they otherwise would, a concern corroborated by labor force participation data (Davis 2021; Schwartz and Marcos 2021; Van Dam 2021; Hsu 2021). Yet we see no obvious increase in retirement withdrawals for those age 60–70. Furthermore, Goda et al. (2021) showed that the number of applications to file for social security retirement benefits also remained largely unchanged during the pandemic. Thus, there is no evidence of near-retirement age individuals decumulating their retirement wealth—whether in the form of social security, pensions, or IRAs—earlier than they otherwise would have. If the pandemic did cause early retirement, then early retirees would have to be financing their consumption through some other source. Perhaps, as suggested by Goda et al. (2021), increased unemployment insurance and other forms of pandemic assistance allowed some to finance an early retirement without needing to dip into retirement wealth.

The increase in workplace pension withdrawals for those of working age likely reflects both a response to policy changes and direct effects of the pandemic. In Figure 6.6, we plot a time series of the total withdrawals from pensions and IRAs (excluding rollovers, Roth conversions, etc.) and total penalized withdrawals for those below age 59½.[11] While total withdrawals increased by $60 billion (25%) in 2020 for this group, the total amount of penalized distributions fell by nearly 50 percent. Thus, it appears that take-up of the penalty suspension was quite high.

There was a smaller take-up of the CARES Act provision that allowed for the income recognition of withdrawals to be spread over three years. In particular, we see that only 1.5 percent of tax units that took withdrawals from retirement accounts reported taxable pension and IRA amounts, approximately equal to one third of total withdrawals from Form 1099-R. Low take-up rates under this provision suggests that the 'hassle' costs of needing to track this information to subsequent tax returns exceeded the value of the deferral of liability or other tax savings.[12]

There is clear evidence that some preretirement age individuals did respond to a combination of these policies. Recall that the penalty suspension and the three-year recognition rule applied to up to $100,000 of withdrawals for any given individual. Figure 6.7 shows bunching at this threshold in 2020: approximately 165,000 individuals (age 20–58) took a

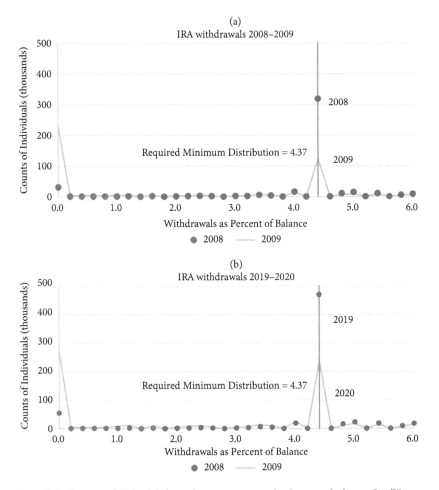

Figure 6.5 Counts of IRA withdrawals as a percent of prior year balance for 75-year-olds

Notes: This figure plots a histogram of IRA withdrawals for 75-year-olds, scaled by prior year IRA balance, separately by year. In each panel, the blue dots represent the series in the years in which RMDs are in effect (2008 and 2019) and the green line represents the series in years in which RMDs have been suspended (2009 and 2020). The vertical line indicates the standard RMD amount for 75-year-olds. Withdrawals are derived from Form 1099-R and exclude rollovers and Roth conversions.

Source: Authors' calculations based on a 5 percent random sample of IRS records derived from tax returns and information returns.

withdrawal within $500 of $100,000, far larger than any nearby bins of the same width. This was not driven by round-number bunching, as we saw no analogous pattern in 2019.[13] Under the extreme assumption that

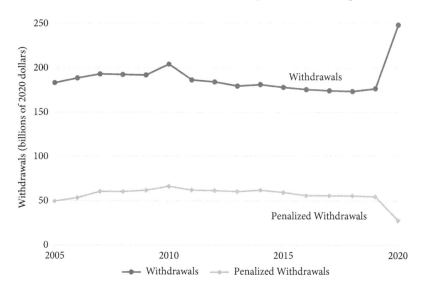

Figure 6.6 Total IRA withdrawals and penalized withdrawals by those under age 59½

Notes: This figure plots withdrawals and (estimated) penalized withdrawals made to tax units with at least one member under age 59½. Withdrawals are derived from Form 1099-R and exclude rollovers and Roth conversions. We estimate penalized withdrawals as equal to the penalty amount on Form 1040 divided by 0.1. All dollar amounts are adjusted to 2020 price levels.

Source: Authors' calculations based on a 5 percent random sample of IRS records derived from tax returns and information returns. All dollar amounts are adjusted to inflation using the chained CPI and expressed in 2020 dollars.

these individuals would not have taken any withdrawals at all in 2020 in the absence of the policy changes, then these bunchers would account for approximately $17 billion of the $65 billion increase in withdrawals from 2019 to 2020 for this age group. We cannot test this assumption directly, but we believe that it is a plausible approximation: only 10 percent of these individuals took a withdrawal of any amount in 2019. Taken together, this suggests that a non-trivial portion of the increase in withdrawals from 2019 to 2020 was driven by policy.

These bunchers could plausibly have been responding to any of the policy changes that applied to coronavirus-related withdrawals. We interpret the bunching mainly to the penalty suspension for two reasons. First, we find that the probability of paying a penalty was substantially lower for those in the bin nearest to $100,000 in withdrawals relative to those in nearby bins. Second, only 7 percent of these bunchers took up the three-year recognition option, using the proxy described above (taxable withdrawals approximately equal to one third of total withdrawals).

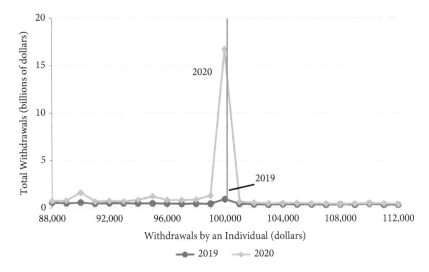

Figure 6.7 Total IRA withdrawals close to a $100,000 threshold, 2019–2020

Notes: This figure plots a histogram of total withdrawals from IRAs and workplace plans made to individuals, broken out by the dollar amount of withdrawals made by an individual. The horizontal axis are thousand-dollar wide bins, and the vertical axis displays the total dollars of withdrawals made within each bin. Withdrawals are measured on Form 1099-R and exclude rollovers and Roth conversions. Only individuals between the ages of 20 and 58 are included. *Source:* Authors' calculations based on a 5 percent random sample of IRS records derived from tax returns and information returns. In this figure, dollar amounts are not adjusted for inflation.

We are particularly interested in the characteristics of those who appeared to be responding to this policy; see Table 6.1. The first column restricts the same to those age 20–58 who took distributions within $500 of $100,000. In column 2, we report the same statistics for the remainder of our 2020 sample within the same age range. In the first row, we find that bunchers had a considerably higher 2019 adjusted gross income (AGI) than average, which is unsurprising given that higher-income individuals are likely to accumulate large retirement account balances. We also find that bunchers were somewhat more likely to have had non-zero business income in 2019, UI income in 2020, and a business loss in 2020. However, bunchers also had a slightly higher wage share of income than the remainder of the sample.

In column 3, we reweight the sample in column 2 within income percentiles to match the 2019 AGI distribution of bunchers (column 1). In this reweighted sample, we can examine whether bunchers differed from others along other dimensions, beyond what can be explained by the fact that

TABLE 6.1 Characteristics of those taking retirement plan distributions close to $100,000 in 2020

	Bunchers	Non-bunchers	Non-bunchers Reweighted
Median AGI in 2019	$129,000	$31,000	$129,000
Share with nonzero business income in 2019	0.199	0.15	0.242
Wage share of income in 2019	0.748	0.71	0.551
Share with UI in 2020	0.232	0.199	0.141
Share with business loss in 2020	0.186	0.063	0.104

Notes: Column 1 reports characteristics of those age 20–58 taking distributions of approximately $100,000 in 2020. Column 2 reports characteristics for all other individuals aged 20–58. In column 3, we report characteristics for the sample in column 2 except that we reweight the sample in order to match the distribution of 2019 AGI of those in column 1. Business income refers to income reported on Schedules C, E, and F. All dollar amounts are adjusted to 2020 price levels.
Source: Authors' calculations based on a 5 percent random sample of IRS records derived from tax returns and information returns. All dollar amounts are adjusted to inflation using the chained CPI and expressed in 2020 dollars.

they were higher earners. We find that bunchers were somewhat less likely than their income-matched peers to have had non-zero business income in 2019, and their wage share of income was much higher. One explanation for this pattern is that retirement savings might be much easier (or a more attractive option for foregone consumption) for wage earners relative to entrepreneurs at a given income level. At the same time, we find that bunchers did appear to experience greater economic distress than their income-matched peers: they were over 60 percent more likely to have UI income and nearly 80 percent more likely to have a business loss, despite being likely to have had non-zero business income in the prior year. This suggests that these bunchers could have used the withdrawals to smooth consumption or provide liquidity to their businesses.

While the evidence on bunching indicates that the relaxation of the early withdrawal penalty played a role in increasing withdrawals in 2020, we also find evidence that many individuals still felt constrained by the penalty, at least to some extent. Following Goda et al. (2016), we examine the probability of taking withdrawals as a function of monthly age in the vicinity of 59½. Consider the series marked with circles (2019) in each panel of Figure 6.8. Individuals indicated with relative age 0 are those who reached age 59½ in January of 2020—they had zero months in 2019 during which to take penalty-free withdrawals. Moving leftward in the graph corresponds to even younger individuals (i.e., who reached age 59½ later in the year) who also had zero penalty-free months in 2019. Moving to the right corresponds to individuals who had more months of penalty-free withdrawals: at relative age 12 months, the entire year was penalty-free. Clearly there were changes in the slope of the probability of taking a non-IRA withdrawal (top panel) or an IRA withdrawal (bottom panel) at relative age 0 and 12 months, suggesting that the probability of taking a non-IRA withdrawal in any given year increased approximately linearly in the number of penalty-free months during that year.

The key empirical test is whether these discontinuous changes in slope were present in 2020 as well. If people perceived the relief for pandemic-related withdrawals as effectively eliminating the penalty for all withdrawals, then there should be no slope change; all individuals would have faced 12 months of penalty-free withdrawals.[14] Yet we see very similar slope changes at 0 and 12 months in 2020 versus 2019. For the non-IRA series, the patterns across the two years are indistinguishable, potentially reflecting measurement error introduced by the fact that both series include DB withdrawals (usually) not subject to the penalty. There is a more noticeable difference in the IRA series: the change in slope in 2020 was statistically significantly smaller than the change in slope in 2019. Yet the difference is modest in magnitude, as the change in slope shrank by only 17 percent.

Figures 6.7 and 6.8 together suggest a nuanced, heterogeneous response to the relief granted to the pandemic-related withdrawals. Figure 6.7 suggests that a select group of about 140,000 people responded to the policy in a sophisticated way, and the behavior of this group was large enough to affect aggregate withdrawals. Meanwhile, Figure 6.8 suggests that most individuals took withdrawals in a manner consistent with the penalty remaining in place, either because they did not deem their distributions to be coronavirus-related (i.e., the penalty would have applied), or because they were unaware of the penalty suspension.

Finally, we note that it is likely that some of the increase in withdrawals by working-age persons in 2020 was not the result of policy, but rather the result of the economic environment. As shown in Goodman et al. (2021), job separation was associated with a substantial increase in the probability of working-age persons taking retirement withdrawals. This could have been caused by the income shock associated with job separation, as well as the choice architecture that often makes withdrawals the default (easiest) option for those with accumulated DC balances in their previous jobs. Thus, the large increase in job separation that occurred in 2020 may have contributed to the increase in withdrawals in this period. In future research, when we are able to observe W-2 data from 2021, necessary for determining whether individuals separated from their employers, we intend to quantify the role of increased job separation on withdrawals in 2020.

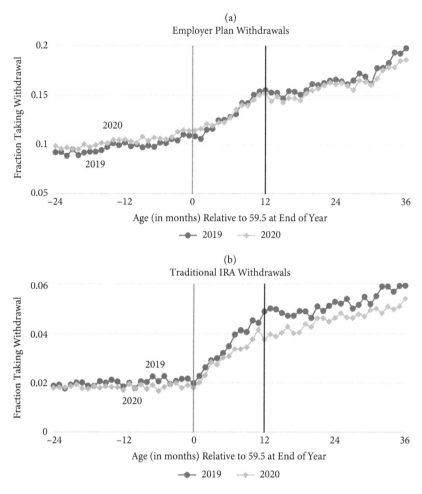

Figure 6.8 Probability of taking retirement plan withdrawals by age, close to age 59½

Notes: This figure plots the mean value of a dummy for taking any withdrawal from a workplace retirement plan (top panel) or IRA (bottom panel) as a function of monthly age, relative to 59½, separately by year. An individual with monthly age one attains 59½ in December of the given year, while an individual with monthly age zero attains 59½ in January of the subsequent year. Withdrawals are derived from Form 1099-R and exclude rollovers and Roth conversions. All dollar amounts are adjusted to 2020 price levels.

Source: Authors' calculations based on a 5 percent random sample of IRS records derived from tax returns and information returns.

Conclusion

The COVID-19 pandemic had many negative consequences that persisted for some time. The sharp increase in unemployment, supply-chain issues, increasing prices, and hesitancy of workers to return to the labor force all produced strains on the economy. Nevertheless, due to the differential impacts of the pandemic across the workforce, aggregate individual contributions to retirement accounts remained largely the same, even increasing beyond what was expected for high-income workers, though contributions by employers did decrease somewhat. Withdrawals by working-age individuals from employer-sponsored retirement accounts did rise substantially during 2020, driven, at least to some extent, by a response to relief granted to certain early withdrawals, including the elimination of the 10 percent early distribution penalty for coronavirus-related reasons. A portion of this increase was also likely driven by the increase in job separations created by the pandemic. Withdrawals from IRAs to those over age 70 dropped precipitously, suggesting a strong response to the suspension of required minimum distribution rules. The source of the asymmetric response in IRAs and employer-sponsored plans to these two policy changes is unclear, but it is likely driven by the co-mingling of DB withdrawals with DC withdrawals in tax data reporting and the age-lifecycle of IRA balances.

In general, the effects of retirement-related policies implemented during the COVID-19 pandemic are ambiguous when it comes to providing relief for people facing financial difficulties, especially in comparison to other targeted policies such as expansions in UI, the Supplemental Nutritional Assistance Program (SNAP), Medicare, and Medicaid. As Moffitt and Ziliak (2024) found, SNAP take-up increased during recessions not only among young, low-income groups but also for older people (particularly for those age 50–61). Moreover, UI claims increased for several groups as well, including the elderly (age 62+) and for the higher-educated. These increases may also help explain why the pandemic did not precipitate a large increase in social security claims (Maestas and Mullen 2024). Similarly, policies directed at lowering costs of health care for those on low income and the elderly have been important, as out-of-pocket medical expenses account for a much larger share of spending in this subpopulation. As Follette and Sheiner (2024) found, changes in Medicare payment policies introduced in the Affordable Care Act (ACA) were also instrumental in slowing the rising cost of health care for older Americans.

Acknowledgments

This research embodies work undertaken for the staff of the Joint Committee on Taxation, but as members of both parties and both houses of

Congress comprise the Joint Committee on Taxation, this work should not be construed to represent the position of any member of the Committee. The views expressed in this chapter are not necessarily those of the US Department of the Treasury. The authors declare that they have no relevant financial interests that relate to the research described in this chapter. The authors thank Thomas Barthold, Edie Brashares, Sally Kwak, Michael Love, and seminar participants at the Penn-Wharton Pension Research Council Online Symposium for helpful comments.

Notes

1. Specifically, the CARES Act allowed plans to increase the section 72(p) loan limit from \$50,000 to \$100,000 for certain loans and allowed plans to elect to suspend certain loan payments. The CARES Act also protected employers from inadvertently generating a 'plan termination' if a large share of its workforce separated from employment.
2. The SECURE Act changed the threshold age from 70.5 to 72. This change would have taken effect in 2020 if Congress had not passed the RMD holiday in the CARES Act.
3. Employers can choose whether to implement these coronavirus-related distribution and loan rules; however, qualified individuals can claim the tax benefits of the coronavirus-related distribution rules even if plan provisions aren't changed (IRS 2022).
4. The tax population—those individuals who appear on a federal income tax return (1040) or information return (e.g., Form W-2)—includes roughly 98% of the Census resident population in each year (Larrimore et al. 2022).
5. These base data have been used in several prior papers (Mortenson et al. 2019; Goodman et al. 2021; Larrimore et al. 2022).
6. For details, see US Department of Labor (nd).
7. Recall that all dollar values in this chapter are indexed to inflation and expressed in 2020 price levels.
8. Large firms did receive relief of various forms, such as the Employee Retention Credit and the ability to carry back tax losses incurred in 2019 or 2020.
9. Wage earnings are defined as box 5 from Form W-2, Medicare Wages.
10. We display the results for 75-year-olds here, but the results are similar for other age groups subject to RMDs.
11. We proxy for penalized distributions, because they are not directly observed in the tax data we use, as retirement-related penalties reported on Form 1040 among people younger than age 59½ divided by 10% (the penalty amount).
12. We currently lack the data to analyze the take-up of the CARES Act provision that allows for subsequent repayment of coronavirus-related withdrawals.
13. We do not inflation-adjust in this figure.
14. Given that the CARES Act passed at the end of March 2020, one might expect a kink at relative age 9 months (i.e., those attaining 59½ around March or April 2020) rather than relative age 12 months. But this should not affect the kink at relative age equal to zero months (i.e., those attaining age 59½ near the end of 2020).

References

Amromin, G. and P. Smith (2003). 'What Explains Early Withdrawals from Retirement Accounts? Evidence from a Panel of Taxpayers.' *National Tax Journal*, 56(3): 595–612.

Argento, R., V. L. Bryant, and J. Sabelhaus (2015). 'Early Withdrawals from Retirement Accounts during the Great Recession.' *Contemporary Economic Policy*, 33(1): 1–16.

Baker, S. R., R. A. Farrokhnia, S. Meyer, M. Pagel, and C. Yannelis (2020). 'Income, Liquidity, and the Consumption Response to the 2020 Economic Stimulus Payments.' NBER Working Paper No. w27097. Cambridge, MA: National Bureau of Economic Research.

Bartik, A. W., M. Bertrand, F. Lin, J. Rothstein, and M. Unrath (2020). 'Measuring the Labor Market at the Onset of the COVID-19 Crisis.' NBER Working Paper No. w27613. Cambridge, MA: National Bureau of Economic Research.

Bershadker, A. and P. A. Smith (2005). 'Cracking Open the Nest Egg: IRA Withdrawals and Retirement Finance.' *Proceedings. Annual Conference on Taxation and Minutes of the Annual Meeting of the National Tax Association*, 98: 73–83.

Brady, P. J. and S. Bass (2019). 'Decoding Retirement: A Detailed Look at Retirement Distributions Reported on Tax Returns.' https://papers.ssrn.com/sol3/papers.cfm?abstract_id=3529682

Brown, J. R., J. Poterba, and D. P. Richardson (2017). 'Do Required Minimum Distribution Rules Matter? The Effect of the 2009 Holiday on Retirement Plan Distributions.' *Journal of Public Economics*, 151: 96–109.

Bui, T. T. M., P. Button, and E. G. Picciotti (2020). 'Early Evidence on the Impact of Coronavirus Disease 2019 (COVID-19) and the Recession on Older Workers.' *Public Policy & Aging Report*, 30(4): 154–159.

Cajner, T., L. D. Crane, R. Decker, A. Hamins-Puertolas, and C. J. Kurz (2020). 'Tracking Labor Market Developments During the Covid-19 Pandemic: A Preliminary Assessment.' Finance and Economics Discussion Series 2020–2030. Washington, DC: Board of Governors of the Federal Reserve System.

Chetty, R., J. N. Friedman, N. Hendren, and M. Stepner (2020). 'How Did COVID-19 and Stabilization Policies Affect Spending and Employment? A New Real-time Economic Tracker Based on Private Sector Data.' NBER Working Paper No. 27431. Cambridge, MA: National Bureau of Economic Research.

Clark, R. L., A. Lusardi, and O. S. Mitchell (2021). 'Financial Fragility During the COVID-19 Pandemic.' *AEA Papers and Proceedings*, 111: 292–296.

Coibion, O., Y. Gorodnichenko, and M. Weber (2020). 'Labor Markets During the COVID-19 Crisis: A Preliminary View.' NBER Working Paper No. 27017. Cambridge, MA: National Bureau of Economic Research.

Coile, C. and H. Zhang (2024). 'Recessions and Retirement: New Evidence from the COVID-19 Pandemic.' In O. S. Mitchell, J. Sabelhaus, and S. Utkus, eds., *Real-World Shocks and Retirement System Resiliency*. Oxford, UK: Oxford University Press, pp. 52–70.

Coile, C. C. and P. B. Levine (2007). 'Labor Market Shocks and Retirement: Do Government Programs Matter?' *Journal of Public Economics*, 91(10): 1902–1919.Davis, O. (2021). 'Employment and Retirement Among Older Workers During the COVID-19 Pandemic.' SCEPA Working Paper 2021-06. New York: Schwartz Center for Economic Policy Analysis (SCEPA), The New School.

Follette, G. and L. Sheiner (2024). 'Retirement Security and Health Costs.' In O. S. Mitchell, J. Sabelhaus, and S. Utkus, eds., *Real-World Shocks and Retirement System Resiliency.* Oxford, UK: Oxford University Press, pp. 180–210.

Forsythe, E., L. B. Kahn, F. Lange, and D. Wiczer (2020). 'Labor Demand in the Time of COVID-19: Evidence From Vacancy Postings and UI Claims.' *Journal of Public Economics* 189: 104–238.

Goda, G. S., E. Jackson, L. H. Nicholas, and S. S. Stith (2021). 'The Impact of Covid-19 on Older Workers' Employment and Social Security Spillovers.' NBER Working Paper No. w29083. Cambridge, MA: National Bureau of Economic Research.

Goda, G. S., D. Jones, and S. Ramnath (2016). 'How Do Distributions from Retirement Accounts Respond to Early Withdrawal Penalties? Evidence from Administrative Tax Returns.' RRC Paper No. NB16-05. Cambridge, MA: National Bureau of Economic Research.

Goda, G. S., J. B. Shoven, and S. N. Slavov (2011). 'What Explains Changes in Retirement Plans During the Great Recession?' *American Economic Review,* 101(3): 29–34.

Goodman, L., K. Mackie, J. Mortenson, and H. R. Schramm (2021). 'The Evolution of Leakage and Retirement Asset Flows in the US.' *National Tax Journal,* 74(3): 689–719.

Guerrieri, V., G. Lorenzoni, L. Straub, and I. Werning (2020). 'Macroeconomic Implications of COVID-19: Can Negative Supply Shocks Cause Demand Shortages?' NBER Working Paper No. 26918. Cambridge, MA: National Bureau of Economic Research.

Hsu, R. (2021). 'These Older Workers Hadn't Planned to Retire So Soon. The Pandemic Sped Things Up.' *National Public Radio,* (updated August 23, 2021) https://www.npr.org/2021/08/23/1028993124/these-older-workers-hadnt-planned-to-retire-so-soon-the-pandemic-sped-things-up.

Hurwitz, A., O. S. Mitchell, and O. Sade (2021). 'Longevity Perceptions and Saving Decisions during the COVID-19 Outbreak: An Experimental Investigation.' *AEA Papers and Proceedings,* 111: 297–301.

Internal Revenue Service (IRS) (2022). 'Coronavirus Relief for Retirement Plans and IRAs.' *Topics in the News* (updated May 31, 2022) https://www.irs.gov/newsroom/coronavirus-relief-for-retirement-plans-and-iras.

The Joint Committee on Taxation (2020). Description of the Tax Provisions of Public Law 116–136, The Coronavirus Aid, Relief, and Economic Security ('CARES') Act. JCX-12R-20. Washington, DC.

Larrimore, J., J. Mortenson, and D. Splinter (2022). 'Earnings Shocks and Stabilization During COVID-19.' *Journal of Public Economics,* 206.

Maestas, N. and K. J. Mullen (2024). 'Economic Conditions, the COVID-19 Pandemic Recession and Implications for Disability Insurance.' In O. S. Mitchell, J. Sabelhaus, and S. Utkus, eds., *Real-World Shocks and Retirement System Resiliency.* Oxford, UK: Oxford University Press, pp. 211–221.

Moffitt, R. A. and J. P. Ziliak (2024). 'The Safety Net Response to the Covid-19 Pandemic Recession and the Older Population.' In O. S. Mitchell, J. Sabelhaus, and S. Utkus, eds., *Real-World Shocks and Retirement System Resiliency.* Oxford, UK: Oxford University Press, pp. 155–179.

Mortenson, J. A., H. R. Schramm, and A. Whitten (2019). 'The Effects of Required Minimum Distribution Rules on Withdrawals from Traditional IRAs.' *National Tax Journal*, 72(3): 507–542.

Neumark, D. and P. Button (2014). 'Did Age Discrimination Protections Help Older Workers Weather the Great Recession?' *Journal of Policy Analysis and Management*, 33(3): 566–601.

Nofsinger, J. R. and A. Varma (2013). 'Availability, Recency, and Sophistication in the Repurchasing Behavior of Retail Investors.' *Journal of Banking & Finance*, 37(7): 2572–2585.

Schwartz, N. D. and C. M. Marcos (2 July 2021). 'They Didn't Expect to Retire Early. The Pandemic Changed Their Plans.' *The New York Times.* July 2: 1.

Stuart, E. and V. Bryant (2021). 'The Impact of Withdrawal Penalties on Retirement Savings.' University of Michigan working paper. http://www-personal.umich.edu/~stuartem/stuart_jmp.pdf

Topoleski, J. J. and E. A. Myers (2020). 'Retirement and Pension Provisions in the Coronavirus Aid, Relief, and Economic Security Act (CARES Act).' *Congressional Research Service: In Focus.* April 1: https://crsreports.congress.gov/product/pdf/IF/IF11482.

Tversky, A. and D. Kahneman (1973). 'Availability: A Heuristic for Judging Frequency and Probability.' *Cognitive Psychology*, 5(2): 207–232.

US Department of Labor, Employee Benefits Security Administration (nd). *Form 5500.* https://www.dol.gov/agencies/ebsa/key-topics/reporting-and-filing/form-5500.

Van Dam, A. (2021). 'The Latest Twist in the "Great Resignation": Retiring but Delaying Social Security.' *The Washington Post.* November 1: https://www.washingtonpost.com/business/2021/11/01/latest-twist-great-resignation-retiring-delaying-social-security/.

Chapter 7

Saving and Wealth Accumulation among Student Loan Borrowers

Implications for Retirement Preparedness

Lisa J. Dettling, Sarena F. Goodman, and Sarah J. Reber

Over the past several decades, student debt has become a large compo-nent of US houschold balance sheets. The implications of this increase for lifecycle wealth accumulation and retirement preparation are ambiguous. Theoretically, the underlying borrowing should support valuable but costly educational investments that potential students otherwise lack the liquidi-ty to make. Even as postsecondary education has increasingly become the norm, the college wage premium has remained substantial and, on aver-age, college graduates enter retirement with more wealth. Still, there are channels through which student borrowers may be left worse off financially. First, there is considerable uncertainty in the labor market return that a giv-en student will see, and the realized return may be insufficient to cover the cost of servicing the debt. Second, the presence of student debt on borrow-ers' balance sheets could constrain other investments, such as purchasing a home or starting a business. This chapter describes the savings of student borrowers over their working years to shed light on whether and where each of these mechanisms dominates, with emphasis on the measurement challenges that must be overcome.

Overview

A nascent student loan literature examines early lifecycle outcomes and illustrates the tension over whether borrowing for education is ultimate-ly helpful or harmful for economic wellbeing. Increased borrowing that results from expanded loan access appears to improve human capital outcomes; for example, Black et al. (2020) found positive effects on edu-cational attainment, earnings, and loan repayment, with little effect on other financial indicators, including homeownership.[1] That said, increased

Lisa J. Dettling, Sarena F. Goodman, and Sarah J. Reber, *Saving and Wealth Accumulation among Student Loan Borrowers*. In: *Real-World Shocks and Retirement System Resiliency*. Edited by: Olivia S. Mitchell, John Sabelhaus, and Stephen P. Utkus, Oxford University Press. © Pension Research Council (2024). DOI: 10.1093/oso/9780198894131.003.0007 borrowing to buffer rising college prices appears to generate some negative downstream effects, such as reduced graduate school enrollment (Chakrabarti et al. 2020) and homeownership (Mezza et al. 2020).

Linking student borrowing to later-life savings and wealth accumulation is difficult, largely due to a lack of data well organized to do so. To date, the best evidence relies on a comparison between otherwise similar young adults around 30 years old based on their student loan borrowing history (Rutledge et al. 2016). The study found that, for those that had borrowed, retirement plan participation was about equal to that of non-borrowers, but balances were lower. Still, early wealth differences need not extend through the lifecycle (e.g., Bottazzi et al. 2015); in particular, at younger ages, retirement contributions are typically low, annual earnings are not well-correlated with lifetime income, and borrowers are still paying down their education debt.

We begin to fill this gap by carefully tracing out student borrowers' lifecycle income and wealth profiles. We analyze two well-known, nationally representative datasets, the Federal Reserve Board's Survey of Consumer Finances (SCF) and the Federal Reserve Bank of New York Consumer Credit Panel/Equifax (CCP/Equifax). The SCF is a triennial survey of US families with rich detail on their current balance sheet, financial characteristics, and demographics. The CCP/Equifax is an administrative panel drawn from the universe of consumer credit records with rich detail on interactions with credit markets and borrowers' age and geography. Both datasets amply cover the increased prevalence of student debt over the past couple of decades; the SCF's core questionnaire has been relatively stable since 1989, with the most recent survey conducted in 2019, and the CCP/Equifax covers student loan debt since the early 2000s.

Our analysis uses the SCF to describe student debt's lifecycle pattern.[2] About half of young families have such debt. This share declines gradually with age, starting when families are in their mid-30s when standard repayment terms typically end. There is some leveling off among families in their 40s and 50s, but at typical retirement ages, a much smaller fraction—no more than 5 percent—hold debt. This general pattern holds when restricting attention to families that have attended college.

Guided by these findings, we compare families with student debt to the general population in four phases of the lifecycle: ages 25–34, 35–44, 45–59, and 60–70. Relative to the population, 60–70-year-olds with student debt display much greater disadvantage than other age groups on measures of education, financial literacy, and family background, and the discrepancy grows when restricting attention to families that attended college. Thus, it appears that families that still have student loan debt at older ages appear to be negatively selected from the population of borrowers. Middle-aged families are not nearly as disadvantaged, but their student loans are much more likely to have financed their children's education rather than their own. Indeed, removing families that are primarily holding others' debt from the lifecycle picture steepens the decline in debt-holding among middle-aged families.

These patterns indicate that families with student loan debt may not be representative of the typical family that financed its education with loans, particularly when families have reached ages at which saving and wealth are more meaningful concepts. To illustrate the central issue, we construct 'naïve' lifecycle wealth profiles, differentiating families in each age group only by their education and whether they currently hold student debt (not whether they *ever* borrowed for education). This analysis indicates that the median wealth of college-educated families with student debt rises anemically with age—well below the trajectory of college-educated families without debt and in lockstep with those that did not attend college.[3] But factoring into this pattern are relatively well-off families paying off their loans earlier in their careers and exiting the population of families with student debt. This compositional shift implies that we cannot reliably measure student borrowers' economic outcomes beyond early-career ages from current student loan debt. That said, one can surmise that families that still have such debt at older ages appear to be no better off financially than those who never went to college.

The remainder of the analysis seeks to understand the long-run economic position of the typical family that financed its education with loans, drawing upon complementary information in each of our datasets. In the SCF, since we cannot observe whether families that lack debt financed their education with loans, we develop a strategy to impute borrowing histories, which we calibrate to cohort-level borrowing rates in historical SCFs. In the CCP/Equifax, we draw on the panel nature of the data and follow individuals who took out loans in their early 20s as they age. Our findings indicate that student loan borrowers follow the earnings, saving, and wealth accumulation trajectories of other college attendees on average. They are also similarly likely to participate in a retirement plan, have similar levels of resources in those plans, and report feeling prepared for retirement. If the alternative for these borrowers was no college, they appear to be much better off financially having borrowed.

Prior Literature

Much public discussion of student debt has centered on its potential harmful impacts on borrowers' future economic wellbeing, due to imperfect information in the higher education market, the ease with which the loans are obtained, and the relative financial naïveté of young adults. This conversation is rarely framed in terms of how student borrowers might have fared in a counterfactual state where they could not borrow at all or could not borrow as much as they did.

Many academic studies have made headway on these questions, and the myriad findings highlight that the circumstances under which borrowing occurs are relevant for its effects on student outcomes, both within and beyond school. Where borrowing is driven by increased access to loans, students generally acquire valuable human capital, which would generally imply improvements in measures of future economic wellbeing, including savings. The best evidence to date for four-year students, who hold the majority of debt, indicates such borrowing leads to increased college completion and higher earnings, with little, if any, negative effects on financial wellbeing later in life (Black et al. 2020).[4] Student borrowers at community colleges experience analogous benefits, although most of the literature has only examined shorter-run educational outcomes (Marx and Turner 2019; Barr et al. 2019; Dunlop 2013; Wiederspan 2016; Denning 2019).[5] Further, when students who have already completed most of college experience increased loan access, they apply the funds toward graduating earlier, housing, and other important lifecycle investments (Denning 2019; Goodman et al. 2021).

Nevertheless, student loan borrowing has been associated with worse outcomes in some contexts, which suggests it could weigh on economic wellbeing. For one, borrowing to buffer price increases appears to negatively affect job choice (Rothstein and Rouse 2011), graduate education (Chakrabarti et al. 2020), entrepreneurship (Krishnan and Wang 2019), and homeownership (Mezza et al. 2020), suggestive of repayment difficulties or credit constraints that might affect saving and investment. Further, students induced to attend for-profit colleges—which tend to serve nontraditional students and offer notoriously low labor market returns (e.g., Cellini and Turner 2019; Darolia et al. 2016; Deming et al. 2012, 2016)— borrow more and see marked increases in default (Armona et al. 2020; Cellini et al. 2020; Goodman and Volz 2020).[6]

A comprehensive review of the student loan literature leaves considerable uncertainty about the implications of the rise in aggregate student debt for longer-term savings and preparation for retirement, with only a handful of studies endeavoring to draw a direct connection. One reason is a lack of data with broad coverage of the population and student loan borrowing histories that extend beyond young adulthood. To a lesser extent, it also reflects the issue that those who borrowed in the past several decades are still relatively young. Studies that have approached this question find evidence of poorer outcomes (e.g., Rutledge et al. 2016; Gicheva and Thompson 2015; Cooper and Wang 2014), but such studies usually suffer from at least one of two measurement issues. The first is that they cannot measure outcomes late enough in a person's life, when the temporary pressure of student debt payments on spending and saving would likely have resolved, and when annual earned income is a better predictor of lifetime earnings. The second is that when analyzing older persons, they condition on the presence of student debt, thereby excluding the experiences of those that have already repaid their student loans. Our analysis attempts to overcome these two issues.

There is also a small but growing literature on the nexus between consumer debt and retirement preparation. Brown et al. (2020) document that the likelihood that older families hold debt has been increasing in recent decades, suggesting understanding this connection could grow in importance. Lusardi et al. (2018) show that holding debt at older ages is related to behavioral biases and a lack of financial literacy, which they argue are likely to be correlated with inadequate retirement preparation. Still, Butrica and Karamcheva (2013, 2018) examine how holding debt at older ages affects the timing of retirement and benefit-claiming behavior, and they find that those with debt work longer and claim social security later, which could offset any negative effects of debt on income during retirement. To our knowledge, this literature does not directly engage on whether debt-financed investments—including, of course, education but also home, business, or vehicle purchases—which could help build wealth or improve labor market opportunities, ultimately aid or detract from retirement preparation.[7]

Background

Key facts about student loans. At $1.6 trillion, US federal student loan debt is the largest source of non-housing debt on households' balance sheets. A majority of these loans were originated under one of two federal lending programs established under Title IV of the Higher Education Act of 1965—the Federal Direct Loan (DL) Program and the (now-defunct) Federal Family Education Loan (FFEL) Program—which grew markedly over time.[8] Adjusting for inflation, the federal programs lent $7.5 billion in 1970–1971 and $94.1 billion in 2018–2019 (Ma and Pender 2021).

About one half of US undergraduates rely on loans to help finance their education.[9] Undergraduate Stafford Loans, the main loan type offered through the DL and FFEL programs, feature standardized terms and a congressionally-set interest rate.[10] Unlike other forms of credit, Stafford Loans can be made to any student who meets the basic eligibility criteria for federal financial aid, even those with thin or adverse credit histories.[11]

Federal student loan programs also exist for graduate and parent borrowers, with the principal differences being that they are not subsidized, they are not subject to the statutory limits, and credit history is relevant for eligibility. These programs have grown in importance over time, with each accounting for around 5 percent of non-consolidated federal student debt in 2021.[12] Our analysis attempts to distinguish borrowing under the parent program. Much of the increase in graduate debt, which we cannot distinguish, is held by students taking out both graduate and undergraduate loans (Looney and Yannelis 2015).

The standard repayment period for a federal student loan is 10 years, beginning in the year after a borrower graduates or leaves college. Thus, a traditional student who begins college immediately after high school and earns a degree in four (six) years is expected to fully repay the loan at around 33 (35) years old. Federal student loan borrowers may enter into alternative repayment plans under certain conditions, in which case the repayment period can be longer. For example, low-income borrowers may be eligible for an income-driven repayment (IDR) plan with either a 20- or 25-year term, reduced payments, and potential loan forgiveness for the remaining balance at the end of the term.

Reflecting the fact that human capital cannot serve as collateral, nonpayment of student loan debt entails different consequences than other types of consumer debt. After 270 days of nonpayment, a federal student loan is in default, and overdue payments can be withheld from tax refunds, federal benefits, and/or wages. It is also relatively difficult to discharge federal student loans in bankruptcy, as it requires a separate proceeding with more stringent hardship rules.

Figure 7.1 plots average college attendance and borrowing rates by birth year in the 1989–2019 SCFs. Although borrowing for college has become more prevalent over time, college students in older cohorts often took student loans as well. Indeed, 17 percent of all families born between 1958 and 1962 borrowed, compared with 43 percent of those born from 1991 to 1995. A large share of the increase—30 percent—reflects increased college attendance; nonetheless, the majority is due to increased reliance on loans to pay for college.

Individual saving and the US retirement system. Over the past 40 years, the US retirement system has changed markedly, with the burden and risk of retirement saving moving from the employer to the individual.[13] Following the introduction of the 401(k) plan in 1978, employers have increasingly replaced traditional defined benefit (DB) pensions with defined contribution (DC) plans (Jacobs et al. 2020).[14] DC plans allow the employee to accumulate tax-advantaged retirement savings in an individual account, typically funded by a combination of employee and employer contributions.[15] With DC plans it is generally the employee's responsibility to choose the level of contributions and the investment mix which will determine the level of benefits the employee will be able to access in retirement and how

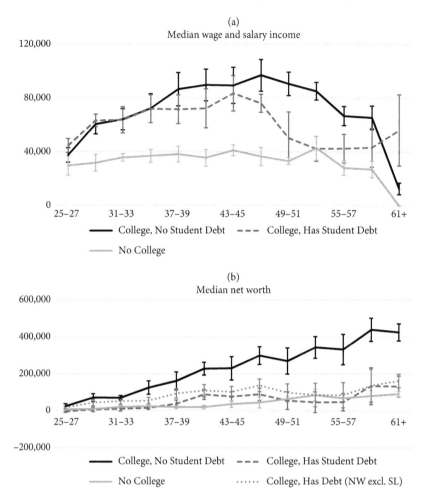

Figure 7.1 Income and wealth by current student debt-holding status and education

Note: Panel (a) plots the median annual salary and wage income and Panel (b) plots the median net worth of families based on their education and own student loan debt status by age of the household reference person. College-educated refers to families in which the reference person attended at least some college, and own student debt refers to families with student loan debt whose largest student loan financed the respondent's (or their partner's) education. The dotted line in Panel (b) excludes student loan debt from net worth.

Source: Authors' calculations from 2016 and 2019 SCF.

long those benefits will last. By contrast, DB plans provided a steady stream of guaranteed benefits in retirement, and it was the employer's responsibility to ensure the plan is sufficiently funded to pay the employee some promised benefit.[16] In addition to DC plans, individuals can save in tax-preferred individual retirement accounts (IRAs).[17] IRAs are generally not connected to a job like a DC plan, but most IRAs are funded by assets rolled over from DC plans when individuals change jobs or retire. As with a DC plan, the individual is responsible for determining contribution levels and how funds are invested.

In addition to savings held in tax-preferred, quasi-liquid retirement accounts (e.g., DC plans, IRAs), many families also plan to support their retirement consumption with other types of assets. Financial assets include those that are highly liquid such as checking and savings accounts, as well as those held in investment accounts, directly-held stocks, bonds, and mutual funds. Nonfinancial assets—such as real estate or closely-held business—are generally illiquid but may still generate income or can otherwise be sold or borrowed against. Of note, the most commonly held nonfinancial asset and largest component of most Americans' net worth is a primary residence. In addition to direct channels through which owning a house might support retirement consumption—for instance, via its sale (if a family downsizes), or a reverse mortgage—it also enables families to divert spending that would otherwise go toward housing to other areas.

Data and Measurement

The Survey of Consumer Finances. Our primary data source is the SCF, a nationally representative, cross-sectional survey of US families produced triennially by the Federal Reserve Board that collects detailed information on their balance sheets, pensions, income, and demographic characteristics.[18] The SCF provides highly reliable statistics on debt and assets broadly distributed in the population, as well as those concentrated in the high end of the wealth distribution. To accomplish this, it employs a two-part sample design—a geographically-based random sample and an oversample of higher wealth families—with weights that combine the two samples to describe the full population (Bhutta et al. 2020). Consistent questionnaire design and methodology from 1989 to 2019 allow meaningful analysis over time.

Central to our analysis, the SCF asks respondents their educational attainment and whether their family has student loan debt. Regarding student loan debt, the SCF collects information on balance, age, and repayment status (on schedule, behind schedule, forbearance, etc.), among other details. The 2016 and 2019 waves of the SCF also included several key questions, including for whose education the debt was obtained, allowing for a distinction between debt that financed one's own or one's partner's education ('own student debt') and debt that financed someone else's education, including children's. They also added questions on parental education, which we use as a proxy for childhood circumstances. Due to the importance of these questions, the analysis here mainly draws from the 2016 and

2019 surveys. Where possible, we supplement the analysis with the larger history and greater statistical power afforded by the 1989–2019 surveys. All dollar values are expressed in 2019 dollars.

The SCF contains a number of quantitative and qualitative measures of saving behavior, wealth accumulation, and overall financial wellbeing which allow for a broad perspective on retirement preparation.[19] To measure wealth, we use SCF's measure of net worth: the difference between a family's gross assets and their liabilities. Due to their importance for retirement, we examine participation in employer-sponsored retirement plans, including both DB and DC plans. We also examine other measures of financial wellbeing and saving behavior, including wage and salary earnings. To study savings in assets earmarked for retirement, we examine the balances of quasi-liquid retirement accounts, including IRAs and employer-sponsored defined contribution (DC) retirement accounts (e.g., 401(k)-type accounts).[20] We also consider other asset classes of interest, such as housing equity.

While these features of the SCF make it well-suited to analyze how the presence of student loan debt interacts with retirement preparedness, the survey is not without shortcomings. Most importantly for this analysis, the SCF does not measure student loan borrowing history for families that do not currently have student loan debt, which we will show is an important impediment to understanding whether the later-life economic wellbeing of families that borrowed for education differs from those that did not. Also, the SCF does not capture the entirety of aggregate student loan balances (Dettling et al. 2015; Appendix Table A1).[21] Because its sampling frame is household-based, it omits student loan debt held b those in institutional settings (e.g., dormitories). In addition, the SCF does not collect detailed balance sheet information for roommates or live-in relatives, including children, who are financially independent of the respondent, so any student loan debt held by such individuals will be omitted. As a result, our analysis will understate the prevalence of student loan debt, especially among younger families, and it will likely also somewhat overstate the financial wellbeing of those that borrowed for college.[22]

Our analytical choices strive for consistency in the unit of observation, but several key questions—such as race, ethnicity, and financial literacy—are asked only of the respondent, while others—such as employment, pensions, and educational attainment—are asked only of the respondent and spouse or partner. Further, for simplicity, our analysis differentiates families by age and educational attainment using characteristics of the family reference person.[23] Any family in which the reference person attended college, even if they did not obtain a degree, is considered college-educated.

Description of CCP/Equifax data. We supplement the SCF findings with an extract of consumer credit records from the Federal Reserve Bank of New

York Consumer Credit Panel/Equifax (CCP/Equifax). The CCP/Equifax is an individual-level panel dataset of consumer credit reports obtained from Equifax—one of the three main credit bureaus in the US—formed from a 5 percent random sample of all US consumers with credit histories. The data are reported quarterly and include detailed information drawn from credit reports, including loan balances and payment status on mortgages, credit cards, student loans, auto loans, and other miscellaneous debt, as well as year of birth.[24] We exploit the panel nature of the CCP/Equifax to follow student loan borrowers and non-borrowers over time. We treat June 2003–June 2007 as the origin and start by restricting the sample to individuals who established a credit record in that period and were between 17 and 20 years old.[25] Our final sample includes over 180,000 borrowers.

We classify these borrowers according to their educational borrowing. In particular, we distinguish between individuals who originated a student loan around the time they established their record and those who did not.[26] We refer to the former group as student borrowers, and the latter as non-student borrowers.[27] Because the dataset does not have information on educational attainment or enrollment, our non-borrower sample will include those who did not attend college and those who attended college but did not borrow. Thus, we further partition the student borrower sample into two groups based on initial borrowing, specifically, whether a student borrower's first academic year of student borrowing was above or below the median for that year. Following analogous logic to our choice to compare college attendees who did and did not borrow in the SCF, this focus helps us draw comparisons between types of people who are similar except for their level of borrowing. Within-cohort differences in borrowing primarily reflect unmet financial need to cover educational expenses (accounting for grants and own resources), the cost of the school, and individual preferences over borrowing and working during school, and thus offer insight into distributional differences.

We follow these cohorts for up to 16 years from when they are first observed in the data—when they would be between 33 and 36 years old—and analyze credit attributes that measure financial wellbeing, including student loan balances, combined credit card limit (a proxy for income), and presence of a mortgage (a proxy for homeownership).[28]

Analysis

General trends. Figure 7.2, panel a plots student debt's implied lifecycle profile, both for all families (unconditional) and restricting to those that have attended college. The figure includes averages computed from the 2016 and 2019 SCFs, as well as from those spanning the 1989–2019 period.

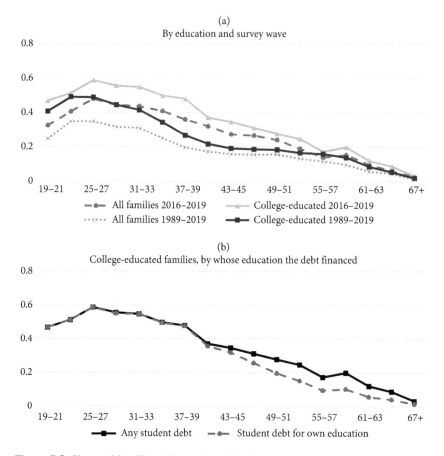

Figure 7.2 Share of families with student debt by age

Note: This figure plots the share of families with student loan debt by age-group of the reference person. Panel (a) plots the share of families with student loan debt by their level of education, where college-educated refers to families in which the reference person attended at least some college. Panel (b) plots the share of college-educated families with student loan debt, according to whether the largest loan financed the respondent (or partner's) education or anyone in the household.

Source: Authors' calculations from 1989–2019 SCF.

There is a clear pattern. Among all households, younger families are much more likely to have student debt, and there is a relatively steady decline as families age, such that only a small fraction of families—less than 5 percent—have student debt during typical retirement ages. This pattern remains after restricting to families that have attended college, but unsurprisingly, such families are more likely to have debt. That said, differences based on education disappear when families are in their 60s, suggesting that the debt held by older families largely finances someone else's education.

Comparing statistics generated from the more recent surveys to those from the full series produces several insights into the time series of student loan borrowing. One, focusing on the youngest families, the propensity to have student debt is quite similar whether one considers the shorter or longer horizon, especially among those that attended college, suggesting conditional borrowing rates are somewhat stable over the full 30-year time series. Second, in the longer time series, the decline in the propensity to have debt begins at younger ages, and there is a more obvious plateau over the 40s and 50s. This likely reflects several interacting phenomena occurring in more recent years (e.g., longer repayment terms owing to expanded availability of and enrollment in alternative repayment programs; increased amount of debt, conditional on borrowing; increased borrowing by graduate students; and increased repayment difficulties). The wedge between the two different time horizons becomes almost negligible once families are in their mid-50s and is, on average, smaller for families who have attended college. Finally, the key takeaway is that the reduced propensity to have debt with age is not exclusively an artifact of cohort differences, as the pattern holds over the full time series. A considerable share of student borrowers paid off these loans by their mid-40s, and most did by their mid-50s.

Driven by these findings, we describe characteristics of families with student debt over different phases of the lifecycle using the 2016 and 2019 surveys. We group families into four age groups: early-career (25–34-year-olds), mid-career (35–44-year-olds), late-career (45–59-year-olds), and near- (or at) retirement (60–70-year-olds). Table 7.1 describes the prevalence of student debt and college attendance among families in these groups and illustrates some unsurprising patterns. About half of early-career families have student debt, and families who went to college are more likely to have student debt. Both college attendance and student debt rates are lower for older segments of the sample, but the decline in student debt is much more marked.

Table 7.2, Panel a characterizes families with student debt in each of these age groups. About one-fifth of families with student debt are Black (non-Hispanic), and just under one-third received or expect an inheritance. These figures are fairly stable across phases of the lifecycle. Older families with debt are more likely than younger families to have served in the military and to come from a less-educated family. They are less likely to have a graduate degree, but a greater share are financially literate.[29]

These comparisons mask cohort differences and/or natural lifecycle progressions. For example, financial literacy improves with experience. To adjust for these factors, Table 7.2, panel b characterizes the different age groups in the general population and Table 7.2, panel d characterizes different age groups of college-educated families. The differences between the corresponding rows in panels a versus b and panels c versus

TABLE 7.1 Student debt and college attendance by age group

	Has student debt	Has student debt for own education	Attended college
All families			
25–34	0.45	0.45	0.69
35–44	0.34	0.33	0.66
45–59	0.20	0.13	0.63
60–70	0.07	0.03	0.62
Families that attended college			
25–34	0.55	0.55	
35–44	0.42	0.41	
45–59	0.25	0.17	
60–70	0.09	0.04	

Notes: Table displays means rates of student debt-holding and college attendance by age group. College attendance refers to families in which the reference person attended at least some college, and own student debt refers to
families with student loan debt whose largest student loan financed the respondent's (or their partner's) education.
Source: Authors' calculations, 2016 and 2019 SCF.

d indicate the degree to which families with debt in each age group are
differentially selected from each population, and whether selection varies
by age.

Through this lens, we see financial literacy improves more over the lifecycle for the overall population than among families with student debt,
leading to a wider gap in financial literacy between the indebted population and the general population for the near-retirement families than
early-career families. We see similar differences for each of the characteristics considered, with near-retirement families who have debt appearing to
be a particularly disadvantaged group with respect to family background
when we restrict the sample to college attendees. These findings echo those
in Lusardi et al. (2018), which found that those experiencing financial distress near retirement have similar traits. This is relevant for policy in that
families still holding student debt as they approach retirement are mea-
surably worse off along observable dimensions than the typical family who
relied on student loans to finance education. Older families with student
debt may benefit from targeted policies, but their experience is not gener-
alizable to the entirety of student borrowers, many of whom will no longer
have debt at retirement.

Table 7.1 also reveals that the gap in the likelihood that a family's student
debt was for their own education widens with age. Among the young-career
families, nearly all families with student loan debt acquired it for their own
education, whereas many of the late-career families with student loan debt
acquired it for another person's education (e.g., their children). Figure 7.1,
panel b plots the lifecycle profile of 'own' student debt and of any student

TABLE 7.2 Characteristics of families, by presence of student debt

	Received or expects an inheritance	Military service	Black (non-Hispanic)	White (non-Hispanic)	Financial literacy	Graduate degree receipt	Mother high school dropout
				All families			
A. With student debt							
25–34	0.26	0.07	0.20	0.58	0.40	0.04	0.12
35–44	0.29	0.10	0.21	0.61	0.44	0.06	0.13
45–59	0.26	0.17	0.22	0.58	0.48	0.04	0.22
60–70	0.38	0.18	0.23	0.57	0.54	0.07	0.29
B. All							
25–34	0.26	0.08	0.17	0.55	0.37	0.02	0.16
35–44	0.25	0.09	0.16	0.56	0.42	0.04	0.20
45–59	0.30	0.14	0.15	0.63	0.47	0.04	0.26
60–70	0.39	0.21	0.14	0.71	0.48	0.05	0.33
				College-educated families			
C. With student debt							
25–34	0.27	0.07	0.19	0.59	0.43	0.04	0.10
35–44	0.30	0.11	0.22	0.62	0.47	0.07	0.11
45–59	0.30	0.18	0.21	0.61	0.54	0.05	0.18
60–70	0.41	0.21	0.22	0.60	0.57	0.09	0.25
D. All							
25–34	0.29	0.09	0.15	0.60	0.45	0.03	0.10
35–44	0.29	0.11	0.16	0.62	0.51	0.07	0.12
45–59	0.36	0.15	0.14	0.69	0.57	0.06	0.18
60–70	0.47	0.23	0.11	0.77	0.60	0.08	0.22

Notes: Table displays means of various characteristics of SCF respondents.
Source: Authors' calculations, 2016–2019 SCF.

debt for families who have attended college. The decline in student debt with age is steeper when restricting attention to one's own debt, indicating that in Figure 7.2, panel a, new parent borrowing masks families continuing to steadily pay off their own student loans, particularly at late-career ages. The remainder of the analysis aims to compare saving and student loan debt between those that financed their own education with loans and those that did not.

Descriptions of the economic positions of those with student debt at various segments of the lifecycle, including older ages, can be useful, yet they do not necessarily inform the broader debate about whether financing education with loans is ultimately helpful or harmful. To illustrate the central issue, Figure 7.2 plots median income and median wealth by age for families with student debt who went to college, families without student debt who went to college, and families who did not go to college. Annual earned income for the typical college-educated family with student debt tracks that for the typical college-educated family without student debt until families are in their late 30s. This is precisely the same age where we start to see a drop-off in the share of families with student debt. Without accounting for the notable share of families that have paid off their debt, we might erroneously conclude that at early-saving ages (i.e., mid-30s), wages of student loan borrowers are not keeping up with those of their peers. This gap grows with age, as more families pay off their debt, so those who do not are increasingly negatively selected. By late-career ages, the wages of the typical college-educated family with student debt are essentially the same as families who did not go to college.

The conclusion is even more striking when considering wealth, as families who went to college and do not have debt have increasingly more wealth with age than families with debt and families that did not go to college. In fact, the naïve wealth profile is essentially the same for those with debt and those who did not go to college. An erroneous interpretation of this picture, without considering the dynamics behind it, is that families who borrowed for college accumulate wealth anemically relative to their college-educated peers who did not borrow, and from a wealth perspective, they are no better off than those who never went to college.

What generates this pattern? We already have insight from the companion discussion of earnings that student loan borrowers paying off their loans distort comparisons beyond mid-career ages, but what is happening at early-career ages when the share of families with loans is stable? First, wealth, by definition, nets any student debt the family has, so all else being equal, early-career student debtors will mechanically have less wealth than those who attended college without borrowing, even if they have similar earnings (as they do). Indeed, the dotted line in Figure 7.2, panel b plots median wealth for those with debt, excluding student loan debt, and the line better tracks college-educated families without debt through the early-career phase. Further, families with student loan debt must spend some of their earned income servicing their debt and are thus less able to save, which likely exacerbates early differences in wealth. It is quite possible that once the student loan debt is paid off, those who borrowed can save more of their earnings, and their wealth accumulation will rise. In Figure 7.2, such families would be included in the calculation of median wealth for those who went to college and do not have debt.

This exercise tells us two things. First, college attendees who still hold student loan debt around retirement are no better off than their peers who did not go to college. The small share of families in this category appear not to have experienced the typical wage boost associated with a college education that would enable them to repay their debt and save, leaving them relatively ill-prepared for retirement. Second, it illustrates the importance of properly accounting for the many borrowers who successfully pay off their student loans in understanding the implications of student loan borrowing for economic wellbeing. The attrition of these borrowers from the set of families with student loan debt, coupled with the increased negative selection with age evidenced in Table 7.2, distorts comparisons that rely on the observation of current debt alone.

Imputing student loan borrowing history from the SCF. Key indicators of economic wellbeing and retirement preparation, such as wealth, lifetime income, and saving behavior, are best measured at ages when many families who borrowed to finance their education would have already paid off their loans. Thus, to be able to examine how the typical family who took student loans fares on these dimensions within the SCF, we need to identify families who paid off their loans.

To do this systematically, we develop an algorithm that imputes families' student loan borrowing histories from their observable characteristics. We first predict the likelihood that families in the 2016 and 2019 SCFs borrowed for college, $\hat{\rho}$, using the observed relationship between own student loan debt and family characteristics among 24–30-year-old families. Families in this age range are unlikely to have paid off their debt or to have acquired debt for others, as their student debt rates are stable, high, and coincide with own student debt rates. The family characteristics in the prediction equation are either fully predetermined or at least minimally likely to change beyond 24 years old.[30] Families with $\hat{\rho}$ above some threshold, $\bar{\rho}$, are classified as student loan borrowers and those below it as non-borrowers.

We calibrate the threshold, $\bar{\rho}$, to cohort borrowing rates derived from the longer 1989–2019 SCF time series, focusing on college-educated families for maximum comparability. These 'true' rates are obtained by stacking 24–30-year-old, college-educated families—an age range over which, if the family had borrowed for college, they would still likely have student loan debt—from these 11 surveys and calculating the share with student debt by birth year. The oldest cohort in the calibration is 57 years old in the 2019 SCF; thus, the imputation cannot accommodate older age groups.[31] Beginning with 0.500, we increment by 0.025 and select the threshold that minimizes the mean squared difference between the imputed rates and truth, which is 0.550.

Figure 7.3 graphs the correspondence between the imputed cohort borrowing rates and those implied by the 1989–2019 SCFs, expressed in 2019 age. For comparison, the figure also includes imputed rates using neighboring thresholds. The imputation does reasonably well approximating truth, especially for younger cohorts. That said, while both series trend downward with age, the imputation does so more gradually and, as a result, modestly overstates borrowing rates for older cohorts. Importantly, the steep decline with age that emerged when relying exclusively on the observation of debt is not visible in the imputation.

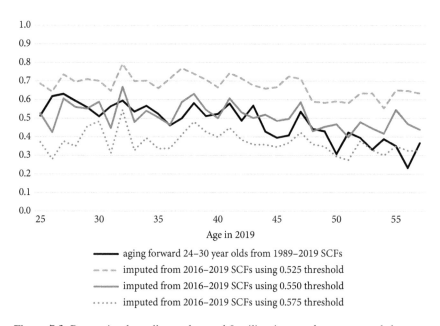

——— aging forward 24–30 year olds from 1989–2019 SCFs
- - - imputed from 2016–2019 SCFs using 0.525 threshold
——— imputed from 2016–2019 SCFs using 0.550 threshold
· · · · · · imputed from 2016–2019 SCFs using 0.575 threshold

Figure 7.3 Borrowing by college-educated families: imputed versus actual share

Notes: This figure plots student loan borrowing rates for college-educated families in the SCF by 2019 age, derived by averaging borrowing rates by cohort among 24–30-year-old families in the 1989–2019 SCFs or by the imputation described in the text. For the imputation, the solid line denotes the best-fit threshold used in the analysis and the dashed and dotted lines denote the two next-best-fit thresholds. College-educated refers to families in which the reference person attended at least some college.
Source: Authors' calculations, 1989–2019 SCF.

While the calibration reduces concerns that our imputation is far from the truth, we note two less-desirable properties. First, our prediction equation does not explain all of the variation in own student loan debt among 24–30-year-old families—just over 13 percent. Second, the imputation assumes that the relationship between a family's observed characteristics and borrowing history is roughly stable across cohorts. This assumption may not hold if, for example, our prediction equation is missing important independently-predictive characteristics (e.g., parental wealth) or if families, conditional on these characteristics, have become more reliant on student loans over time, which based on the calibration appears likely to be at least somewhat true.

Comparisons between student loan borrowers and non-borrowers. Figure 7.4 plots various economic indicators of interest for college-educated families based on their imputed borrowing histories, grouped in three-year age bins. In each case, we plot both the mean or median of the variable and accompanying 95 percent confidence intervals, where the standard errors were adjusted to account for both multiple imputation and sampling variability (Bricker et al. 2015).[32]

Annual income from wages and salaries for the typical student loan borrower roughly coincides with that for the typical non-student loan borrower for all ages and is modestly higher in most instances (Figure 7.4, panel a). Importantly, there is no meaningful divergence with age.

What we see for wealth reflects the similar patterns for income (Figure 7.4, panel b). In general, wealth accumulates at similar rates for the typical borrower and the typical non-borrower. At younger ages, median wealth among borrowers is slightly lower than for non-borrowers, which at least partially reflects differences in student loan debt.[33] These differences accumulate somewhat over the lifecycle, with the gap between borrowers and non-borrowers growing over mid-career ages; nonetheless, the gap disappears by late-career ages. At all ages, the confidence intervals between the two groups overlap.

If we include an estimate for the value of DB pension assets, it raises wealth and steepens implied accumulation over the lifecycle for both groups (Dettling et al. 2022). That said, the gap at mid-career ages widens, which is consistent with findings that student borrowers are less likely to enter public sector jobs (Rothstein and Rouse 2011), where DB plans are more commonly offered, and indicates that retirement consequences of student loan borrowing can emerge through features of jobs beyond earnings.

Focusing on retirement plans, there is little distinction between borrower and non-borrower families in terms of their likelihood of participating in an employer-sponsored retirement plan (Figure 7.4, panel c).[34] Thus the findings from Rutledge et al. (2016) appear to extend to later ages. There is some evidence that borrowers have more savings in a quasi-liquid retirement

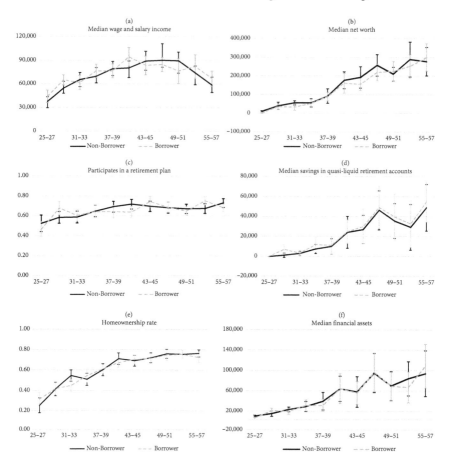

Figure 7.4 Wealth and retirement preparation for college-educated families, by imputed student borrower status

Notes: This figure plots various economic indicators for college-educated families by imputed student loan borrowing history and age of the household reference person in three-year age bins. College-educated refers to families in which the reference person attended at least some college. Bars indicate 95 percent confidence intervals.
Source: Authors' calculations from 2016 and 2019 SCF.

account like a 401(k) or IRA (Figure 7.4, panel d), but the differences are tiny and confidence intervals overlap.

Turning to other types of assets and portfolio allocation decisions, median financial assets are similar between borrowers and non-borrowers (Figure 7.4, panel e).[35] Homeownership rates are also similar between borrowers and non-borrowers (Figure 7.4, panel f). Similar homeownership between borrowers and non-borrowers is consistent with findings in Black et al. (2020) and from the CCP/Equifax (shown in the next section). All in all, the imputed lifecycle comparisons imply that income and wealth follow similar trajectories for college-educated borrowers and non-borrowers, and differences in any given indicator are quite minimal. Together with evidence from Figure 7.4, the analysis suggests borrowers would be financially worse off forgoing the education that borrowing afforded them.

Evidence from the CCP/Equifax. An important limitation in using the SCF to study lifecycle outcomes is that the time series is formed from repeated cross-sections rather than observing the same individuals over time. To try to disentangle cohort differences from true lifecycle differences, we turn to the CCP/Equifax, which offers a shorter time series but allows us to corroborate our earlier findings for several key outcomes as well as offer insight into distributional considerations. Figure 7.5 graphs: (a) average student loan balances; (b) average credit card limits; and (c) proportion with a mortgage by years since college entry.[36] These outcomes are plotted for three groups based on their initial level of student loan borrowing: those with above-median borrowing, those with below-median borrowing, and those with no borrowing.

Figure 7.5, panel a plots average student loan balances.[37] By construction, the non-borrowers have an average balance of zero throughout, while above-median borrowers initially have a higher average balance than below-median borrowers. Throughout the analysis horizon, these initial differences persist, but the slopes change over time. Average balances among above-median borrowers grow quickly over the first decade and decline thereafter (at about age 27–30), whereas average balances among below-median borrowers grow less quickly over the first decade and stabilize thereafter. In other words, above-median borrowers eventually start to pay off their debt at a faster rate than below-median borrowers, suggesting that increased borrowing is associated with higher returns to education that better permit borrowers to pay down their principals. This interpretation is consistent with Black et al. (2020).

Panel b of Figure 7.5 plots average credit card limits, a proxy for income. Initially, average limits exhibit similar levels and growth rates for all three groups, reflecting lengthening credit records. Over time, average limits among above-median borrowers exhibit more growth than the other two groups, so that by 15 years out, their average limits are well above those of the other two groups, which remain fairly similar to one another. Consistent with panel a, this pattern suggests that above-median borrowers see increased returns. Finally, panel c plots the share of each group that has a mortgage, a proxy for homeownership. Homeownership rates grow over time for all groups, but initially, non-borrowers are more likely to be homeowners than borrowers, and below-median borrowers are more likely to be homeowners than above-median borrowers. Then, about eight years

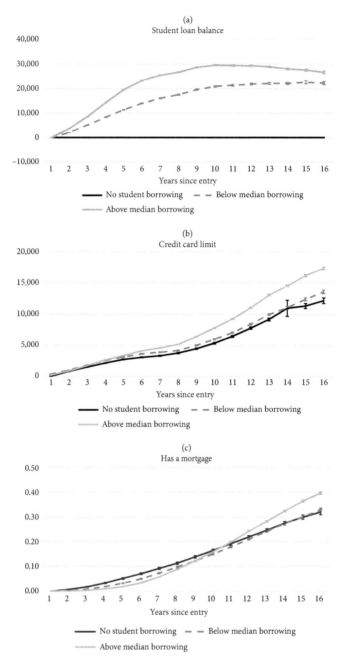

Figure 7.5 Credit report characteristics by student borrower status

Notes: Panels display means and 95 percent confidence intervals of each outcome across the three groups (above-median first year student borrowing, below-median first year student borrowing, and no student borrowing) by year since entry into the sample.

Source: Authors' calculations from CCP/Equifax.

out (about age 25–28), the pattern reverses and above-median borrowers become more likely to own homes. Through the remainder of the analysis horizon, their homeownership rates grow faster than the other two groups. This suggests that above-median borrowers are less likely to purchase a home as they complete their schooling and begin to service their debt, but they quickly catch up and ultimately surpass their peers that borrowed less, likely reflecting the higher labor market returns suggested by our other metrics. Overall, our analysis of the CCP/Equifax corroborates the pattern of results from the SCF and provides evidence that borrowing for education is associated with improved financial positions.

Conclusions

The accumulation of wealth over the lifecycle feeds into retirement wellbeing along several important dimensions, including the resources available in retirement, retirement age, and health. In the US, the retirement system currently places much of the burden and risk of saving and planning for retirement on the individual, a shift from an earlier era in which the government and employers bore most of this responsibility. Against this backdrop, this chapter examines whether the rise in student loan borrowing over the past several decades may have impinged on families' ability to save and accumulate wealth over the lifecycle and to prepare for retirement.

Our analysis documents several findings which may be useful for setting policy in this area. We find that student loan borrowers tend to follow the lifecycle earnings and savings trajectories of other similarly-educated families into late-career ages. Both groups are wealthier entering retirement than those who did not attend college at all. If the appropriate counterfactual is that in the absence of the student loan program, student loan borrowers would have lacked the resources to attend college, they are better off having borrowed on nearly all dimensions. Student loans appear to finance valuable human capital investments that translate into long-run improvements in families' economic wellbeing on average, suggesting that the program is largely having its intended effect. Given this, policies aimed at improving retirement preparation that target resources toward reducing student loan balances or increasing saving among student borrowers are likely to be regressive.

We also show that the small subset of borrowers who carry student debt into near-retirement ages are observably worse off than the full population of student loan borrowers and much less prepared for retirement than their peers on average. Such families likely have other problems contributing to

lower saving and wealth accumulation and they are ultimately not comparable to those with similar education that have repaid their student loan debt.
Highly targeted support for this small subgroup—for example, loan forgiveness at a certain age threshold—could be a cost-effective policy to improve
retirement security for this subset.

From a methodological perspective, our analysis is instructive about the
pitfalls of statistics that derive from observed student debt beyond early-
career ages. We demonstrate that such statistics do not generalize to the
experience of the typical student loan borrower and could lead to misleading conclusions about the role of student debt in financial wellbeing.

Our analysis demonstrates that one should not judge the efficacy of the
federal student loan program by considering only the financial positions
of older households with student loan debt, as it excludes a large share of
households who take student loans and repay them earlier in the lifecycle.
While it also implies that after adjusting for these households in the data,
wealth accumulation among student loan borrowers largely resembles non-
borrowers at each stage of the lifecycle, there are several limitations to the
analysis that should be addressed in future work. First, the majority of the
analysis relies on implied lifecycle profiles from the SCF, constructed by
deriving either a mean or median value of various indicators within the relevant age group, rather than repeated observations of the same households
over time. These pictures do not necessarily forecast future financial positions of younger borrowing cohorts or future differences between younger
borrowers and their non-borrowing peers because differences between age
groups reflect a combination of lifecycle patterns and circumstances specific
to each cohort, including with respect to educational, borrowing, and retirement regimes.[38] Further, all of our findings are predicated on conditions
today that may change as younger cohorts who borrowed in different conditions age toward retirement. Thus, inferences regarding the overall posture
of more recent cohorts of student loan borrowers as they enter retirement
are limited to the extent to which they follow a similar trajectory as their
older peers. In particular, the analysis cannot rule out whether the vulnerable group of households with student loan debt entering retirement will
grow in size, especially as parents have increasingly acquired student loan
debt on behalf of their children.

A second, related limitation is that the chapter primarily focuses on the
extensive margin of student loan borrowing and largely leaves intensive margin considerations, such as the implications of rising student loan debt loads
over time as well as distributional differences among those that borrowed,
for future work. That said, some groundwork is laid. Per the former, the similarities in wealth between borrowers and non-borrowers in each age group,
including those who would have attended school within the last 10–20 years,
is suggestive that larger student loan balances have not come at the expense

of wealth building. Per the latter, the longitudinal analysis of credit records considers borrowing intensity and suggests those with greater initial borrowing experience improved financial wellbeing along several dimensions. Indeed, within the more recent cohorts, borrowers with smaller debt loads, who often have less or lower quality education, appear to struggle the most (Mezza and Sommer 2016).

Finally, our statements concerning retirement preparedness and economic wellbeing more generally reflect student loan borrowers' relative positions rather than their absolute positions. It is possible that the different groups that drive our comparisons, even on average, have different expectations for their retirement consumption and/or realization of consumption needs in retirement.

Acknowledgments

The authors thank John Sabelhaus and Alice Volz for generously sharing estimates of defined benefit plan asset values.

Appendix

TABLE 1 Student loan aggregates by age ($T)

	18–29	30–39	40–49	50–59	60–69	70+	TOTAL
FRBNY Household Debt and Credit Report (2019:Q1)	0.35	0.5	0.32	0.21	0.09	0.02	1.49
SCF (2019)	0.24	0.43	0.21	0.15	0.07	0.01	1.11
difference	0.11	0.07	0.11	0.06	0.02	0.01	0.38

	<=24	25–34	35–49	50–61	62+	N/A	All
Federal Student Loan Portfolio (FY2019:Q2)	0.12	0.50	0.56	0.23	0.07	0.00	1.48
SCF (2019)	0.05	0.41	0.41	0.17	0.06	#N/A	1.11
Difference	0.08	0.08	0.14	0.06	0.01	#N/A	0.37

Sources: Authors' calculations, 2019 SCF; page 21 of the supplemental data file from the FRBNY Household Debt and Credit Report 2019:Q1 publication; the US Department of Education Federal Student Loan 'Portfolio by Age' file accessible at: https://studentaid.gov/sites/default/files/fsawg/datacenter/library/Portfolio-by-Age.xls.

Notes

1. Expanded loan access also increases household formation (Goodman et al. 2021). A possible exception is borrowing to finance a for-profit education, which primarily serves nontraditional students but is highly debt-financed and has notoriously low returns (e.g., Looney and Yannelis 2015; Cellini and Turner 2019).

2. We primarily analyze the 2016 and 2019 SCFs which added several valuable questions, although the 1989–2019 surveys produce similar student debt curves. These SCF 'lifecycle' pictures reflect age-specific averages across multiple cross-sections and thus may be influenced by cohort differences. In particular, the decrease in the fraction of families with student debt that coincides with age likely reflects a combination of paydowns over the lifecycle and reduced educational attainment and borrowing rates for earlier cohorts (Looney and Yannelis 2019). Government-backed student loans were first available to select students in 1958 (an 18-year-old then would be 79 years old in 2019) under the National Defense Education Act and available broadly in 1965 (an 18-year-old then would be 72 years old in 2019).

3. Median wages of college-educated families with student debt track those of college-educated families without debt and remain well above families that did not attend college until their mid- to late 30s; thereafter, they move toward the wages of those that did not attend college.

4. Gervais and Ziebarth (2019) also provide suggestive evidence that borrowing leads to higher wages. In related work, Solis (2017) finds access to education loans in Chile improves academic outcomes.

5. Even though this sector is large, it is relatively inexpensive and students tend to be less reliant on loans for financing. Calculations that include all students who began their borrowing careers at community colleges—many of whom continue on to a four-year college—imply the sector accounts for only a little over one-tenth of outstanding debt (Looney and Yannelis 2015).

6. This sector constitutes a small fraction of enrollment but one-fifth of outstanding student debt (Looney and Yannelis 2015).

7. See, e.g., Baum (2009) and Herbert et al. (2013) on the importance of a vehicle or home for labor market advancement and wealth accumulation.

8. There is also a small private student loan market, representing less than 10 percent of outstanding student debt. Private student loans do not entail standardized terms and rates and often require an established credit record or a cosigner. Our analysis will not distinguish private student loan borrowing, but the vast majority of students who finance their education with private loans also use federal loans (Department of Education, *Digest of Education Statistics 2020*: Table 331.60). Thus, our discussion here will focus on federal loans.

9. See https://nces.ed.gov/programs/digest/d19/tables/dt19_331.20.asp.

10. Most student borrowers receive a more favorable interest rate than the market would offer them. Stafford Loans come in two varieties: subsidized loans, which are need-based, and unsubsidized loans, which are not. For subsidized loans,

interest that accrues early in the life of the loan is paid by the government. Annual Stafford Loan borrowing is subject to a statutory limit that varies with academic level and student dependency status.

11. To receive financial assistance through these programs, students must complete the Free Application for Federal Student Aid (FAFSA), which collects demographic, asset, and income information for students and their households for the calendar year prior to enrollment and computes a student's Expected Family Contribution (EFC) for college, a key factor in addition to the statutory limit and the cost of college that determines the amount of subsidized loan a student may receive. Continuing students must reapply each year.

12. See https://studentaid.gov/sites/default/files/fsawg/datacenter/library/PortfoliobyLoanType.xls.

13. This section omits a discussion of an important component of the US retirement system—government-sponsored social security retirement benefits. We will generally omit social security from our analysis because expected benefits are difficult to estimate (especially at younger ages) and because on average social security only covers about 40 percent of preretirement income so that most families will also need to save to plan for retirement.

14. In 1975, 11.2 million private sector workers actively participated in DC plans and 27.2 million participated in DB plans; by 2019, there were over 85 million DC plan participants, compared to just 12.6 million DB plan participants (Myers and Topoleski 2021).

15. Examples of DC plans include 401(k) plans, 403(b) plans, 457 plans, and Employee Stock Ownership Plans (ESOPs).

16. Some DB plans allow the participant to take the benefits as a lump sum amount at retirement.

17. IRAs were initially introduced in 1974 to encourage retirement savings among individuals without pensions, but eligibility was expanded in 1981. Keoghs, SEP-IRAs, and other qualified retirement plans are similar to IRAs, except they are used by self-employed individuals as an alternative to employer-sponsored DC plans.

18. Detailed information is collected for the household's primary economic unit (PEU)—the economically dominant single person or couple and all other persons in the household who are financially interdependent with that economically dominant person or couple—and limited information is collected for financially independent adults in the household.

19. Our chapter will not attempt to quantify whether an individual's retirement income is adequate. For a discussion of retirement adequacy, see, e.g., Jacobs et al. (2020).

20. The SCF collects the asset value of DC plans but does not collect an analogous measure for traditional DB pensions, as their market value is less salient to the respondent. Dettling et al. (2022) considers an alternative measure of retirement assets that adds imputed DB plan values based on earnings and employment histories from Sabelhaus and Volz (2022). These calculations require stronger assumptions for younger families who will have typically completed a smaller portion of their employment and earnings history.

21. Student debt growth over time in the SCF matches other aggregates (Bricker et al. 2015).
22. Young adults not captured in the data tend to be less well-off (Dettling and Hsu 2014), and student borrowers are more likely to live with their parents and thus will be omitted from the sample of SCF borrowers (Dettling and Hsu 2018; Bleemer et al. 2017).
23. The reference person is the male in a mixed-sex couple or the older person in a same-sex couple, who need not be the survey respondent.
24. For more information on the CCP/Equifax, see Lee and van der Klaauw (2010).
25. Following our work in Black et al. (2020), we restrict the set of student loan borrowers to individuals whose initial student loans did not exceed the statutory first-year federal borrowing limit to try to isolate traditional students that began borrowing at entry. We also restrict the sample to those that maintained a credit report for at least 10 years. This process removes any incorrectly duplicated records, which can appear (typically for a limited period) when new accounts are opened and have not yet been linked to an existing credit record. That said, because the CCP/Equifax sampling is based on social security numbers, it will also remove individuals who pass away over this period or whose credit file is too thin to populate. We focus on cohorts that began borrowing in mid-2003, because that is the first cohort for whom we can reliably observe first-year borrowing in the CCP/Equifax.
26. The CCP/Equifax tends to slightly undercount younger individuals because it takes time to establish a credit record and enter the sample. Lee and van der Klaauw (2010) find that by age 25, population estimates from the CCP/Equifax are similar to those from other sources.
27. We exclude individuals that first take a student loan in subsequent years.
28. Credit card companies determine credit card limits partly based on borrowers' incomes and credit scores, which reflect their overall financial wellbeing. Few young people purchase their homes outright, making the presence of a mortgage a good proxy for homeownership.
29. Following the literature, a financially literate respondent answers all of the 'big three' financial literacy questions correctly (Lusardi and Mitchell 2011).
30. Specifically, the equation includes indicators for whether a family receives or expects an inheritance, whether at least one of the respondent's parents completed college, whether the respondent's mother completed high school, whether the respondent believes borrowing for education is okay, and whether the respondent has served in the military, as well as a set of indicators for the respondent's race or ethnicity and the reference person's educational attainment (whereby potential categories are less than high school, high school, some college, or college degree).
31. For a cohort to be included in the calibration, its borrowing rate must derive from more than 150 observations.
32. These standard errors were calculated using 200 bootstrap replications and the SCF replicate weights. They do not account for additional error introduced by the imputation of borrowing status, and thus, they could be viewed as a lower bound.

33. This gap narrows upon excluding student debt from the calculation of wealth, but some remains, potentially owing to income diverted from savings toward servicing the debt (Dettling et al. 2022).
34. Dettling et al. (2022) also analyzes retirement expectations. The question probing expectations for retirement income yields a noisy picture, although near retirement age, it seems that borrower families, on average, feel more financially prepared. That said, the average borrower family plans to retire later than the average non-borrower family, which is consistent with Butrica and Karamcheva (2013, 2018). Finally, differences in wealth accumulation are well reflected in saving behavior reported by borrower and non-borrower families. Non-borrower families are much more likely to report saving through mid-career ages, on average, which is a phase over which the wealth gap widens. Borrower families are more likely to do so in late-career ages, when the gap disappears.
35. Stock ownership—including stocks that are either directly-held or held in a retirement or investment account—is somewhat higher for borrowers, as are balances, which could suggest a preference among borrowers toward holding their wealth in riskier assets (Dettling et al. 2022).
36. Technically, we use the year the credit record was established, which is a proxy for college entry within our sample of individuals whose credit record was established at traditional college entry ages.
37. We also examined the propensity to have a positive student loan balance. The results are similar to the mean balances: the higher balance sample has more debt throughout, but the two groups appear to be converging and by 16 years out, are about equally as likely to have paid off their loans completely.
38. Restricting attention to families with a college education helps minimize the extent to which increased borrowing rates among more recent cohorts reflect broader access to college over time; however, the analysis does not disentangle increased borrowing rates among attendees or borrowing volumes among borrowers.

References

Armona, L., R. Chakrabarti, and M. Lovenheim (2020). 'Student Debt and Default: The Role of For-Profit Colleges.' Federal Reserve Bank of New York Staff Reports No. 811, Rev. Oct. 2021. New York, NY: Federal Reserve Bank of New York.

Barr, A., K. Bird, B. Castleman, and W. Skimmyhorn (2019). 'A Comparison of Postsecondary Outcomes for Army Service Members, Veterans, and Civilians.' EdWorking Paper 19–50. Providence, RI: Brown University.

Baum, C. L. (2009). 'The Effects of Vehicle Ownership on Employment.' *Journal of Urban Economics*, 66(3): 151–163.

Bhutta, N., J. Bricker, A. C. Chang, L. J. Dettling, S. F. Goodman, J. W. Hsu, K. B. Moore, S. Reber, A. H. Volz, and R. Windle (2020). 'Changes in US Family Finances from 2016 to 2019: Evidence from the Survey of Consumer Finances.' *Federal Reserve Bulletin*, 106(5). Washington, DC: Board of Governors of the Federal Reserve System.

Black, S. E., J. T. Denning, L. J. Dettling, S. Goodman, and L. J. Turner (2020). 'Taking it to the Limit: Effects of Increased Student Loan Availability on Attainment, Earnings, and Financial Well-being.' NBER Working Paper No. w27658. Cambridge, MA: National Bureau of Economic Research.

Bleemer, Z., M. Brown, D. Lee, and W. van der Klaauw (2017) 'Tuition, Jobs, or Housing: What's Keeping Millennials at Home?' Federal Reserve Bank of New York Staff Reports No. 700. New York, NY: Federal Reserve Bank of New York.

Bottazzi, R., T. F. Crossley, and M. Wakefield (2015). 'First-Time House Buying and Catch-up: A Cohort Study.' *Economica*, 82: 1021–1047.

Bricker, J., M. Brown, S. Hannon, and K. M. Pence (2015). 'How Much Student Debt is Out There?' *FEDS Notes* 2015-08. Washington, DC: Board of Governors of the Federal Reserve System.

Brown, M., D. Lee, and W. van der Klaauw (2020). 'The Graying of American Debt.' In O. S. Mitchell and A. Lusardi, eds., *Remaking Retirement: Debt in an Aging Economy*. Oxford, UK: Oxford University Press, pp. 35–59.

Butrica, B. A. and N. S. Karamcheva (2013). 'Does Household Debt Influence the Labor Supply and Benefit Claiming Decisions of Older Americans?' CRR WP 2013-22. Chestnut Hill, MA: Center for Retirement Research at Boston College.

Butrica, B. A. and N. S. Karamcheva (2018). 'In Debt and Approaching Retirement: Claim Social Security or Work Longer?' *AEA Papers and Proceedings*, vol. 108, pp. 401–406.

Cellini, S. R., R. Darolia, and L. J. Turner (2020). 'Where Do Students Go When For-profit Colleges Lose Federal Aid?' *American Economic Journal: Economic Policy*, 12(2): 46–83.

Cellini, S. R. and N. Turner (2019). 'Gainfully Employed? Assessing the Employment and Earnings of For-profit College Students Using Administrative Data.' *Journal of Human Resources*, 54(2): 342–370.

Chakrabarti, R., V. Fos, A. Liberman, and C. Yannelis (2020). 'Tuition, Debt, and Human Capital.' Federal Reserve Bank of New York Staff Reports No. 912. New York, NY: Federal Reserve Bank of New York.

Cooper, D. H. and J. C. Wang (2014). 'Student Loan Debt and Economic Outcomes.' *Current Policy Perspectives No. 14-7*. Boston, MA: Federal Reserve Bank of Boston.

Darolia, R., C. Koedel, P. Martorell, K. Wilson, and F. Perez-Arce (2016). 'Race and Gender Effects on Employer Interest in Job Applicants: New Evidence from a Resume Field Experiment.' *Applied Economics Letters*, 23(12): 853–856.

Deming, D. J., C. Goldin, and L. F. Katz (2012). 'The For-profit Postsecondary School Sector: Nimble Critters or Agile Predators?' *Journal of Economic Perspectives*, 26(1): 139–164.

Deming, D. J., N. Yuchtman, A. Abulafi, C. Goldin, and L. F. Katz (2016). 'The Value of Postsecondary Credentials in the Labor Market: An Experimental Study.' *American Economic Review*, 106(3): 778–806.

Denning, J. T. (2019). 'Born Under a Lucky Star: Financial Aid, College Completion, Labor Supply, and Credit Constraints.' *Journal of Human Resources*, 54(3): 760–784.

Dettling, L. J., S. Devlin-Foltz, J. Krimmel, S. Pack, and J. P. Thompson (2015). 'Comparing Micro and Macro Sources for Household Accounts in the United

States: Evidence from the Survey of Consumer Finances.' Finance and Economics Discussion Series 2015-08. Washington, DC: Board of Governors of the Federal Reserve System.

Dettling, L. J., S. F. Goodman, and S. J. Reber (2022). 'Saving and Wealth Accumulation among Student Loan Borrowers: Implications for Retirement Preparedness.' FEDS Working Paper No. 2022-019. Washington, DC: Board of Governors of the Federal Reserve System.

Dettling, L. J., and J. W. Hsu (2014). 'The State of Young Adults' Balance Sheets: Evidence from the Survey of Consumer Finances.' *Federal Reserve Bank of St. Louis Review*, 96(4): 305–330.

Dettling, L. J. and J. W. Hsu (2018). 'Returning to the Nest: Debt and Parental Co-Residence among Young Adults.' *Labour Economics*, 54(C): 225–236.

Dunlop, E. (2013). 'What Do Stafford Loans Actually Buy You? The Effect of Stafford Loan Access on Community College Students.' National Center for Analysis of Longitudinal Data in Education Research Working Paper 94. Washington, DC: CALDER, American Institutes for Research.

Gervais, M. and N. L. Ziebarth (2019). 'Life after Debt: Postgraduation Consequences of Federal Student Loans.' *Economic Inquiry*, 57(3): 1342–1366.

Gicheva, D. and J. Thompson (2015). 'The Effects of Student Loans on Long-term Household Financial Stability.' In B. Hershbein and K. M. Hollenbeck, eds., *Student Loans and the Dynamics of Debt*. Kalamazoo, MI: W. E. Upjohn Institute for Employment Research, pp. 287–316.

Goodman, S., A. Isen, and C. Yannelis (2021). 'A Day Late and a Dollar Short: Liquidity and Household Formation among Student Borrowers.' *Journal of Financial Economics*, 142(3): 1301–1323.

Goodman, S. and A. H. Volz (2020). 'Attendance Spillovers between Public and For-profit Colleges: Evidence from Statewide Variation in Appropriations for Higher Education.' *Education Finance and Policy*, 15(3): 428–456.

Herbert, C. E., D. T. McCue, and R. Sanchez-Moyano (2013). 'Is Homeownership Still an Effective Means of Building Wealth for Low-income and Minority Households? (Was it ever?)' *Homeownership Built to Last*, 10(2): 5–59.

Jacobs, L., E. Llanes, K. Moore, J. P. Thompson, and A. H. Volz (2020). 'Wealth Distribution and Retirement Preparation among Early Savers.' Research Department Working Papers No. 20-4. Boston, MA: Federal Reserve Bank of Boston.

Krishnan, K., and P. Wang (2019). 'The Cost of Financing Education: Can Student Debt Hinder Entrepreneurship?' *Management Science*, 65(10): 4522–4554.

Lee, D. and W. van der Klaauw (2010). 'An Introduction to the New York Fed Consumer Credit Panel.' Federal Reserve Bank of New York Staff Reports 479. New York, NY: Federal Reserve Bank of New York.

Looney, A. and C. Yannelis. (2015) 'A Crisis in Student Loans? How Changes in the Characteristics of Borrowers and in the Institutions They Attended Contributed to Rising Loan Defaults.' Brookings Papers on Economic Activity No. 2. Washington, DC: Brookings Institution.

Looney, A. and C. Yannelis (2019). 'How Useful are Default Rates? Borrowers with Large Balances and Student Loan Repayment.' *Economics of Education Review*, 71: 135–145.

Lusardi, A. and O. S. Mitchell (2011) 'Financial Literacy and Planning: Implications for Retirement Wellbeing.' NBER Working Paper No. 17078. Cambridge, MA: National Bureau of Economic Research.

Lusardi, A., O. S. Mitchell, and N. Oggero (2018). 'The Changing Face of Debt and Financial Fragility at Older Ages.' *AEA Papers and Proceedings*, 108: 407–411.

Ma, J. and M. Pender (2021). *Trends in College Pricing and Student Aid.* New York, NY: College Board. https://research.collegeboard.org/media/pdf/trends-college-pricing-student-aid-2021.pdf.

Marx, B. M. and L. J. Turner (2019). 'Student Loan Nudges: Experimental Evidence on Borrowing and Educational Attainment.' *American Economic Journal: Economic Policy*, 11(2): 108–141.

Mezza, A., D. Ringo, S. Sherlund, and K. Sommer (2020). 'Student Loans and Homeownership.' *Journal of Labor Economics*, 38(1): 215–260.

Mezza, A. and K. Sommer (2016). 'A Trillion Dollar Question: What Predicts Student Loan Delinquencies?' *Journal of Student Financial Aid*, 46(3): 14–54.

Myers, E. and J. Topoleski (2021). 'A Visual Depiction of the Shift from Defined Benefit (DB) to Defined Contribution (DC) Pension Plans in the Private Sector.' *In Focus*. Washington, DC: Congressional Research Service.

Rothstein, J. and C. E. Rouse (2011). 'Constrained After College: Student Loans and Early-Career Occupational Choices.' *Journal of Public Economics*, 95(1–2): 149–163.

Rutledge, M., G. Sanzenbacher, and F. Vitagliano (2016). 'How Does Student Debt Affect Early-Career Retirement Saving?' CRR WP 2016-9, Rev. 2018. Chestnut Hill, MA: Center for Retirement Research at Boston College.

Sabelhaus, J, and A. H. Volz (2022). 'Social Security Wealth, Inequality, and Lifecycle Saving.' In R. Chetty, J. N. Friedman, J. C. Gornick, B. Johnson, and A. Kennickell, eds., *Measuring and Understanding the Distribution and Intra/Inter-Generational Mobility of Income and Wealth.* NBER Book Series Studies in Income and Wealth. Chicago, IL: The University of Chicago Press.

Solis, A. (2017). 'Credit Access and College Enrollment.' *Journal of Political Economy*, 125(2): 562–622.

Wiederspan, M. (2016). 'Denying Loan Access: The Student-level Consequences when Community Colleges Opt Out of the Stafford Loan Program.' *Economics of Education Review*, 51: 79–96.

Part III

Real-World Shocks and Policy Developments

Chapter 8

The Safety Net Response to the COVID-19 Pandemic Recession and the Older Population

Robert A. Moffitt and James P. Ziliak

The US has an extensive safety net designed to provide support to individuals and families with low income, and also to provide support during economic downturns. The Unemployment Insurance (UI) system is directly intended to provide such cyclical relief, but the other programs in the safety net—for example, the Supplemental Nutrition Assistance Program (SNAP), the Supplemental Security Income (SSI) program, Medicaid, subsidized housing, and the Temporary Assistance for Needy Families (TANF) programs—also provide relief during economic downturns because more families are in economic need, even if only temporarily. There is an extensive literature documenting the degree to which the safety net system as a whole, and the specific programs within it, respond to cyclical increases in the unemployment rate and decreases in employment (Ziliak et al. 2000; Ziliak et al. 2003; Bitler and Hoynes 2010; Moffitt 2013; Anderson et al. 2015; Maestas et al. 2015; Bitler and Hoynes 2016; Ziliak 2016; Bitler et al. 2017; Ganong and Liebman 2018; Hershbein and Stuart 2022). This literature shows that some programs are more cyclically responsive than others and some are not very responsive at all, but the overall system is strongly responsive.

The recent pandemic recession has raised new questions about responsiveness of the safety net, and a significant body of evidence has accumulated for that topic (Bitler et al. 2020a, Bitler et al. 2020b; Ganong et al. 2020; Moffitt and Ziliak 2020; Rees-Jones et al. 2020; Hembre 2021; Larrimore et al. 2022). This work has demonstrated a very strong response to the pandemic by the UI and SNAP programs. Moreover, much of the strong response has been the result of specific Congressional actions providing support via these

Online appendix for this chapter will be available at www.oup.com/real-world_shocks.

Robert A. Moffitt and James P. Ziliak, *The Safety Net Response to the COVID-19 Pandemic Recession and the Older Population*. In: *Real-World Shocks and Retirement System Resiliency*. Edited by: Olivia S. Mitchell, John Sabelhaus, and Stephen P. Utkus, Oxford University Press. © Pension Research Council (2024).
DOI: 10.1093/oso/9780198894131.003.0008

programs over and above what would automatically be provided through normal operation of eligibility and benefit payments.

One topic that has not been examined in the pandemic literature is the responsiveness of the safety net for older workers and early retirees. Poverty rates among the older population are high and many older individuals who enter poverty stay for long periods, longer than younger individuals (Clark et al. 2022; Larrimore et al. 2022). Programs that are most relevant for that population are not necessarily the same as those for the general population. For instance, programs designed for low-income families with children are unlikely to be of major importance. Yet the SSI program, which provides benefits not only to individuals with disabilities but also to low-income aged individuals, is likely to be more relevant to the older population. We would also expect older workers who have not yet retired to be eligible for more UI benefits than the younger population, because of their presumed higher earnings. The social security retirement program is obviously most relevant to the older population and may respond to recessions if older individuals change their decisions about when to take up retirement benefits. SNAP is already known to provide major benefits to low-income seniors, as has been well documented, although take-up rates of SNAP benefits by older persons fall well below those of the younger population (USDA FNS 2021). Medicaid may also be important for older workers who are laid off and lose private health insurance coverage but are not yet eligible for Medicare, as well as for those who have passed the Medicare eligibility age but are low income and eligible for supplemental Medicaid coverage.[1]

This chapter fills this gap by investigating the receipt of safety net and social insurance benefits by the older population in the pandemic recession. We also compare the receipt of benefits by this population in the Great Recession to that in the pandemic recession. We consider the population age 50–74, including both workers and retirees, and we document how benefit receipt changes with age. We also consider most major safety net programs, including those particularly important to the older population. In addition to UI and SNAP, we examine receipt of social security retirement benefits, SSI, Social Security Disability Insurance (SSDI), and Medicaid.[2]

The data set we employ to study the question is the Current Population Survey Annual Social and Economic Supplement (CPS-ASEC), perhaps the most frequently used dataset in the safety net literature. The ASEC has information on demographic characteristics of US households as well as receipt of all major forms of income in the prior calendar year. We use data from the 2001–2021 surveys, which have information on benefit receipt in calendar years 2000–2020; thus, the first year of the pandemic is covered. In our multivariate work, we heavily utilize cross-sectional and over time state-specific variation in unemployment rates and employment declines to identify the effects of the economic downturns, both the pandemic recession and the Great Recession.

In what follows, we first review the major US safety net programs, with a focus on those used by the older population. We discuss both the pandemic recession response as well as that in the Great Recession, and we review how the US programs have evolved over time. Next, we discuss the data used and provide descriptive statistics on the sample and its characteristics. We then turn to the main results of our analysis on benefit receipt among the older population in the pandemic recession, and how that receipt compared to the Great Recession. A summary, and a discussion of open questions, concludes.

The US Social Safety Net and Its Cyclical Responsiveness

We begin with a review of the history of safety net programs since 2000, with a focus on the six programs whose participation status are salient to the older population: UI, SNAP, social security, SSI, SSDI, and Medicaid.[3] We note that we discuss the cyclical responsiveness of these programs while recognizing that the pandemic recession was also a health crisis that affected older individuals disproportionately. Accordingly, one should not necessarily expect the responsiveness of the safety net to be the same as in past recessions. In addition, the pandemic recession differed from past recessions in its pattern of employment declines. Whereas in most recessions, employment declined relatively slowly as the downturn began and then, after the trough was reached, it rose relatively slowly during a recovery, the pandemic recession in contrast was shorter than most, with a very rapid decline in the first two to three months, followed by a recovery which was relatively rapid by the standards of past recessions. This may also generate differences in individual employment responses and in safety net responses.

In the US, the UI program is a state-level contributory social insurance program for individuals who have become involuntarily unemployed. Eligibility requires certain minimums for weeks worked and/or earnings levels in the quarters preceding the occurrence of unemployment. The exact eligibility requirements and benefit provisions vary by state. There has also been a long-run trend toward reduced take-up of UI benefits among the unemployed, with the pre-pandemic take-up rate at about 28 percent. Extra weeks of benefits are automatically provided during times of high unemployment, but Congress typically adds additional coverage during recessions. During the Great Recession, this support was primarily in the form of additional weeks of potential benefits funded by the federal government. In the pandemic recession, a smaller number of extra weeks of benefits was added, but Congress also added an additional $600 per week to all UI receipts for several months after March 2020 as well as extending coverage to the self-employed, independent contractors, and part-time workers, ordinarily not covered by typical state UI programs. We anticipate the UI response to be greater in the pandemic recession than in the Great Recession. We should expect the impact of the pandemic on UI receipt to decline with age within the older population because employment also declines.

The SNAP program is federal, with the federal government setting benefit levels and income and asset eligibility rules, but it is administered by the states. The program is distinguished from all others by its near-universal demographic eligibility, since it covers all individuals with sufficiently low economic resources, whether aged or non-aged, childless or with children, and married or nonmarried. Over the last three decades, the program has seen the liberalization, by many states, of a variety of eligibility and income reporting rules; one of the most important changes has been in asset tests (including equity value of vehicles), which limit eligibility for individuals laid off during recessions who often have significant assets and thus are not poor by that measure. While several states started that relaxation in the early 2000s, many more did so during the Great Recession, with some doing away with those tests altogether. Most states did not return to their prior levels after the recession was over, at least not completely. This relaxation of asset limits would be expected to increase the responsiveness of SNAP caseloads to recessions, and we expect that the older population would exhibit significant participation response to such recessions.

Congress temporarily increased SNAP maximum benefits by 13 percent in the Great Recession. SNAP changes to benefits during the pandemic recession were quite different. Initially, Congress allowed states to issue emergency allotments which provided all eligible recipients the maximum benefit amount. The December 2020 Bill temporarily increased SNAP benefits for all recipients by 15 percent, and a permanent 21 percent increase in benefits was effectuated by the Administration to take effect in October 2021. Lastly, to aid the lowest income families, legislation in January 2021 provided an additional $95 emergency allotment to SNAP families that previously qualified for the maximum benefit amount, amounting to a 21 percent benefit increase for a family of two. Our data only cover the first pandemic year, 2020, and we expect the SNAP response in that year to be less than in the Great Recession.

Social security retirement benefits provide cash support to older individuals who have worked a sufficient number of quarters over their lifetimes and earned above certain minimal levels in covered jobs. While there is a segment of the low-income population that does not qualify for benefits, most of the low-income population does and, in fact, social security is the largest anti-poverty program in the country in terms of numbers of individuals moved over the poverty line by the program (this reflects how many retirees have almost nothing other than social security benefits). Benefits can be claimed as early as age 62, but there is a downward actuarial adjustment to those early retirement benefits which has grown in magnitude as the normal retirement age for benefits has risen from age 65 to 67 over the last decade. While Congress during the Great Recession provided a small one-time top-up of retirement benefits, it did not do so during the pandemic recession, so we expect the response to be greater in the former, although the difference is likely to be small.

SSI is a federal program that provides cash benefits to two distinct populations: the disabled, and the 65+ population with low income. While applications for disability programs are mildly countercyclical, the stringent disability requirements in the program limit the degree to which the program can respond to declines in employment per se. In addition, after application, decisions on enrollment can often take long periods of time, making it unlikely that caseloads respond very much in the short run. Nevertheless, the second eligibility group is more likely to respond to downturns because the main criterion is low income. Benefits and eligibility are means-tested and social security retirement benefits are counted against the SSI benefit, which means that the primary dual beneficiary group for SSI (i.e., those receiving both SSI and social security) are those with low (or no) social security benefits. However, SSI also has fairly rigid asset tests (which are not indexed to inflation), and this can limit its cyclical responsiveness. While a small one-time top-up to the SSI benefit was provided during the Great Recession, Congress did not do so in the pandemic recession, although it did mandate that Economics Impact Payments (which many SSI recipients received) not be counted against the benefit (or other programs like SNAP). We do not expect large differences in the Great Recession and the pandemic recession.

The SSDI provides cash benefits and health insurance coverage—Medicaid during the first two years of enrollment, and Medicare thereafter—for under-age-65 individuals who have a qualifying, rather severe, disability. Very few SSDI recipients work, and hence should not be much affected by cyclical downturns. As noted for SSI, while applications to SSDI have shown some countercyclicality, it is not large (Maestas et al. 2015; Cutler et al. 2015). Again, decisions on applications often take place only after a long lag. In addition, after many years of growth, applications to the program have been declining in recent years. The expectation should not be that it is very responsive to the pandemic recession, although given that the pandemic was a health shock, there could be a longer-term response for those suffering from extended health problems. But we have no priors on whether the response should be any different than in the Great Recession.

The Medicaid program is the nation's program for providing subsidized medical care to a variety of low-income recipients, including low-income disabled adults, low-income seniors for supplements to Medicare, nursing home care, and all families and individuals without private health insurance who are on low income. Medicaid recipients also enrolled in Medicare must use Medicare as the first payer for services covered by both programs. States have great leeway in setting both, and hence program generosity varies widely across states. Its main role in the business cycle is to provide medical care coverage to workers who have lost their jobs and their health insurance. Prior to the 2010 Affordable Care Act, the program had asset tests which could have reduced its cyclical sensitivity, and application procedures were fairly onerous. But most asset tests disappeared around 2012–2014, following the passage of the Affordable Care Act, which also simplified eligibility conditions. Congress provided additional emergency aid during the Great Recession, and increased the federal matching rate; it also provided subsidies to laid-off workers to purchase private health insurance, which could have reduced the demand for Medicaid. In the pandemic recession, March 2020 legislation required states not to terminate from the rolls any current recipients, and it also increased the matching rate to accommodate increased expenditures. This had a major impact on increasing caseloads beyond what would normally have been expected in a recession. We expect responsiveness to be greater in the pandemic.

Appendix Figure A1 shows a time series of expenditures from our six programs. Medicaid and social security completely dominate the other programs in terms of expenditure. Among the other programs, SNAP and Medicaid have, on average, the largest expenditures, and SSI the smallest. UI expenditure fluctuates with the business cycle but, in the good economic period 2012–2019, was smaller than SNAP and Medicaid.

Data

To analyze our questions of interest, we use the Current Population Survey Annual Social and Economic Supplement (ASEC), an annual supplement to the CPS which asks about receipt of transfers during the prior calendar year. We use the 2001–2021 surveys, so our information on transfer receipt covers the years 2000–2020. The 2020 observation is taken as the initial pandemic year, even though the first two months were prior to the pandemic. We examine individuals age 50–74, but we also split the sample into those age 50–61 and 62–74, as a rough approximation to retirement dates. Transfer receipt is a binary indicator equal to 1 if the individual received the benefit at any time during the year. All transfers are recorded at the individual level, except for SNAP which is asked at the household level, but we assign all persons in the household as recipients. We also examine employment, defined as a binary variable equal to 1 if the individual worked at any time during the year. In addition to examining patterns separately by the two age groups, we also examine patterns separately by gender.

It is well known that survey respondents underreport program participation in the ASEC. To address this, we use a model-based approach to predict program participation as a flexible function of household demographics, following the method of Moffitt and Pauley (2018) for the SIPP and extended to the ASEC by Moffitt and Ziliak (2020). We then randomly assign participation to those nonparticipants with a high *ex ante* predicted probability of participation until the population weighted participation counts align with administrative totals.[4] The other adjustment we make after first predicting program participation for likely participants as explained above is to drop individuals with either their entire ASEC imputed, or those with labor force variables imputed. Census imputes missing data on individual questions on the ASEC, whereby observations with missing information are assigned the values from a randomly matched 'donor' based on a set of observed demographic characteristics. A similar random match method is employed for individuals with their entire supplements imputed. Bollinger et al. (2019) show that rates of supplement nonresponse have been on the rise in recent years, with nearly 25 percent of all households receiving a completely imputed ASEC record. To retain population representativeness, we use inverse probability weights (IPW) as a way to adjust for this subsampling. For each gender and year, we predict the probability of not having a whole impute or imputed labor force variables as a rich function of demographics, and then we divide the ASEC person weight by the fitted probability of not being imputed.[5] Weighted summary statistics of men and women are presented in Appendix Tables A1 and A2.

Results

We will present our results first in graphical form and then with multivariate regressions. Preliminary analysis showed that transfer program receipt is very small among those with a college degree or more, so we restrict our analysis to those without a college degree.

Graphical analysis. We show trends in per capita transfer program receipt for men and women, separately for those age 50–61 and 62–74, for the six major programs we study. Figure 8.1 shows trends for men age 50–61. The most cyclically sensitive program is UI, experiencing large jumps in both the Great Recession and the pandemic recession. This is not surprising, given the normal operation of the program during downturns combined with the additional Congressional support in those two periods described above. Online Appendix Figure OA1 shows that employment rates for less educated men in this age bracket experienced the cyclical employment patterns

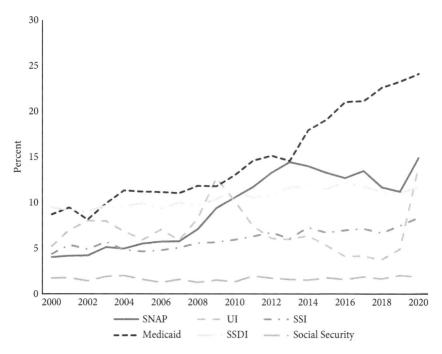

Figure 8.1 Transfer program participation rates of men age 50–61

Source: Authors' calculations from the Current Population Survey Annual Social and Economic Supplement, 2001–2021.

consistent with this UI receipt (see Coile and Zhang 2024 for further evidence on employment and retirement in the pandemic). The second most notable increase in the pandemic was for the SNAP program, whose participation rate jumped about four percentage points in 2020. Less of a cyclical response is visually evident in the Great Recession, but this is primarily because receipt experienced an increase during that period that also continued afterward. The continued increase in SNAP receipt after the Great Recession ended has been noticed previously and has been partly ascribed to the reforms adopted by the program which were kept in place afterward (Ganong and Liebman 2018).

The other programs responded very little during the pandemic, although SSDI experienced a slight uptick, very small in magnitude. The SSI, social security, and Medicaid programs experienced no visual jump, although in some cases (like Medicaid) increases occurred which appear to be continuations of pre-pandemic trends. During the Great Recession, SSDI again experienced a small increase, but the other programs' receipt was mostly stable.

Figure 8.2 shows the same program trends for women 50–61. In terms of general shape and patterns, women's program participation experienced similar cyclical responsiveness to that of men.[6] The largest cyclical changes in both the Great Recession and the pandemic occurred for the UI and SNAP programs, for example, with very little evidence of response for the other programs (with, again, SSDI something of an exception). However, there is a significant difference in magnitudes of UI receipt overall, and in the magnitude of the responsiveness of that receipt during the Great Recession for the two genders. UI receipt is generally lower for women in all periods, presumably because women have lower employment rates by men and may be less likely to work in covered jobs when working (see Online Appendix Figure OA1 for employment rates for women). But the jump in UI receipt during the Great Recession was much larger for men than for women, while during the pandemic, receipt jumped by about the same amount for the two. This is probably because, as has been noted elsewhere, the Great Recession was characterized by layoffs in traditionally-male sectors like manufacturing, whereas during the pandemic the hard-hit

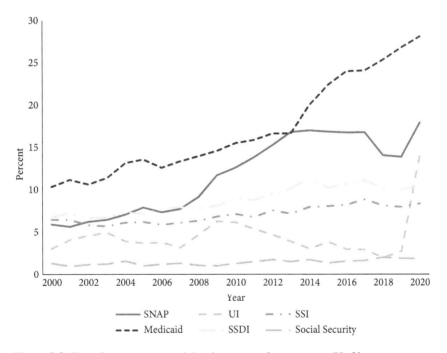

Figure 8.2 Transfer program participation rates of women age 50–61

Source: Authors' calculations from the Current Population Survey Annual Social and Economic Supplement, 2001–2021.

industries included those employing women, such as leisure and hospitality, transportation, and retail trade (Alon et al. 2020).

Figures 8.3 and 8.4 show trends for men and women age 62–74. Again, the patterns for men and women are generally quite close to one another, but both show some differences from the results for the 50–61 age group. UI receipt, for example, is much lower for older men and women than for their younger counterparts, no doubt because (full-time) employment rates are lower as well (see Online Appendix Figure OA2 for employment rates for this age group). But sufficient numbers of older men and women are still working after age 61 to experience UI upticks during the pandemic and Great Recessions similar in shape to those for younger individuals. SNAP receipt also shows the same increase during the Great Recession, continuing into the post-recession period, and receipt jumped during the pandemic, as was found for those age 50–61. However, unlike those age 50–61, older men and women experienced small declines during the pandemic in the receipt of Medicaid, SSDI, and SSI (the last mostly for women). This is

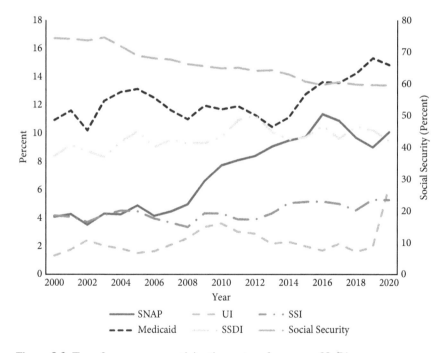

Figure 8.3 Transfer program participation rates of men age 62–74

Source: Authors' calculations from the Current Population Survey Annual Social and Economic Supplement, 2001–2021.

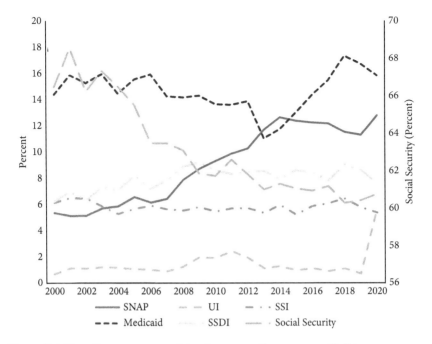

Figure 8.4 Transfer program participation rates of women age 62–74

Source: Authors' calculations from the Current Population Survey Annual Social and Economic Supplement, 2001–2021.

consistent with the findings of Goda et al. (2021), noted earlier, who speculated that one reason could have been the closure of SSA offices during the early months of the pandemic, making application more difficult.

Regression results. We estimate Probit regressions for our six binary program receipt indicators over the period 2000–2020 for men and women, age 50–61 and 62–74 separately, in line with our graphical analysis, and again just for the population with less than a college degree. We enter dummy variables for the Great Recession period and the COVID period (i.e., 2020), for the state unemployment rate, and for interactions between the unemployment rate and the two recession indicators to test for differences in responsiveness to the severity of the two recessions. We enter a year variable to pick up long-term trends (which are evident for some programs in Figures 8.1–8.4) and we control for demographic characteristics, including age, race/ethnicity, education level, marital status, household size, and home-owning (we will test for differential impacts for some of these demographic groups below). We also control for state fixed effects.

Table 8.1 has the results for men age 50–61, showing marginal effects evaluated at the means of the regressors (standard errors computed using

TABLE 8.1 Marginal effects of transfers: Male age 50–61 Probit models

	(1) SNAP	(2) UI	(3) SSI	(4) Medicaid	(5) SSDI	(6) Social Security
Trend/10	0.050***	−0.015***	0.008***	0.065***	0.010***	−0.000
	(0.003)	(0.002)	(0.001)	(0.004)	(0.002)	(0.001)
COVID-19	−0.018	0.069**	0.061**	−0.051***	0.005	0.011
	(0.017)	(0.033)	(0.030)	(0.018)	(0.031)	(0.014)
Great Recession	0.012	0.007	0.002	−0.006	0.003	−0.002
	(0.009)	(0.009)	(0.007)	(0.014)	(0.012)	(0.004)
State Unemployment Rate	0.685***	0.619***	0.004	−0.426***	0.130**	0.002
	(0.066)	(0.050)	(0.050)	(0.152)	(0.056)	(0.027)
Unemployment Rate x COVID	−0.096	0.122	−0.426**	0.935***	−0.151	−0.094
	(0.270)	(0.232)	(0.177)	(0.303)	(0.382)	(0.097)
Unemployment Rate x Great Recession	−0.294***	0.210*	−0.009	0.033	−0.106	0.007
	(0.108)	(0.115)	(0.086)	(0.172)	(0.144)	(0.059)
Age	0.001**	−0.002***	0.002***	0.004***	0.008***	0.002***
	(0.000)	(0.000)	(0.000)	(0.000)	(0.000)	(0.000)
Black	0.048***	−0.006**	0.030***	0.067***	0.001	0.009***
	(0.005)	(0.003)	(0.004)	(0.005)	(0.005)	(0.002)
Other Race	0.027***	−0.005	0.007	0.046***	−0.023***	−0.001
	(0.006)	(0.004)	(0.004)	(0.008)	(0.007)	(0.001)
Hispanic Ethnicity	−0.001	−0.002	−0.016***	−0.005	−0.050***	−0.000
	(0.006)	(0.004)	(0.003)	(0.005)	(0.004)	(0.001)
Less than High School	0.100***	0.004	0.087***	0.191***	0.100***	0.007***
	(0.006)	(0.003)	(0.005)	(0.006)	(0.007)	(0.001)
High School Only	0.028***	0.009***	0.020***	0.052***	0.027***	0.003***
	(0.003)	(0.002)	(0.002)	(0.004)	(0.002)	(0.001)
Married	−0.109***	−0.000	−0.084***	−0.156***	−0.078***	0.002**
	(0.005)	(0.003)	(0.003)	(0.004)	(0.006)	(0.001)
Widowed, Divorced, or Separated	−0.014***	0.012***	−0.022***	−0.050***	−0.023***	0.003***
	(0.003)	(0.004)	(0.002)	(0.003)	(0.005)	(0.001)
Number of persons in household	0.019***	−0.002***	−0.002**	0.012***	−0.003***	−0.002***
	(0.001)	(0.001)	(0.001)	(0.001)	(0.001)	(0.000)
Own Home	−0.100***	−0.006**	−0.042***	−0.117***	−0.047***	0.004***
	(0.005)	(0.003)	(0.003)	(0.007)	(0.005)	(0.001)
Observations	129,950	129,950	129,950	129,950	129,950	129,950
Pseudo R2	0.188	0.038	0.156	0.161	0.079	0.056
Ave. Pred. Prob.	0.100	0.069	0.061	0.151	0.107	0.016
Effect of Ave. COVID UR on Pred. Prob.	0.018	0.024	−0.014	0.014	0.000	−0.003
Effect of Ave. Great Recession UR on Pred. Prob.	0.008	0.015	−0.004	0.009	0.000	−0.001

Notes: Robust standard errors in parentheses. *** p<0.01, ** p<0.05, * p<0.1
Source: Authors' calculations from the Current Population Survey Annual Social and Economic Supplement, 2001–2021.

the delta method and clustered at the state level).[7] The results for SNAP, for example, show a positive time trend and no statistically significant impact of the Great Recession or COVID per se, but positive effects of the state unemployment rate on receipt. The insignificance of the Great Recession and COVID indicators means that the response during those downturns can be entirely ascribed to the unemployment rate itself, and that participation did not deviate from what would be expected from that business cycle indicator alone (see Online Appendix Table OA1 for regression results for the employment rate, showing its cyclical sensitivity). However, the interaction terms show that the response of SNAP participation to the unemployment rate during the pandemic was insignificantly different from its non-recessionary response, but the response during the Great Recession, while positive, was considerably lower. Thus we find that the cyclical responsiveness of SNAP was much greater during the pandemic than during the Great Recession, at least for men age 50–61, somewhat contrary to our expectations noted in the last section.

The UI results are different, with an increase during COVID over and above what would have been expected from the unemployment rate alone, but not during the Great Recession. That additional impact was also large in magnitude (6.9 percentage points) relative to the 2000–2020 mean (6%). Again, COVID changes were greater than those during the Great Recession in this sense, but the responsiveness of UI to the state unemployment rate was greater during the Great Recession than during the pandemic. One possible reason for this difference is that, during the Great Recession, Congress allocated extra weeks of benefits in a way that differed across states, whereas during the pandemic Congress added a $600 weekly supplement regardless of the state unemployment rate. Thus, we find that UI was more responsive to the unemployment rate per se in the Great Recession than during the pandemic, but there was greater separate support through the UI system in the pandemic.

For the other four programs, little responsiveness is indicated for the SSDI and social security programs, consistent with the graphical analysis (the unemployment rate effects in both the Great Recession and the pandemic are close to zero; different patterns are found for SSI and Medicaid, however. SSI receipt experienced a long-term upward trend (this can be seen in Figure 8.1) but a positive deviation from that trend during COVID, sizable in magnitude (6.1 percentage points). But SSI receipt actually fell in states with higher unemployment rates. Medicaid receipt also exhibited a strong long-term upward trend (again evident in Figure 8.1) but a negative deviation (5.1 percentage points) from that trend during the pandemic. Medicaid receipt did increase more in states with higher unemployment rates, however. The response was greater during the pandemic than during the Great Recession in that sense.

TABLE 8.2 Marginal effects of transfers: Female age 50–61 Probit models

	(1) SNAP	(2) UI	(3) SSI	(4) Medicaid	(5) SSDI	(6) Social Security
Trend/10	0.057***	−0.007***	0.010***	0.075***	0.023***	0.003**
	(0.002)	(0.001)	(0.002)	(0.004)	(0.003)	(0.001)
COVID-19	−0.017	0.094***	0.039*	−0.043*	−0.006	0.028*
	(0.018)	(0.030)	(0.022)	(0.022)	(0.017)	(0.016)
Great Recession	0.010	0.005	−0.003	−0.012	0.011	0.001
	(0.009)	(0.006)	(0.006)	(0.016)	(0.013)	(0.004)
State Unemployment Rate	0.625***	0.428***	−0.066	−0.573***	0.056	0.000
	(0.067)	(0.046)	(0.045)	(0.109)	(0.068)	(0.017)
Unemployment Rate x COVID	−0.162	0.007	−0.373**	0.910**	−0.061	−0.209***
	(0.256)	(0.145)	(0.167)	(0.371)	(0.218)	(0.073)
Unemployment Rate x Great Recession	−0.258**	−0.001	0.054	0.170	−0.200	−0.040
	(0.103)	(0.070)	(0.080)	(0.202)	(0.129)	(0.050)
Age	0.001**	−0.001***	0.002***	0.003***	0.005***	0.002***
	(0.000)	(0.000)	(0.000)	(0.000)	(0.000)	(0.000)
Black	0.055***	0.003	0.021***	0.066***	0.008*	0.008***
	(0.006)	(0.002)	(0.003)	(0.007)	(0.004)	(0.002)
Other Race	0.007	0.001	0.002	0.039***	−0.026***	−0.001
	(0.006)	(0.002)	(0.004)	(0.007)	(0.003)	(0.001)
Hispanic Ethnicity	0.001	−0.001	−0.018***	−0.005	−0.043***	−0.002**
	(0.008)	(0.003)	(0.006)	(0.008)	(0.003)	(0.001)
Less than High School	0.114***	−0.006***	0.110***	0.215***	0.064***	0.009***
	(0.007)	(0.002)	(0.005)	(0.006)	(0.006)	(0.002)
High School Only	0.026***	0.003**	0.022***	0.051***	0.013***	0.004***
	(0.002)	(0.002)	(0.002)	(0.004)	(0.002)	(0.001)
Married	−0.126***	−0.015***	−0.080***	−0.157***	−0.068***	−0.004***
	(0.004)	(0.002)	(0.003)	(0.007)	(0.005)	(0.001)
Widowed, Divorced, or Separated	−0.001	0.004*	−0.011***	−0.020***	−0.005	0.002*
	(0.003)	(0.003)	(0.002)	(0.005)	(0.004)	(0.001)
Number of persons in household	0.020***	−0.002***	−0.004***	0.013***	−0.003***	−0.001***
	(0.001)	(0.000)	(0.001)	(0.001)	(0.001)	(0.000)
Own Home	−0.130***	−0.003	−0.063***	−0.154***	−0.054***	0.004***
	(0.006)	(0.002)	(0.003)	(0.008)	(0.004)	(0.001)
Observations	148,261	148,261	148,261	148,261	148,261	148,261
Pseudo R2	0.236	0.047	0.178	0.190	0.085	0.057
Ave. Pred. Prob.	0.122	0.044	0.072	0.174	0.092	0.016
Effect of Ave. COVID UR on Pred. Prob.	0.014	0.022	−0.014	0.009	0.000	−0.007
Effect of Ave. Great Recession UR on Pred. Prob.	0.006	0.007	−0.005	0.005	0.000	−0.001

Notes: Robust standard errors in parentheses. *** p<0.01, ** p<0.05, * p<0.1
Source: Authors' calculations from the Current Population Survey Annual Social and Economic Supplement, 2001–2021.

The contribution of the unemployment rate per se during the Great Recession and the pandemic is shown at the bottom of the table, where rows are given that multiply the (Probit) unemployment coefficients by the increase in the unemployment rate (relative to non-recessionary periods) to numerically indicate the contribution of increases in that rate per se. Those rows show that the responsiveness to the unemployment rate was very strong for SNAP and UI (increases of 1.8 and 2.4 percentage points, respectively), and somewhat strong for Medicaid, but small for the other three programs (and negative for SSI and social security, and large relative to the mean participation rate for the former). Further, for those three programs where responsiveness was strong, it was greater during the pandemic than during the Great Recession. We should nevertheless note that the Great Recession responsiveness to the unemployment rate was generally positive and, in fact, constituted the main channel of response, since most of the Great Recession dummies themselves are insignificant.

The coefficients on the demographic variables are often very statistically significant. Age has a positive impact except for UI, Black men usually have higher rates of receipt except (again) for UI, education is negatively correlated with receipt, and unmarried men as well as those not owning a home have higher rates of receipt. These results are consistent with the large literature on transfer program receipt in the US.

Table 8.2 shows the regression results for women age 50–61. We noted in our discussion of the Figures that those for women appeared generally consistent with those of men for this age group, except for a larger responsiveness in the Great Recession for men, likely a result of the greater impact of that downturn on industries predominantly occupied by men. Table 8.2 is similarly consistent with the Table 8.1 results for men, with much less of a change in responsiveness of UI receipt to the unemployment rate in the Great Recession for women; but the last two rows of the table show that, for women, we again find that the responsiveness of women's SNAP, UI, and Medicaid receipt to the unemployment rate was greater during the pandemic than during the Great Recession (with the same SSI result noted above for men).

Tables 8.3 and 8.4 show regression results for men and women age 62–74, respectively. We noted in our discussion of the figures that program receipt followed the same general patterns for these older individuals as those for younger men and women except for lower rates of UI receipt, and with some indications of declines in receipt of SSI, SSDI, and Medicaid during the pandemic. The latter does not appear as statistically significant in the regressions, as the coefficients on the COVID indicators do not reach statistical significance and are not even always negative in sign. But the regression

TABLE 8.3 Marginal effects of transfers: Male age 62–74 Probit models

	(1) SNAP	(2) UI	(3) SSI	(4) Medicaid	(5) SSDI	(6) Social Security
Trend/10	0.034***	0.000	0.003	0.008**	0.008***	−0.082***
	(0.002)	(0.001)	(0.002)	(0.004)	(0.002)	(0.006)
COVID-19	−0.034***	0.029	0.016	−0.012	−0.001	0.011
	(0.007)	(0.020)	(0.019)	(0.027)	(0.021)	(0.044)
Great Recession	0.003	0.002	−0.006	−0.003	0.008	0.007
	(0.009)	(0.004)	(0.004)	(0.013)	(0.011)	(0.017)
State Unemployment Rate	0.252***	0.212***	−0.043	−0.319***	0.129*	0.053
	(0.066)	(0.025)	(0.027)	(0.096)	(0.075)	(0.142)
Unemployment Rate x COVID	0.408*	−0.026	−0.142	0.397	−0.167	0.028
	(0.213)	(0.101)	(0.139)	(0.378)	(0.253)	(0.487)
Unemployment Rate x Great Recession	−0.135	0.015	0.076	0.098	−0.155	−0.276
	(0.113)	(0.041)	(0.064)	(0.184)	(0.150)	(0.258)
Age	−0.001***	−0.004***	−0.002***	−0.006***	−0.011***	0.064***
	(0.000)	(0.000)	(0.000)	(0.000)	(0.000)	(0.001)
Black	0.033***	−0.001	0.019***	0.061***	0.019***	−0.057***
	(0.004)	(0.001)	(0.003)	(0.005)	(0.005)	(0.009)
Other Race	0.016***	0.000	0.033***	0.080***	−0.017**	−0.099***
	(0.004)	(0.002)	(0.003)	(0.007)	(0.007)	(0.010)
Hispanic Ethnicity	0.021**	0.002	0.003	0.036***	−0.021***	−0.049***
	(0.010)	(0.002)	(0.005)	(0.010)	(0.004)	(0.017)
Less than High School	0.073***	−0.003*	0.057***	0.143***	0.086***	−0.057***
	(0.005)	(0.002)	(0.002)	(0.005)	(0.006)	(0.005)
High School Only	0.013***	−0.000	0.011***	0.036***	0.020***	−0.004
	(0.002)	(0.001)	(0.002)	(0.005)	(0.003)	(0.004)
Married	−0.087***	0.003**	−0.060***	−0.118***	−0.062***	0.119***
	(0.005)	(0.002)	(0.003)	(0.008)	(0.005)	(0.011)
Widowed, Divorced, or Separated	−0.015***	0.004	−0.017***	−0.039***	−0.010**	0.080***
	(0.003)	(0.003)	(0.001)	(0.003)	(0.004)	(0.011)
Number of persons in household	0.017***	−0.000	−0.001*	0.010***	0.001	−0.036***
	(0.001)	(0.000)	(0.000)	(0.001)	(0.001)	(0.003)
Own Home	−0.097***	−0.002	−0.047***	−0.116***	−0.053***	0.083***
	(0.005)	(0.002)	(0.006)	(0.006)	(0.005)	(0.008)
Observations	94,017	94,017	94,017	94,017	94,017	94,017
Pseudo R2	0.202	0.074	0.180	0.150	0.094	0.193
Ave. Pred. Prob.	0.076	0.024	0.045	0.124	0.097	0.650
Effect of Ave. COVID UR on Pred. Prob.	0.019	0.009	−0.006	0.002	−0.001	0.001
Effect of Ave. Great Recession UR on Pred. Prob.	0.014	0.004	−0.003	0.001	−0.001	0.001

Notes: Robust standard errors in parentheses. *** p<0.01, ** p<0.05, * p<0.1
Source: Authors' calculations from the Current Population Survey Annual Social and Economic Supplement, 2001–2021.

TABLE 8.4 Marginal effects of transfers: Female age 62–74 Probit models

	(1) SNAP	(2) UI	(3) SSI	(4) Medicaid	(5) SSDI	(6) Social Security
Trend	0.040***	−0.000	0.001	−0.003	0.011***	−0.031***
	(0.003)	(0.001)	(0.001)	(0.004)	(0.002)	(0.005)
COVID-19	−0.042***	0.028**	0.009	−0.029	0.006	−0.049
	(0.010)	(0.012)	(0.012)	(0.020)	(0.022)	(0.053)
Great Recession	0.022**	0.001	−0.003	−0.028***	0.028***	−0.010
	(0.010)	(0.003)	(0.005)	(0.010)	(0.009)	(0.019)
State Unemployment Rate	0.353***	0.138***	−0.036	−0.517***	0.166***	−0.084
	(0.073)	(0.018)	(0.037)	(0.093)	(0.052)	(0.079)
Unemployment Rate x COVID	0.557	0.001	−0.123	0.749**	−0.284	0.681
	(0.339)	(0.048)	(0.118)	(0.301)	(0.247)	(0.669)
Unemployment Rate x Great Recession	−0.337***	−0.004	0.032	0.496***	−0.217**	0.014
	(0.101)	(0.040)	(0.066)	(0.156)	(0.093)	(0.281)
Age	−0.002***	−0.002***	−0.002***	−0.006***	−0.008***	0.056***
	(0.000)	(0.000)	(0.000)	(0.001)	(0.000)	(0.001)
Black	0.052***	−0.002***	0.026***	0.080***	0.023***	−0.049***
	(0.006)	(0.001)	(0.003)	(0.005)	(0.004)	(0.005)
Other Race	0.016***	0.000	0.029***	0.079***	−0.015***	−0.119***
	(0.006)	(0.002)	(0.005)	(0.007)	(0.005)	(0.007)
Hispanic Ethnicity	0.040***	−0.003***	0.013	0.057***	−0.011*	−0.070***
	(0.011)	(0.001)	(0.011)	(0.015)	(0.006)	(0.022)
Less than High School	0.081***	−0.004***	0.076***	0.157***	0.060***	−0.091***
	(0.005)	(0.001)	(0.004)	(0.006)	(0.005)	(0.007)
High School Only	0.011***	−0.003***	0.013***	0.031***	0.013***	0.006
	(0.002)	(0.001)	(0.002)	(0.003)	(0.003)	(0.005)
Married	−0.075***	−0.007***	−0.050***	−0.103***	−0.060***	0.140***
	(0.006)	(0.002)	(0.005)	(0.009)	(0.004)	(0.011)
Widowed, Divorced, or Separated	0.003	0.001	−0.008***	−0.014***	−0.006*	0.032***
	(0.004)	(0.001)	(0.002)	(0.005)	(0.004)	(0.007)
Number of persons in household	0.015***	−0.000	0.000	0.009***	0.000	−0.036***
	(0.001)	(0.000)	(0.000)	(0.001)	(0.001)	(0.001)
Own Home	−0.116***	0.001	−0.069***	−0.148***	−0.049***	0.075***
	(0.006)	(0.001)	(0.006)	(0.009)	(0.003)	(0.011)
Observations	123,971	123,971	123,971	123,971	123,971	123,971
Pseudo R2	0.222	0.100	0.202	0.173	0.100	0.157
Ave. Pred. Prob.	0.095	0.015	0.057	0.144	0.080	0.627
Effect of Ave. COVID UR on Pred. Prob.	0.026	0.011	−0.004	0.005	−0.003	0.011
Effect of Ave. Great Recession UR on Pred. Prob.	0.021	0.003	−0.003	0.005	−0.002	0.008

Notes: Robust standard errors in parentheses. *** p<0.01, ** p<0.05, * p<0.1
Source: Authors' calculations from the Current Population Survey Annual Social and Economic Supplement, 2001–2021.

results confirm the first results, showing much lower responsiveness of UI receipt for women, both by smaller or insignificant results on the coefficient on the COVID indicator and on the coefficients for the responsiveness of UI receipt for the unemployment rate. This is confirmed by the last rows of the table for UI, which show a lower contribution of the unemployment rate to UI receipt for these older individuals compared to those for younger individuals. One difference between older and younger individuals appears for SNAP receipt, where older individuals experienced a larger responsiveness of receipt to the unemployment rate during the pandemic than during the Great Recession, but also a reduction in receipt relative to that induced by the unemployment rate in the pandemic. This may be because those age 62–74 are more likely to be poor and have more negative employment effects than those age 50–61, and SNAP is perhaps the most important means-tested anti-poverty program for older nonworking individuals and their families. On the other hand, it should be kept in mind that those age 62–74 also generally have social security and Medicare benefits, and this may reduce their need for other transfer programs.

We tested for heterogeneity of business cycle response by education, marital status, and race. For men age 50–61, SNAP and UI recipiency responded the most to the unemployment rate for more educated men, those who were never married, and (often, but not always) among Black men. For women age 50–61, a similar pattern followed by race but recipiency responded the most for women who were divorced, widowed, or separated, possibly because of greater need. Among older women, the responses of SNAP and UI receipt were also greatest among widowed, separated, and divorced women, and among Black women. For both men and women, recipiency responded the most among the least educated, perhaps again reflecting greater need.

Conclusions

How the safety net affected the older population during recessions has been little examined in the literature, nor have prior studies explored how it responded to the pandemic recession. Our analysis yields several new findings. First, we have established that the UI program and the SNAP program are quite important for the less educated older population of men and women, just as they are for prime age persons. In recessions in general and in the pandemic recession, these programs provided significant support to older men and women. Second, these programs provided support to those age 62 and older, as well as to those age 50–61, especially SNAP. Even with programs like social security and SSI, low-income individuals after retirement are eligible for SNAP benefits, and many apply and receive benefits during recessions. Although to a lesser extent than younger individuals, people age 62 also receive UI benefits. Third, we find that receipt in both programs responded more strongly in the pandemic recession than in the Great Recession. Fourth, we find some evidence that the Medicaid program provides countercyclical assistance during recessions and when the unemployment rate is high in general, but in magnitudes much smaller than those for SNAP and UI. Fifth, we find some evidence, though not conclusive and small in magnitude, of countercyclical effects on SSI and/or SSDI, but more in the Great Recession than in the pandemic recession, and receipt may even have fallen in the latter. Sixth and finally, we find consistent evidence of greater countercyclical assistance to women who are widowed, divorced, or separated, compared to married or never-married women.

There are a number of policy issues that our findings suggest need further discussion. One is the weak response of SSI receipt to the business cycle, at least that portion of the program that provides assistance to low-income older individuals (as opposed to the disabled). SSI should be a major program for low-income older individuals, yet it responds very little to the unemployment rate, when hardship within the older population rises. It is likely that part of this lack of response is the stringent asset tests, which have been held fixed in nominal dollars since 1989. This prevents those who ordinarily do not need assistance because of higher-than-minimal assets from receiving assistance during a temporary downturn. Temporary reductions in those asset tests, as the SNAP program implemented during the Great Recession, should be considered.

The SSDI and SSI programs for the disabled population have some evidence of countercyclical assistance, but very little. What responsiveness there is may not be socially beneficial, because individuals with disabilities who may have the capacity to work may be drawn into long-term recipiency only because of a temporary downturn in the economy. This is related to the long-noted issue with the US DI and SSI programs, that they are aimed at those with severe and not partial disabilities. Reforms to the program which provide more benefits to the partially disabled, and even on a temporary basis during downturns, could address both of these problems and would make the program more flexible in providing assistance during recessions (Maestas 2019).

Finally, a general issue with many transfer programs in the US is that they do not have built-in, automatic responses to major downturns like the pandemic recession and the Great Recession. Typically, Congress responds with ad hoc legislation to increase benefits in some programs and not others and, because it is acting quickly to provide relief as soon as possible, enacts programs that are poorly designed. The temporary relaxation of asset tests is usually not considered as well. Better-designed programs which would provide quicker relief and assistance could be accomplished by legislation which provides for automatic temporary increases in benefits and temporary relaxation of asset limits without time-consuming acts by Congress after a major downturn has begun (Chodorow-Reich et al. 2022).

Acknowledgments

The authors thank Olivia S. Mitchell, David Splinter, and Christopher Wheat for comments, and Shria Holla for research assistance.

Appendix

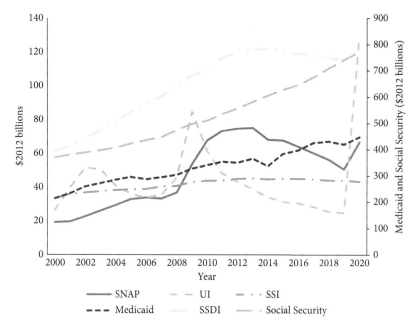

Figure A1 Trends in real transfer program spending among adults

Notes: Data are for adults age 18 and older, except for the UI series that includes 16- and 17-year-olds. Data are deflated using the 2012 personal consumption expenditure deflator.
Source: Authors' calculations from administrative data, various sources available upon request.

TABLE A1 Summary statistics of men

Variable	Ages 50–74 Mean	Std. Dev.	Ages 50–61 Mean	Std. Dev.	Ages 62–74 Mean	Std. Dev.
Age	60.13	6.89	55.21	3.43	67.26	3.64
White	0.84	0.37	0.83	0.38	0.85	0.36
Black	0.10	0.30	0.11	0.31	0.09	0.29
Other Race	0.06	0.24	0.07	0.25	0.06	0.23
Hispanic	0.10	0.30	0.11	0.31	0.08	0.27
Less than High School	0.12	0.33	0.11	0.31	0.14	0.35
High School	0.31	0.46	0.31	0.46	0.30	0.46
Some College	0.25	0.43	0.26	0.44	0.24	0.42
College or More	0.32	0.47	0.32	0.47	0.32	0.47
Married	0.71	0.45	0.70	0.46	0.74	0.44

Continued

TABLE A1 *Continued*

Variable	Ages 50–74 Mean	Std. Dev.	Ages 50–61 Mean	Std. Dev.	Ages 62–74 Mean	Std. Dev.
Widowed, Divorced, or Separated	0.19	0.39	0.19	0.39	0.20	0.40
Never Married	0.10	0.29	0.12	0.32	0.06	0.24
Household Size	2.49	1.31	2.69	1.39	2.21	1.11
Own Home	0.81	0.39	0.79	0.41	0.84	0.36
Employed	0.59	0.49	0.76	0.43	0.34	0.47
SNAP	0.07	0.25	0.07	0.26	0.06	0.23
UI	0.04	0.21	0.06	0.24	0.02	0.15
SSI	0.04	0.20	0.04	0.21	0.03	0.18
Medicaid	0.11	0.31	0.11	0.32	0.10	0.29
Social Security	0.26	0.44	0.01	0.12	0.63	0.48
SSDI	0.08	0.27	0.08	0.27	0.07	0.26
State Unemployment Rate	0.06	0.02	0.06	0.02	0.06	0.02

Note: Sample consists of men ages 50–74 with less than a college education.
Source: Authors' calculations from the Current Population Survey Annual Social and Economic Supplement, 2001–2021.

TABLE A2 Summary statistics of women

Variable	Ages 50–74 Mean	Std. Dev.	Ages 50–61 Mean	Std. Dev.	Ages 62–74 Mean	Std. Dev.
Age	60.37	6.94	55.27	3.43	67.36	3.68
White	0.82	0.38	0.81	0.39	0.83	0.37
Black	0.11	0.32	0.12	0.32	0.11	0.31
Other Race	0.07	0.25	0.07	0.25	0.06	0.24
Hispanic	0.10	0.30	0.11	0.31	0.09	0.28
Less than High School	0.12	0.33	0.10	0.31	0.15	0.35
High School	0.33	0.47	0.31	0.46	0.35	0.48
Some College	0.27	0.44	0.28	0.45	0.25	0.43
College or More	0.28	0.45	0.31	0.46	0.25	0.43
Married	0.62	0.49	0.65	0.48	0.58	0.49
Widowed, Divorced, or Separated	0.30	0.46	0.26	0.44	0.36	0.48
Never Married	0.08	0.27	0.09	0.29	0.06	0.23
Household Size	2.38	1.28	2.57	1.33	2.11	1.16
Own Home	0.80	0.40	0.79	0.41	0.82	0.38
Employed	0.47	0.50	0.64	0.48	0.25	0.43
SNAP	0.09	0.28	0.09	0.29	0.08	0.27
UI	0.03	0.17	0.04	0.19	0.01	0.12
SSI	0.05	0.22	0.05	0.22	0.05	0.21

Table A2

Variable	Ages 50–74		Ages 50–61		Ages 62–74	
	Mean	Std. Dev.	Mean	Std. Dev.	Mean	Std. Dev.
Medicaid	0.13	0.33	0.13	0.34	0.12	0.32
Social Security	0.27	0.44	0.01	0.12	0.61	0.49
SSDI	0.07	0.25	0.07	0.26	0.07	0.25
State Unemployment Rate	0.06	0.02	0.06	0.02	0.06	0.02

Note: Sample consists of women ages 50–74 with less than a college education.
Source: Authors' calculations from the Current Population Survey Annual Social and Economic Supplement, 2001–2021.

Notes

1. Medicaid also provides nursing home care, but we exclude the institutionalized population in the empirical work below.
2. See Goda et al. (2021) for a study of the impact of the pandemic recession on retirement but with an additional examination of DI and SSI applications. The authors found a slight dropoff in applications. See Maestas and Mullen (2024) for a study showing no increase in DI applications in the pandemic recession.
3. Each of these programs, and recent policy developments, are covered in greater detail in Moffitt and Ziliak (2019). The TANF program is omitted from our discussion because eligibility for cash assistance requires the presence of a dependent child under age 18 residing in the household, and this is rare for the older population. In results not presented we found that fewer than 0.5 percent of persons age 50–74 participated in TANF, and thus we drop it from our analysis. Housing assistance is a benefit received by older persons, but quality measurement of the program is lacking in the ASEC.
4. The administrative totals we match are adult participants in each program ages 18 and older, and thus we use an expanded ASEC sample of persons ages 18 and older in order to match administrative counts prior to restricting the sample to 50–74-year-olds.
5. The whole supplement imputes are retained for the adjustment for underreporting of transfer programs in order to match population weighted totals to administrative counts.
6. Although program receipt is measured at the family level, the male and female receipts do not have to exactly coincide because unmarried men and women are included in each gender's sample.
7. The regressions are weighted by the inverse probability of remaining the sample after imputed values are excluded.

References

Alon, T., M. Doepke, J. Olmstead-Rumsey, and M. Tertilt (2020). 'This Time It's Different: The Role of Women's Employment in a Pandemic Recession.' NBER Working Paper 27660. Cambridge, MA: National Bureau of Economic Research.

Anderson, P. M., K. F. Butcher, and D. W. Schanzenbach (2015). 'Changes in Safety Net Use During the Great Recession.' *American Economic Review*, 105(5): 161–165.

Bitler, M. and H. Hoynes (2016). 'The More Things Change, the More They Stay the Same? The Safety Net and Poverty in the Great Recession.' *Journal of Labor Economics*, 34(1): S403–444.

Bitler, M., H. Hoynes, and E. Kuka (2017). 'Child Poverty, the Great Recession, and the Social Safety Net in the United States.' *Journal of Policy Analysis and Management*, 36(2): 358–389.

Bitler, M. P. and H. W. Hoynes (2010). 'The State of the Social Safety Net in the Post-Welfare Reform Era.' *Brookings Papers on Economic Activity*, 2: 71–127.

Bitler, M. P., H. W. Hoynes, and J. Iselin (2020a). 'Cyclicality of the US Safety Net: Evidence from the 2000s and Implications for the COVID-19 Crisis.' *National Tax Journal*, 73(3): 759–780.

Bitler, M. P., H. W. Hoynes, and D. W. Schanzenbach (2020b). 'The Social Safety Net in the Wake of COVID-19.' *Brookings Papers on Economic Activity*, Summer: 119–145.

Bollinger, C., B. T. Hirsch, C. M. Hokayem, and J. P. Ziliak (2019). 'Trouble in the Tails? What We Know about Earnings Nonresponse Thirty Years after Lillard, Smith, and Welch.' *Journal of Political Economy*, 127(5): 2143–2185.

Chodorow-Reich, G., P. Ganong, and J. Gruber (2022). 'Should We Have Automatic Triggers for Unemployment Duration and How Costly Would It Be?' *AEA Papers and Proceedings*, 112: 112–116.

Clark, R., A. Lusardi, and O. S. Mitchell (2022). 'Movements In and Out of Poverty at Older Ages: Evidence from the HRS.' Pension Research Council Working Paper PRC WP2022-11. Philadelphia, PA: Wharton School, University of Pennsylvania.

Coile, C. and H. Zhang (2024). 'Recessions and Retirement: New Evidence from the COVID-19 Pandemic.' In O. S. Mitchell, J. Sabelhaus, and S. Utkus, eds., *Real-World Shocks and Retirement System Resiliency*. Oxford, UK: Oxford University Press, pp. 52–70.

Cutler, D., E. Meara, W. Powell, S. Richards-Shubik, and S. Stewart (2015). 'Why Do Disability Insurance Claims Increase During Recessions?' NBER Working Paper DRC NB15-03. Cambridge, MA: National Bureau of Economic Research.

Ganong, P. and J. Liebman (2018). 'The Decline, Rebound, and Further Rise in SNAP Enrollment: Disentangling Business Cycle Fluctuations and Policy Changes.' *American Economic Journal: Economic Policy*, 10(4): 153–176.

Ganong, P., P. Noel, and J. S. Vavra (2020). 'US Unemployment Replacement Rates During the Pandemic.' Becker-Friedman Institute Working Paper 2020-62. Chicago, IL: University of Chicago.

Goda, G. S., E. Jackson, L. H. Nicholas, and S. S. Stith (2021). 'The Impact of COVID-19 on Older Workers' Employment and Social Security Spillovers.' NBER Working Paper 29083. Cambridge, MA: National Bureau of Economic Research.

Hembre, E. (2021). 'Examining SNAP and TANF Caseload Trends, Responsiveness, and Policies during the COVID-19 Pandemic.' http://dx.doi.org/10.2139/ssrn.3693339

Hershbein, B. and B. A. Stuart (2022). 'Place-Based Consequences of Person-Based Transfers: Evidence from Recessions.' Federal Reserve Bank of Philadelphia Working Paper WP 22-08. Philadelphia, PA: Federal Reserve Bank of Philadelphia.

Larrimore, J., J. Mortenson, and D. Splinter (2022). 'Earnings Shocks and Stabilization During COVID-19.' *Journal of Public Economics*, 206: 1–9.

Larrimore, J., J. Mortenson, and D. Splinter (2022). 'Presence and Persistence of Poverty in U.S. Tax Data.' In R. Chetty, J. N. Friedman, J. C. Gornick, B. Johnson, and A. Kennickell, eds., *Measuring the Distribution and Mobility of Income and Wealth*. Cambridge, MA: National Bureau of Economic Research, pp. 383–409.

Maestas, N. (2019). 'Identifying Work Capacity and Promoting Work: A Strategy for Modernizing the SSDI Program.' *Annals of the American Academy of Political and Social Science*, 686 (1): 93–120.

Maestas, N. and K. J. Mullen (2024). 'Economic Conditions, the COVID-19 Pandemic, and Implications for Disability Insurance.' In O. S. Mitchell, J. Sabelhaus, and S. Utkus, eds., *Real-World Shocks and Retirement System Resiliency*. Oxford, UK: Oxford University Press, pp. 211–221.

Maestas, N., K. J. Mullen, and A. Strand (2015). 'Disability Insurance and the Great Recession.' *American Economic Review*, 105(5): 177–182.

Moffitt, R. A. (2013). 'The Great Recession and the Social Safety Net.' *Annals of the American Academy of Political and Social Science*, 650 (November): 143–166.

Moffitt, R. A. and G. Pauley (2018). 'Trends in the Distribution of Social Safety Net Support after the Great Recession.' *Stanford Center on Poverty and Inequality Issue Brief, March 2018*. Stanford, CA: Stanford Center on Poverty and Inequality.

Moffitt, R. A. and J. P. Ziliak, eds. (2019). 'Entitlement Reform.' *The ANNALS of the American Academy of Political and Social Science*, 686 (November).

Moffitt, R. A. and J. P. Ziliak (2020). 'COVID-19 and the US Safety Net.' *Fiscal Studies*, 41(3): 515–548.

Rees-Jones, A., J. D'Attoma, A. Piolatto, and L. Salvadori (2020). 'COVID-19 Changed Tastes for Safety-Net Programs.' NBER Working Paper No. 27865. Cambridge, MA: National Bureau of Economic Research.

US Department of Agriculture, Food and Nutrition Service, Office of Policy Support (USDA FNS) (2021). *Characteristics of Supplemental Nutrition Assistance Program Households: Fiscal Year 2019*. Alexandria, VA: USDA FNS.

Ziliak, J. P. (2016). 'Why Are So Many Americans on Food Stamps?' In J. Bartfeld, C. Gundersen, T. M. Smeeding, and J. P. Ziliak, eds., *SNAP Matters: How Food Stamps Affect Health and Well-Being*. Stanford, CA: Stanford University Press, pp. 18–48.

Ziliak, J. P., D. N. Figlio, E. E. Davis, and L. S. Connolly (2000). 'Accounting for the Decline in AFDC Caseloads: Welfare Reform or the Economy?' *Journal of Human Resources*, 35(3): 570–586.

Ziliak, J. P., C. Gundersen, and D. N. Figlio (2003). 'Food Stamp Caseloads over the Business Cycle.' *Southern Economic Journal*, 69(4): 903–919.

Chapter 9

Retirement Security and Health Costs

Glenn Follette and Louise Sheiner

Despite virtually universal health insurance coverage through Medicare, household spending on health care in the US accounts for a larger share of income for the elderly than it does for the non-elderly (Carman et al. 2020). In addition, Medicare beneficiaries face larger out-of-pocket costs when faced with a health shock than do many non-elderly, because traditional Medicare and, to some extent, Medicare Advantage impose high cost-sharing requirements. Furthermore, Medicare does not cover long-term care expenses. As a result of the structure of our health care system, private health care expenses rise sharply with age.

In addition to high expected costs of health care and vulnerability to health spending shocks, the elderly are also vulnerable to rising health care costs over time. Health care spending has increased faster than GDP on average for decades. Although it has slowed in recent years, both the Congressional Budget Office (CBO) and the Centers for Medicaid and Medicare Services (CMS) project that per capita Medicare spending will continue to rise at a faster pace than income over coming decades. Rising costs affect the elderly in two dimensions: by pushing up costs for individuals as they age, and by increasing the costs faced by each succeeding cohort.

Many analysts have examined the effects of health care cost growth on the sustainability of the federal budget (e.g., CBO 2016), but less attention has been paid to the vulnerability of elderly households to such cost increases and what that vulnerability implies for retirement security. In a previous paper, we examined long-term health spending trends by income quintile for the elderly and the non-elderly (Follette and Sheiner 2008). We noted that, despite significant increases in national health care spending as a share of national income, household health spending had increased much less because of expansions in the share of spending financed by public programs. We argued that public policy was quite responsive to falling health care affordability, and that there would likely be pressure to further expand public financing of health care over time, presenting a risk to the long-term federal budget projections. In this chapter, we update that analysis, focusing

Glenn Follette and Louise Sheiner, *Retirement Security and Health Costs*. In: *Real-World Shocks and Retirement System Resiliency*. Edited by: Olivia S. Mitchell, John Sabelhaus, and Stephen P. Utkus, Oxford University Press.

solely on the elderly. We examine what the slowdown in health spending observed in recent years has meant for retirement security and assess how vulnerable the elderly are to future increases in health spending. An innovation in our analysis relative to other efforts (e.g., Cubanski et al. 2018 and Hatfield et al. 2018) is that we allow health care spending growth to differ between Medicare and national health spending, and we also consider the extent to which rising health care prices will boost the income of the elderly through their impact on the CPI used to adjust social security and other government transfer programs.

We show that the slowdown in health care cost growth over the past decade has had a major impact on the wellbeing on the low- and middle-income elderly, boosting the income available to finance non-health consumption by up to 15 percent. To a large extent, this slowdown is attributable to changes in Medicare payment policy enacted as part of the Affordable Care Act (ACA). Without an expansion of public financing, however, health care is likely to become increasingly unaffordable for those in the lowest two income quintiles.

The effect of increased health spending on the elderly will be somewhat muted, to the extent that higher health costs filter into the CPI and thus raise benefits paid to the elderly; yet we find that this offset is only partial, because health care spending by the elderly is a much higher fraction of their income than it is for the population in general. In addition, not all increases in health spending are the result of faster growth of prices, also muting the benefits of the CPI adjustment.

Our metric of elderly retirement security is the amount of income available for non-health care expenditures.[1] Assuming that health spending continues to increase faster than income, retirement security will decline for each succeeding cohort and within each cohort as it ages, increasing the vulnerability of the elderly to health-cost shocks. Of course, rising health expenditures may improve wellbeing even if they crowd out other consumption, if they are the result of improved treatments that boost the quality and length of life. Thus, our analysis cannot speak to overall welfare. Nevertheless, our analysis sheds light on the extent to which high health spending will strain household budgets.

Increasing unaffordability of health care for the elderly is likely to give rise to pressures to expand programs, while at the same time pressures to rein in government budget deficits will give rise to pressures to lower federal spending. An important question is the extent to which policy can continue to rely on provider cuts, which are a way of both cutting federal spending and increasing affordability.

In what follows, we first examine the structure of Medicare to explain why the elderly face such high expenses despite nearly universal health insurance coverage. Next, we discuss the evolution of health costs over time and projections from the Congressional Budget Office and the Centers on

Medicare and Medicaid Services over the next decades. After describing the data we use to examine the vulnerability of households to health shocks, we examine how the burden of health care has evolved over time and the impact of the recent slowdown in health spending on the budgets of elderly households by income quintile. Next, we present simulations showing how projected health cost increases are likely to affect retirement security of current and future beneficiaries. A final section concludes.

The Structure of Health Insurance for the Elderly

Most elderly (roughly 96%) in the US are covered by Medicare. Americans who turn age 65 receive premium-free Medicare Part A, which covers inpatient hospital costs, if they or their spouse have completed 40 quarters of work in which they paid social security taxes.[2] Medicare beneficiaries pay a Part B premium, which for most people is set to cover 25 percent of average Part B costs; since 2007, high-income beneficiaries have had to pay a higher Part B premium (covering up to 85% of average Part B costs, depending on income). Similarly, Part D premiums cover about 25 percent of expected costs, with high-income beneficiaries paying more (Cubanski and Neuman 2018).

Traditional Medicare has high out-of-pocket payments and no out-of-pocket maximum. For example, in 2022, the hospital deductible was $1,556 paid per hospitalization episode. There were no other charges for the first 60 days of hospitalization, but there was a daily charge of $389 for days 61–90, and $778 per day after 91 days.[3] In 2022, the Part B premium was $2,041 per year for most beneficiaries and the Part B deductible was $233.[4] Once the deductible is met, beneficiaries pay 20 percent of the Medicare-approved amount for most doctor services, outpatient therapy, and medical equipment.

Beneficiaries have the option of choosing Medicare Advantage instead of traditional Medicare. Under Medicare Advantage, Medicare pays private plans which then provide insurance that covers the services otherwise covered by Parts A and B. Medicare Advantage plans can charge additional premiums, but many of them do not, and some even pay all or part of the Part B premium for beneficiaries. Medicare Advantage plans are required to have out-of-pocket maximums, which in 2022 were $7,550 for in-network and $11,300 for out-of-network providers; yet these plans typically do require considerable cost sharing, sometimes exceeding those of traditional Medicare (Freed et al. 2021).

Medicare Part D is an optional add-on to Medicare. Beneficiaries choosing Part D coverage choose among a set of private plans approved by

Medicare. Beneficiaries pay a monthly premium which averaged $400 per year in 2022, although there was wide variation across plans. Part D also has a deductible (which varies by plan and averaged less than $25 in 2022) and coinsurance (which varies by plan, but was no more than 25%), and an out-of-pocket maximum of $7,050 in 2022.

Low-income beneficiaries. About 12 percent of elderly Medicare beneficiaries are also enrolled in Medicaid. About 85 percent of these 'dual eligibles' qualify for full Medicaid benefits, which pays for Medicare premiums and cost sharing and provides insurance coverage for services not covered by Medicare, including, importantly, nursing home care, as well as things like eyeglasses and dental services. The remaining 15 percent of dual eligibles qualify for lesser benefits.[5]

Eligibility for these different levels of coverage depends on income and assets. There are differences across the states in eligibility categories, but to qualify for full Medicaid in many states, income must be less than the federal poverty line and assets—excluding the primary home and other personal property—must be lower than $2,000. In some states (so called 'medically-needy states'), people with income too high to qualify for Medicaid but with large medical expenses can qualify for Medicaid if their income less their Medicaid expenses is low enough, and if they meet the assets tests. There are also special low-income subsidies for Medicare Part D, which also have both income and asset limits.

Thus, Medicaid is a much more important source of coverage for lower-income elderly: in 2019, according to the Medicare Current Beneficiary Survey, 50 percent of elderly Medicare beneficiaries in the lowest income quintile were covered by Medicaid, and about 6 percent of beneficiaries in the second income quintile.

With Medicare beneficiaries potentially exposed to large out-of-pocket expenditures as well as a lack of coverage for dental and other services, it is not surprising to find that most elderly Medicare beneficiaries have supplemental coverage. For example, in 2018, among the 60 percent of Medicare enrollees with traditional Medicare, 83 percent have other coverage (MEDPAC 2021). The added forms of coverage include Medigap (41%), employer-sponsored insurance (20%), and Medicaid (9%). Some people with Medicare Advantage are also enrolled in other programs, including Medicaid and employer-sponsored insurance.

National Health Spending Trends over Time

Health care spending has exceeded income growth for decades, rising from 5 percent of GDP in 1960 to 17.6 percent in 2019.[6] As discussed in Follette and Sheiner (2008), the rate of increase in health spending's share of

GDP slowed over the 1960–2005 period, and that rate of growth has slowed even more markedly since. Indeed, the increase over the most recent decade has been the smallest since before 1960. There was an even more dramatic slowing in real spending per capita, as per capita GDP growth also slowed significantly.[7]

Medicare spending slowed considerably over this period. Lower reimbursement rates enacted as part of the ACA were the main driver, but lower utilization rates and much lower spending on drugs were also important. Regardless of whether expressed in nominal dollars or as a share of GDP, by 2019, Medicare spending was about 20 percent lower than projected by the Congressional Budget Office in 2009 (Figure 9.1). This saved the federal government roughly $1 trillion from 2010 to 2019.

A key question is whether the slowdown in overall health spending and Medicare spending growth is likely to persist. As we discuss below, both CMS and CBO assume that the recent slowdown is largely transitory, but both predict eventual slowdowns in health spending growth. Before discussing these long-run projections, we first detail the source of the slowdown.

Factors influencing spending growth. Table 9.1 reports CMS's estimates of national health expenditure growth adjusted for changes in the demographic composition of the population (CMS 2021a). The first row of the table shows that growth in real health spending per capita (using the GDP deflator to inflation adjust) has been declining gradually over time. In

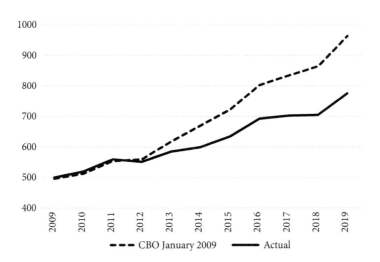

Figure 9.1 Medicare spending, projected as of 2009, and actual

Source: Authors' calculations using CBO Budget Projections, January 2009; CBO Historical Budget Data, February 2021.

TABLE 9.1 Decomposition of health spending 1980–2019

	1980–1990	1990–2000	2000–2010	2010–2019	Estimate of Excess Cost Growth Under 'Normal' Economic Conditions
CMS Adjusted Real Health Spending Growth per Capita	4.5	2.3	2.5	0.9	
Real GDP Growth Per Capita	1.3	1.3	-0.1	0.9	
CMS Excess Cost Growth	3.2	1	2.6	0	
Contributions					
Approximation of CMS Factor Model					
Income	2.4	1.9	2.7	0.5	0.6
Relative Prices	2.4	1.1	0.6	-0.1	0.5
Insurance	0.4	0.5	0.3	0.1	0.0
Other	-2.0	-2.5	-1.0	-0.5	-0.4
Total	*3.2*	*1.0*	*2.6*	*0.0*	*0.7*
Alternative Decomposition					
Income	0.0	0.0	0.0	0.0	0.6
Relative Prices (0.2)	3.2	1.5	0.8	-0.1	0.6
Insurance	0.4	0.5	0.3	0.1	0.1
Other	-0.4	-1.0	1.5	0.0	0.5
Total	*3.2*	*1.0*	*2.6*	*0.0*	*1.2*

Note: The middle panel denoted 'Approximation of CMS Factor Model' uses the income and price elasticities used by CMS to decompose changes in Excess Cost Growth over time. The bottom panel uses an alternative set of elasticities from the literature (income elasticity of 1 and a relative price elasticity of 0.2) to create an alternative decomposition. In the column marked 'Normal' Economic Conditions, we estimate excess cost growing forward assuming that health prices increase 0.75 percentage points faster than GDP prices, GDP rises x percent a year, increases in insurance coverage have the same effect going forward as over the last decade, and 'other' contributes the same amount as it did on average from x to y.
Source: Authors' calculations using Centers for Medicaid and Medicare Services (CMS 2021a, 2021c) National Health Expenditure Data, 2021, and Bureau of Economic Analysis (BEA) 2022.

describing health spending growth, economists typically focus on excess cost growth—defined here as the difference between per capita GDP growth and demographically-adjusted per capita health spending growth.[8] The third row of the table reports CMS's estimates of excess cost growth over time. While the decline over time is clear, the pattern is a bit volatile, suggesting that a clear signal of the underlying trend can be difficult to ascertain.[9]

As discussed in Heffler et al. (2021), the key contributors to excess health spending growth are increased demand owing to technological advances, more rapid increases in measured health prices compared to other goods and services, the falling price for care faced by consumers owing to insurance expansions, and population aging.[10] In the following discussion, we review how each of these factors has changed over time. The middle and bottom panels of Table 9.1 present two different numerical decompositions of excess cost growth based on these factors. These decompositions reflect two different set of price and income elasticities: those used by CMS and an alternate set that is reasonable given the literature.

Income and technology. There is considerable uncertainty about the relationship between health care spending and income. Looking across countries at a point in time, spending does rise with income, and an income elasticity of about 1 seems reasonable. With a unit elasticity, changes in GDP growth have no effect on excess cost growth, as shown in the bottom panel of Table 9.1. But elasticities estimated from cross-country studies may understate the effect of income on health spending that occurs through the availability of new technology that might be related to income, yet is available to all countries at any given time. To account for this potential relationship between health technology and income growth, CMS assumes a time varying income elasticity that averages 1.6 over 1980–2020 (Heffler et al. 2021). The middle panel of Table 9.1 uses this elasticity to estimate the contribution of income growth on excess cost growth over time.[11]

Insurance. Insurance coverage can affect health spending growth by affecting the price paid by consumers at the time of purchase of health care. Since 1960, there has been rising coverage of individuals through several channels, including the expansion of government programs, an increase in the types of health services that are insured, as well as the changing structure of insurance contracts. The share of health spending paid out-of-pocket (i.e., spending excluding premiums) fell from 24 cents on the dollar in 1990 to 17 cents in 2005, and then to 14 cents in 2020. Applying a demand elasticity to changes in insurance coverage of –0.2 used by the CMS, the reduction in out-of-pocket spending share may have raised demand by roughly 0.1 percentage point per year over the past 25 years (middle and bottom panels of Table 9.1).

TABLE 9.2 Relative health care inflation

	Average Relative Inflation Rate, Ten Years Ending							2019 less 2010
	1990	1995	2000	2005	2010	2015	2019	
Excess Inflation Relative to GDP Prices	4.0	3.5	1.8	0.8	1.0	0.4	0.0	−1.0
Medical products, appliances, and equipment	2.9	2.1	1.1	0.9	0.8	0.7	0.6	−0.2
Outpatient services	3.0	2.9	1.5	0.3	0.3	−0.2	−0.6	−0.9
Hospital and nursing home services	5.1	4.4	2.1	1.2	1.7	0.8	0.3	−1.4

Source: Authors' calculations using Bureau of Economic Analysis (BEA) 2022, Table 2.4.4.

Health care prices. Another source of excess growth has been faster increases in health care prices than overall inflation—Table 9.2.[12] Over the 2010–2020 period, health care inflation slowed markedly, even more than overall inflation. As a result, health prices increased 0.1 percentage point slower than GDP prices, compared to increasing 1.0 percentage point faster over 2000–2010, with even much larger wedges in earlier decades.

Many factors can move relative prices over time. For example, the consolidation of providers can lead to higher prices, and more aggressive negotiating by health insurance companies can lower prices. Changes to Medicare pricing policies also have a large effect on overall health prices, both because Medicare makes up about 25 percent of total health spending, and because Medicare reimbursement rates also affect non-Medicare health prices. Some states specify Medicaid payments as a percentage of Medicare's prices (Fiedler 2022). In addition, evidence suggests that Medicare reimbursement rates also have a large effect on the negotiated rates between providers and private health insurance (Clemens and Gottlieb 2017; White 2013).

Higher prices generally lower utilization, so the rise in prices contributes less than one-for-one to increased nominal spending. Using CMS's assumed price elasticity of −0.4, over the 2000–2010 period, the 1.0 average rise in relative health care prices raised excess growth by 0.6 percentage point annually, which fell to 0.1 percentage point over 2010–2019. Yet this price elasticity is higher than other estimates.[13] As an alternative, the bottom panel of Table 9.1 uses an elasticity of −0.2, which raises the contribution of excess health costs during the first decade from 0.6 to 0.8 percentage point.

With a lower price elasticity, the slowdown in relative prices makes a larger contribution to the deceleration in excess cost growth.

Other factors affecting excess cost growth. As shown in Table 9.1, the decompositions do not fully account for excess cost growth. The residual (labeled 'Other') can stem from many factors, including changes in the availability and cost of new technologies or new drugs over time, and shifts in sources of coverage not picked up by measured prices. In addition, there is huge uncertainty about the elasticity assumptions (and the model itself), and these may vary over time.

What does the recent slowdown imply about health spending going forward? Looking at the sources of the slow excess cost growth in 2010–2019, it seems likely that continued insurance expansions are not likely to have much effect on excess cost growth going forward, given that the share of health spending paid out of pocket is already so small. By contrast, relative prices could revert to playing a larger role, in line with historical experience. A shift to relative price increases of 1.5 percent per year, the average from 1990 to 2005, would lead to excess cost growth of about 0.9 to 1.2 percentage points, depending on the assumed price elasticity.

Nevertheless, with Medicare continuing to allow only modest increases in reimbursement rates over time, it is possible that relative prices growth will stay muted. In addition, it is also possible that other forces beside Medicare payment policy have held private health prices down, and these other (unexplained) forces could persist.

In the column under 'normal' economic conditions in Table 9.1, we assume health prices increase 0.75 percentage points faster than GDP prices, in line with CMS's estimate. With CMS's estimate of the income elasticity in 2020 of about 1.4, a return to normal GDP growth would lead to excess cost growth of about 0.6 percentage point. In the bottom decomposition, income affects spending growth, but has no effect on 'excess' spending growth.

In the middle decomposition that attempts to approximate CMS's factors model, the residual 'other factors' component is generally negative but shrinks over time. CMS assumes this residual fully dissipates over 25 years, and that it subtracts about 0.5 percentage point from excess cost growth in the near term. In the bottom decomposition, health spending growth has on average been higher than accounted for simply by relative price and insurance cost increases over the past 20 years, but this residual disappeared in the most recent decade. A reasonable estimate going forward might be 0.5, which would yield an equilibrium excess cost growth of 1.2 percent.

CMS and CBO projections of excess cost growth. Both CMS and CBO use a detailed bottom-up approach to project Medicare spending over the next decade, meaning that they project trends in utilization and reimbursement rates for each type of health service, and then they account for very detailed projections of reimbursement rates. Yet, they do take somewhat different approaches to projecting spending after that first decade.

For the final 50 years of its 75-year projection period, CMS uses the 'factors model' described above to project National Health Expenditures, along with a variety of assumptions, and factoring in the Medicare's payment rules. Altogether, CMS assumes that excess cost growth for Medicare averages roughly 0.5 percentage point from 2031 to 2051, and 0.8 percentage points for NHE.[14]

Rather than trying to model the underlying forces giving rise to excess cost growth, CBO recently has taken a more mechanical approach for the longer-term projection, factoring in the historical excess cost growth experience along with a number of assumptions. In its March 2021 Long-Term Budget Outlook, average excess cost growth from 2031 to 2051 was assumed to be 1.15 percentage points for Medicare and 1.27 percentage points for Medicaid and private health insurance premiums (CBO 2021a, 2021b).

Reasonable parameters for our simulations. In our view, there is some possibility that excess cost growth remains relatively low over time. This would have the effect of enhancing retirement security of the current and future elderly, and also shaping the long-run fiscal outlook for the federal government. Yet, it is also plausible that the recent lull will not persist. Furthermore, it is unclear whether the CMS projection, which assumes lower Medicare price growth and hence lower overall spending growth than non-Medicare spending, will prove correct, or whether the CBO approach, which has almost the same levels of excess cost growth for Medicare as for Medicaid and private health spending, will.

As we discuss below, the extent to which excess cost growth comes from relative (measured) prices versus from increased utilization also matters. As a result of these considerations, we assess the implications of 0 and 1 percent excess cost growth for NHE and Medicare, allowing the rates to move separately (e.g., 1% excess cost growth for NHE and 0% for Medicare.) We examine 2 percent excess cost growth—probably an upper bound—in the appendix.

Data Used in this Analysis

Our main source of data is the Medicare Current Beneficiary Survey (MCBS) (CMS 2022); in our analysis, we examine spending in 1996, 2000, 2005, 2009, 2015, and 2016. The MCBS includes information on premiums paid by the elderly, which include premiums for Medicare (either through traditional Medicare or a Medicare Advantage Plan) as well as any private premiums paid for supplemental insurance through Medigap or other private plans, including plans from a former employer to which they contribute. The MCBS also contains information on the source of funds that providers receive—for example, private insurance, Medicaid, or Medicare.

In the MCBS, total health spending, or the total amount paid to providers, is equal to the sum of amounts paid by Medicare and Medicaid, amounts paid directly by beneficiaries (copayments, deductibles, coinsurance), amounts paid by private insurance, and uncollected bills (bad debts). This decomposition of health spending does not account for the fact that Medicare beneficiaries pay premiums that cover some of the payments by Medicare and private insurance. Accordingly, to gauge the burden on the household, we decompose health spending as the sum of amounts paid by Medicare beneficiaries (premiums, copayments, deductibles, and coinsurance), publicly-financed spending (Medicare and Medicaid less premiums), and other spending (private payments less private premiums paid directly by Medicare beneficiaries, and bad debt).

In our decomposition, other spending includes spending financed by previous employers (the part of retiree health insurance not paid for directly by Medicare beneficiaries, as well as insurance profits or losses in a particular year and monies owed but not paid to hospitals, physicians, and other providers).

Adjustment of income. The main focus of the MCBS is on capturing health spending, and there is less focus on accurately measuring income; in fact, the income measures used are known to understate income (Cubanski et al. 2018). In addition, the questions used to capture income have changed over the course of the years that we analyze, making comparisons difficult. As discussed in Chen et al. (2018), the income measures in the Health and Retirement Study (HRS) are reasonably accurate. We therefore use income measured in the HRS to adjust the MCBS income. In particular, because the composition of the MCBS and the HRS populations are somewhat different (even with sample weights), we adjust as follows: for each year, we calculate adjustment factors by quintile, marital status, and age group equal to the ratio of HRS income to MCBS income, and we then multiply MCBS income by that adjustment factor.[15] We are assuming that the ranking of income in the MCBS matches the ranking of income in the HRS, which should be reasonably accurate at the quintile level of aggregation.

The MCBS includes measures of income for respondents and spouses, if present. For households where the respondent is married, we create an equivalence-adjusted per capita income measure by dividing household income by 1.7, following Follette and Sheiner (2008) and De Nardi et al. (2016).

Health care budget shares. The slowdown in aggregate health care spending described above shows through to real health spending per beneficiary. Figure 9.2 illustrates the rise and flattening of spending per beneficiary,

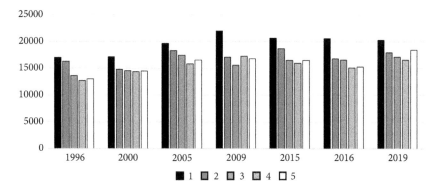

Figure 9.2 Real health expenditures by income quintile (2021 $), age adjusted

Note: Real health expenditures are adjusted according to the age distribution of Medicare beneficiaries over the full sample period.

Source: Authors' calculations using the Medicare Current Beneficiary Survey.

adjusted for the changing age distribution, since 1996, which is apparent for all income quintiles. It also shows that health spending generally declines as household income rises, reflecting the fact that age-adjusted health spending is actually highest for those in the lowest income quintiles and relatively flat across the other quintiles (not shown). Health spending tends to be higher for lower-income people because they are on average in worse health. Those with life-long health problems are likely to have low income, and low education is thought to contribute both to low income and poor health. Furthermore, lower-income elderly may have experienced more physically demanding jobs and more stressful lives, which could also affect health status later in life.

Panel (a) of Figure 9.3 shows the evolution of private health spending (the amount paid by beneficiaries through premiums for Medicare and other health insurance plans and other out-of-pocket payments like coinsurance and deductibles) as a share of income by quintile over time.

Two results are noteworthy. First, the private share of health spending has been declining over time, reflecting the relative stability in spending per beneficiary since about 2005, a small decline in the share of spending paid privately, and rising income. Second, despite the fact that the average share of health spending paid privately is much lower for those in the lowest income quintiles because of Medicaid, private health spending accounts for a larger share of income for those in the lowest income quintiles. This reflects the fact that health spending is actually somewhat higher for those in the lowest income quintiles, as we discussed above, income is much lower, and Medicaid coverage is far from universal even among the poor elderly.

Panel (b) of Figure 9.3 shows the distribution of spending on premiums for Medicare (either through traditional Medicare or a Medicare Advantage Plan) as well as any private premiums for supplemental insurance through Medigap or other private plans. Overall, beneficiaries in the lowest two income quintiles pay about 10 percent of income in premiums alone.

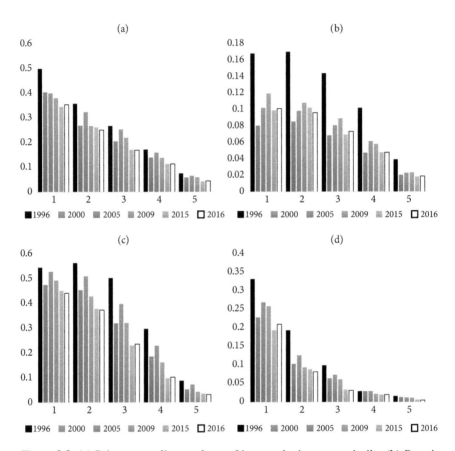

Figure 9.3 (a) Private spending as share of income by income quintile. **(b)** Premiums as a share of income by income quintile. **(c)** Cost burdened share of beneficiaries by income quintile (private spending > 20% income). **(d)** Cost burdened share of beneficiaries by income quintile (private spending > 50% income)

Note: Private spending includes premiums, co-pays, and deductibles. Premiums include premiums for Medicare (either through traditional Medicare or a Medicare Advantage Plan), and any private premiums paid for supplemental insurance. Income is adjusted using the Health and Retirement Study.

Source: Authors' calculations using the Medicare Current Beneficiary Survey and Health and Retirement Study.

These *average* out-of-pocket shares significantly understate the burden of health care spending for elderly households in poor health. Panels (c) and (d) of Figure 9.3 show the shares of beneficiaries who are cost burdened and severely cost burdened, which we define as private spending (premiums, co-pays, and deductibles) exceeding 20 percent and 50 percent of income, respectively. About 40 percent of beneficiaries in the two lowest income quintiles spent more than 20 percent of their income on health care in 2016. Twenty one percent of the lowest income beneficiaries and 8 percent of those in the second quintile spent more than 50 percent of income on health care in 2016. Of course, it is not likely that the same individuals will continue to spend this much year after year. Yet, as shown by De Nardi et al. (2016), health costs can be quite persistent.

Because health status deteriorates over time, and because the elderly face significant cost sharing, total health expenditures and private health spending increase with age. In addition, the ratio of health spending to income rises with age because income falls with age (for social security, e.g., the initial benefit is indexed to wages, but benefits thereafter are indexed to prices, meaning that benefits do not rise overtime as quickly as wages). Consequently, out-of-pocket spending as a share of income rises with age (see Figure 9.4).

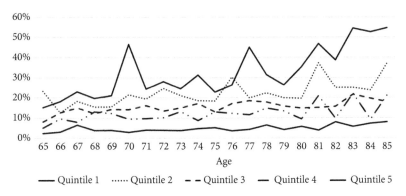

Figure 9.4 Out-of-pocket spending by age as a share of income in 2016

Note: Income quintiles are defined based on the income distribution of 65-year-olds in 2016. Out-of-pocket spending includes premiums, co-pays, and deductibles.
Source: Authors' calculations using the Medicare Current Beneficiary Survey, 2016.

Evaluating Changes in Real Income Available for Non-Health Consumption

Our measure of retirement security is real income available for non-health consumption—that is, after paying for health care, how much do households have left and how does this change over time? This differs from changes in budget shares, for two reasons. First, any increase in health spending as a share of the budget will have a larger effect on non-health consumption the larger is the share of health spending in the budget. Second, income itself may be affected by changes in health prices in such a way as to limit the effect of higher health spending on consumption of other goods and services. For example, if health prices increase but income increases by enough to offset that rise, health spending will increase as a share of nominal income, but income available for non-health expenditures will be unaffected.[16]

The key channel for the interaction of health prices and income is the annual CPI adjustment in social security and many defined benefit (DB) retirement programs. In the simulations below, we account for these interactions and also allow for differences between Medicare and private sector health prices. The appendix shows the derivation of our burden measure and our inflation adjustment. The intuition for the inflation adjustment is straightforward: If overall health care prices are increasing, the CPI adjustment will hold households harmless in the face of health prices increases, if their health spending share of income is the same as the health spending share in the CPI basket and if the prices they face—Medicare prices—are rising as quickly as overall health prices. Of course, elderly households typically spend more on health care than households in general, and health spending rises not just because of rising prices, and thus the CPI adjustment will be inadequate to protect the elderly from a rising burden of health spending over time.

The effect of the recent Medicare slowdown on retirement security. Figure 9.5 reports the effects of slower Medicare growth from 2009 to 2019 discussed above on income available for non-health expenditures. Because virtually all health expenditures of the elderly are tied to Medicare spending, it is reasonable to assume that the 20 percent drop in Medicare spending will result in a roughly 20 percent drop in beneficiary out-of-pocket spending. With that assumption, we estimate that the slower growth of Medicare expenditures over the 2009–2019 period provided a significant increase in resources available for non-health care consumption by 2019, amounting to a 16 percent increase for the lowest quintile, 9 percent for the second quintile, falling to only 1 percent for the highest quintile.

To the extent that the value of health care received hasn't been affected, the Medicare slowdown since 2009 represents a substantial increase in living standards for poor elderly households. This seems likely to be largely the

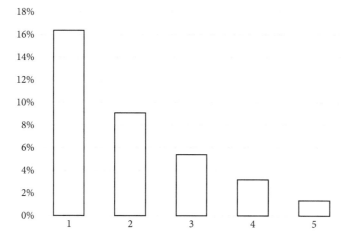

Figure 9.5 Increase in non-health consumption by 2019 from slower growth of Medicare savings since 2009, by income quintile

Note: Income quintiles are defined based on the income distribution of 65-year-olds in 2016.
Source: Authors' calculations using the Medicare Current Beneficiary Survey, 2016.

case. Most of the slowdown reflects cuts to payments to health care providers rather than reductions in utilization, and very few physicians have opted out of Medicare, suggesting that access to providers for Medicare beneficiaries has not deteriorated as a result of these cuts to provider payments (Ochieng et al. 2020). But some of the reduction is because of lower utilization, which might be associated with a reduction in the quality of care. Others have noted that Medicare Advantage—which covers a growing share of Medicare beneficiaries—often denies needed care, which also suggests the possibility of some reduction in the quality of care (Abelson 2022), though not necessarily associated with the slowdown in spending.

Looking Forward

To gauge the importance of future health care costs to elderly retirement security, we undertake two sets of simulations. In the first, we follow individuals of age 65 in 2019 and evaluate how the income available to finance non-health spending over time depends on the rate of increase in overall health care spending, health prices, and overall Medicare spending. In the second set of simulations, we examine the same set of issues through the lens of different cohorts by comparing retirees of the same age over time—that is, a retiree who is 65 in 2019, in 2029, in 2039, and 2049.

Our analysis takes into account increases in health spending over time as a function of quintile, age, and time. To measure the effects of aging on out-of-pocket expenditures, we use the average growth rates of health spending for each year of age by income quintile and Medicaid status (for bottom two quintiles) from 2009, 2015, 2016, and 2019.[17] We redefine quintiles for this exercise as the distribution of income of 65-year-olds, in order to capture the trajectory of out-of-pocket spending for people with the same real income over time.

Given that we are following people who are mostly retired, we assume that income rises with inflation. Health spending increases depend on our assumptions. We follow the Social Security Trustees (2021) by assuming that nominal per capita GDP growth will be roughly 3.5 percent, and that real per capita GAP growth (using the CPI-W deflator that rises 2.3% per year) is 1.2 percent. Thus, with 0 excess cost growth, real health spending rises 1.2 percent per year.

In order to isolate the effects of rapid health spending increases, in all our results we measure the income available for non-health spending relative to what it would be if health spending (Medicare and NHE) increased with overall inflation. In this base case, health spending rises as someone ages only because health status deteriorates with age. Our simulations capture the effects of rising relative prices or changes in health technology or practices.

Following current 65-year-olds over time. Table 9.3 presents our results. The first set of columns 'NHE Prices Rise with Overall Inflation' shows the results when any NHE excess health spending growth is the result of higher utilization, not measured prices; NHE spending growth therefore has no effect on the CPI and, as a consequence, no effect on the elderly for any given Medicare excess cost growth.

Examining the bottom quintile, Medicare excess cost growth of 0 percent—which means that Medicare costs are rising with GDP while income is rising with inflation—has little effect on the young elderly, because they spend a smaller share of their income on health costs and because the impact of faster health spending growth accumulates over time. By the time they are 75–79, however, income available for non-health goods and services is 12 percent lower than it would be if health costs rose with inflation, and the effect is much larger by the time they are in their 80s. Looking across Table 9.3, the third column shows what happens if there is no excess cost growth in Medicare but NHE excess cost growth is 1 percent and it is all due to relative price growth. The effects are just a bit more muted. Changes in the NHE prices only have a modest effect on people in the bottom quintile because the share of health spending in the CPI—roughly 7 percent—is much smaller than the share of out-of-pocket health spending for those in the bottom quintile, particularly at later ages.

A 1 percent rate of excess cost growth in Medicare—still below the average expected by CBO over the next 30 years—has a larger effect on the income available for non-health consumption, lowering it by almost 25

TABLE 9.3 Difference in real non-health consumption share of income relative to baseline scenario where Medicare costs increase with inflation

Medicare Excess Cost Growth	NHE Prices Rise with Overall Inflation		NHE Excess Cost Growth = 1%, All Prices	
	0%	1%	0%	1%
Quintile 1				
70–74	–5%	–9%	–3%	–7%
75–79	–12%	–24%	–10%	–22%
80–84	–61%	–123%	–60%	–124%
Quintile 2				
70–74	–5%	–9%	–3%	–7%
75–79	–12%	–22%	–10%	–21%
80–84	–29%	–57%	–26%	–56%
Quintile 3				
70–74	–2%	–3%	0%	–2%
75–79	–4%	–8%	–2%	–6%
80–84	–8%	–16%	–5%	–13%
Quintile 4				
70–74	–1%	–2%	0%	–1%
75–79	–2%	–4%	0%	–2%
80–84	–5%	–10%	–2%	–7%
Quintile 5				
70–74	0%	–1%	1%	1%
75–79	–1%	–2%	1%	0%
80–84	–2%	–3%	2%	0%

Source: Authors' calculations using the Medicare Beneficiary Survey, 2009–2016.

percent for 75–79-year-olds in the bottom quintile, compared to 12 percent for the case with no excess cost growth. And, again, the assumptions about how fast NHE prices rise has only modest effects.

The results for Quintile 2 are remarkably similar to those for Quintile 1, except for when people reach their 80s. The similarity reflects the fact that, while income is higher in Quintile 2, fewer people have Medicaid and thus private health spending is a similar share of income. The differences for those in their 80s reflects the much higher income shares of health spending for 80 year-olds in Quintile 1.

Of course, as one moves up the income quintiles, health spending as a share of income falls, meaning that any given increase in health costs has less effect on the resources available for non-health consumption. For people in the middle quintile, income available for non-health consumption is about 4 percent lower by their early 70s, assuming 0 excess cost growth, and 8 percent lower for 1 percent excess cost growth. Changes in NHE prices have a larger effect on those in Quintile 3 and above, however, because any offset from a CPI adjustment has a constant effect as a share of income across the quintiles, and thus provides a bigger relative reduction in the harm of higher health prices the smaller that effect is.

Turning to the bottom rows of the table, for Quintile 5, we see that rapid health spending growth has only very small effects on income available for non-health consumption. If NHE prices are increasing as well, higher health spending growth can even make them better off. (In addition, the assumption that income rises with the CPI for people in the top quintile is probably too restrictive for this group; their income likely rises faster than that over time, owing to their significant asset income.)

The main reason that the burdens differ so much by quintiles has to do with the fact that out-of-pocket health spending is a much larger share of income for lower income people (see Appendix Table A2). The actual dollar amounts of health spending do not differ much by income quintile, and the main reason that the burden increases with age is that health spending increases so much with age.

In sum, low-income elderly are quite vulnerable to rising health care costs. As we discuss below, we assume here that Medicaid rates do not vary over time—given that income or asset limits generally are not indexed to inflation, this might overstate the protection offered by Medicaid coverage. But because Medicaid take-up is fairly low, it is possible that as a result of increasing cost burden, take-up could increase. If not, there will undoubtedly be pressure to further expand the federal role in financing health costs for the elderly.[18]

The lack of importance of the CPI for the low-income elderly is also notable. That implies that any changes made to the CPI to better account for health care quality would have only small effects on the retirement security of the low-income elderly. The variation in the income share of private health spending by income quintile also means that measures like the CPI-E that attempt to capture the inflation experienced by the elderly will still not fully compensate the low-income elderly for increases in health costs.

Comparing different cohorts over time. The second set of simulations compare retirees of the same age over time—that is, a retiree who is 65 in 2019, in 2029, in 2039, and 2049—to gauge how different cohorts are affected by health care utilization and prices. We assume income before retirement grows at the rate assumed in the Social Security Trustees projections, and health spending rises at the pace described above. We account for changes in the CPI in the same manner as described above. When health spending rises faster than wages, health spending will be a larger share of income, but to the extent that increase is in the form of relative prices, some of the effect is offset by lower prices for non-health consumption items.

Table 9.4 presents our results, comparing different cohorts 10 years (2026) and 20 years (2036) after our most recent data. We examine only the effects of 1 percent excess cost growth, because with no excess cost growth

Table 9.4 Difference in non-health consumption share of income compared to 2016 cohort

NHE Prices Rise with Overall Inflation

| | 0% Excess Medicare Cost Growth | | | | 1% Excess Medicare Cost Growth | | | |
	65–69	70–74	75–79	80–85	65–69	70–74	75–79	80–85
				Quintile 1				
2026	0%	0%	0%	0%	–3%	–6%	–6%	–12%
2036	0%	0%	0%	0%	–7%	–13%	–13%	–25%
				Quintile 2				
2026	0%	0%	0%	0%	–3%	–3%	–4%	–5%
2036	0%	0%	0%	0%	–6%	–7%	–8%	–11%
				Quintile 3				
2026	0%	0%	0%	0%	–2%	–2%	–3%	–3%
2036	0%	0%	0%	0%	–4%	–5%	–5%	–6%
				Quintile 4				
2026	0%	0%	0%	0%	–1%	–1%	–2%	–2%
2036	0%	0%	0%	0%	–3%	–3%	–4%	–5%
				Quintile 5				
2026	0%	0%	0%	0%	–1%	–1%	–1%	–1%
2036	0%	0%	0%	0%	–1%	–1%	–1%	–2%

NHE Excess Cost Growth = 1%, All Prices

| | 0% Excess Medicare Cost Growth | | | | 1% Excess Medicare Cost Growth | | | |
	65–69	70–74	75–79	80–85	65–69	70–74	75–79	80–85
				Quintile 1				
2026	2%	2%	2%	2%	–1%	–4%	–4%	–10%
2036	5%	5%	5%	5%	–2%	–8%	–8%	–21%
				Quintile 2				
2026	2%	2%	2%	2%	0%	–1%	–1%	–3%
2036	5%	5%	5%	5%	–1%	–3%	–3%	–6%
				Quintile 3				
2026	2%	2%	2%	2%	0%	0%	0%	0%
2036	5%	5%	5%	5%	1%	0%	–1%	–1%
				Quintile 4				
2026	2%	2%	2%	2%	1%	1%	0%	0%
2036	5%	5%	5%	5%	2%	2%	1%	0%
				Quintile 5				
2026	2%	2%	2%	2%	2%	2%	2%	1%
2036	5%	5%	5%	5%	4%	4%	4%	3%

Source: Authors' calculations using the Medicare Beneficiary Survey, 2016

in Medicare and no change in NHE prices, future cohorts spend the same share of income on health spending as current cohorts.

Looking at the right column of the top panel, with 1 percent excess cost growth in Medicare owing to higher utilization and no change in the relative price of non-health goods, the burden of health spending in the bottom quintile increases sharply over time. For 70–74-year-olds in the bottom quintile, the income available for non-health spending falls 6 percent over the 10 years from 2016 to 2026 and 13 percent after 20 years; for the 80–85 cohort, the estimated reduction in income for non-health is dramatic, and would likely result in sizable pressures for government relief.

The bottom panel of the table analyzes the effects when NHE prices rise 1 percent, and therefore, relative prices of non-health goods and services fall. With 1 percent excess Medicare cost growth, real income available for non-health consumption still declines for those in the bottom two quintiles, albeit a bit less. But for those in the top income quintiles, real resources for non-health consumption are actually higher, because the fall in non-health prices is large enough to more than offset the rise in spending on health.

Conclusions and Policy Implications

Our earlier work showed that the higher the share of health spending in income, the more an increase in health care spending affected income available for other consumption (Follette and Sheiner 2008). We also noted, however, that despite rapid increases in health spending from 1980 to 2005, private health spending over that period had been relatively stable as a share of income because public policy had responded when health care threatened to become unaffordable to lower-income households. Our earlier study also focused on policy responses that expanded health coverage by increasing the government share of health spending, and it argued that such responsiveness created an upside risk to long-term federal budget projections, which assume no such expansions.

These policy expansions have continued in recent years, most notably by the introduction of Medicare Part D and the ACA. But for the elderly, an even more important development has been the slowdown in health spending growth. While the source of the slowdown is not fully understood, a large part of it is no doubt due to lower reimbursement rates in the ACA— essentially requiring *providers* to make health care more affordable, rather than simply increasing the federal share of health spending. Other ACA innovations, like the Hospital Readmissions Reductions Program and the introduction of the various Medicare Shared Savings Programs, may also have led to a reduction in utilization by making health care more efficient.

An important question is whether these provider cuts will remain sustainable over the long run, and whether even greater reductions may be possible in the future if health spending starts increasing rapidly again. The pace of health spending growth has significant implications for the federal budget, but as we showed, it is also a key determinant of retirement security, especially for low-income elderly households. With zero excess cost growth, retirees will still face increasing health spending as a share of income over time, both because of aging, and also because their income rises with inflation instead of GDP. For those in the lowest quintile, excess cost growth of zero—that is where health care spending rises with per capita GDP—still results in lower resources available for non-health consumption by 5 percent at age 70–74, and 12 percent at age 75–79, relative to a counterfactual where health spending only increased with inflation. Even if the CPI does adjust to reflect rapid health costs, and even if the health prices tracked by the CPI increase much faster than Medicare's, low-income elderly will receive only modest protection from higher health spending, because health spending represents a much larger share of their budget than the weight in the CPI.

With 1 percent excess cost, still modest by historical standards and below CBO's projections, resources for those in the bottom quintile are projected to decline 9 percent over the next 10 years, and 24 percent for 75–79-year-olds. If excess cost growth remains high, future cohorts will be at a further disadvantage, because they have more years during which health spending growth will exceed income growth. It is worth remembering that it is not just the rate of excess cost growth that determines the effect on resources available to support non-health consumption, but also the share of health spending in income. While excess cost growth has been higher in the past, the share of health spending in income was lower. The high share of health care in household budgets now implies that even modest excess cost growth could have material effects on affordability going forward.

Even assuming that the CMS projections of fairly modest excess cost growth are correct, pressure will likely grow over time for policymakers to take steps to preserve or increase affordability. If further cuts in provider payments are possible (including, e.g., negotiating drug prices), affordability could be increased without much effect on the federal budget. But if there are limits to the extent to which provider payments can be cut without impairing access to quality health care, then the pressure to increase federal financing of health care for the elderly will increase overall pressures on the budget.

Acknowledgments

We are extremely grateful for the excellent research assistance from Sophia Campbell and Nasiha Salwati.

Appendix

This appendix provides detail on our measure of health care burden and the additional simulation Appendix Tables A1–A3. To measure the changing burden of health care spending, it is important to model how changes in health costs affect both health spending and real income.

In our simulations, we measure the burden of health care spending as follows:

Let R be the percent change in real income available for non-health expenditures =

$$R_t = \frac{\frac{(Y_t - H_t)}{(1+\pi_c)}}{(Y_{t-1} - H_{t-1})} - 1,$$

TABLE A1 Difference in real non-health consumption share of income relative to baseline scenario where Medicare costs increase with inflation

	NHE Prices Rise with Overall Inflation	NHE Excess Cost Growth = 1%, All Prices	NHE Excess Cost Growth = 2%, All Prices
Medicare Excess Cost Growth	2%	2%	2%
		Quintile 1	
70–74	–12.8%	–11.7%	–11.1%
75–79	–37.0%	–35.6%	–34.7%
80–84	–195.7%	–199.4%	–201.9%
		Quintile 2	
70–74	–12.9%	–11.7%	–11.1%
75–79	–34.5%	–33.0%	–32.1%
80–84	–90.7%	–90.5%	–90.3%
		Quintile 3	
70–74	–4.8%	–3.6%	–2.9%
75–79	–11.8%	–9.7%	–8.6%
80–84	–26.0%	–23.4%	–21.8%
		Quintile 4	
70–74	–2.9%	–1.6%	–0.9%
75–79	–6.6%	–4.5%	–3.2%
80–84	–16.4%	–13.5%	–11.6%
		Quintile 5	
70–74	–1.1%	0.2%	0.9%
75–79	–3.0%	–0.7%	0.6%
80–84	–5.5%	–2.2%	0.0%

Source: Authors' calculations using the Medicare Beneficiary Survey, 2009–2016.

TABLE A2 Difference in resources available for non-health consumption relative to baseline scenario where Medicare costs increase with inflation (2016 $)

	NHE Prices Rise with Overall Inflation			NHE Excess Cost Growth = 1%, All Prices			NHE Excess Cost Growth = 2%, All Prices		
Medicare Excess Cost Growth	2%	1%	0%	2%	1%	0%	2%	1%	0%
				Quintile 1					
65–69	−153	−104	−56	−127	−77	−29	−113	−64	−15
70–74	−832	−554	−292	−757	−475	−210	−718	−433	−166
75–79	−1996	−1294	−666	−1914	−1195	−552	−1866	−1137	−485
80–84	−5143	−3234	−1616	−5223	−3245	−1570	−5276	−3254	−1540
				Quintile 2					
65–69	−388	−264	−142	−342	−218	−96	−319	−195	−72
70–74	−1608	−1070	−565	−1466	−922	−410	−1390	−842	−326
75–79	−3714	−2409	−1240	−3549	−2213	−1017	−3453	−2098	−886
80–84	−7617	−4791	−2395	−7585	−4659	−2177	−7567	−4574	−2037
				Quintile 3					
65–69	−321	−218	−118	−207	−104	−3	−151	−48	54
70–74	−1469	−978	−517	−1089	−591	−124	−885	−384	88
75–79	−3426	−2222	−1144	−2834	−1601	−498	−2487	−1238	−120
80–84	−6989	−4394	−2196	−6292	−3604	−1327	−5844	−3096	−767
				Quintile 4					
65–69	−346	−235	−127	−143	−32	77	−43	69	178
70–74	−1595	−1062	−561	−897	−357	151	−522	22	534
75–79	−3564	−2312	−1191	−2404	−1123	25	−1726	−426	737
80–84	−8210	−5163	−2581	−6742	−3585	−910	−5796	−2568	167
				Quintile 5					
65–69	−427	−290	−157	145	283	417	430	568	703
70–74	−1775	−1181	−624	260	862	1427	1353	1959	2528
75–79	−4568	−2961	−1524	−1096	549	2020	936	2604	4095
80–84	−8371	−5265	−2631	−3305	−87	2640	−37	3254	6043

Source: Authors' calculations using the Medicare Beneficiary Survey, 2009–2016.

where Y is nominal income, H is health expenditures, and π_c is inflation for consumer items excluding health. When R is 0, households can afford the same basket of non-health consumption as in the previous period.

TABLE A3 Difference in non-health consumption share of income compared to 2016 cohort

		NHE Prices Rise with Overall Inflation				NHE Excess Cost Growth = 1%, All Prices			
		2% Excess Medicare Cost Growth				2% Excess Medicare Cost Growth			
		65–69	70–74	75–79	80–85	65–69	70–74	75–79	80–85
Quintile 1	2026	-7%	-13%	-13%	-24%	-4%	-11%	-10%	-23%
	2036	-15%	-29%	-28%	-54%	-10%	-25%	-24%	-51%
Quintile 2	2026	-5%	-7%	-8%	-11%	-3%	-5%	-6%	-8%
	2036	-12%	-16%	-18%	-23%	-8%	-12%	-13%	-20%
Quintile 3	2026	-4%	-5%	-5%	-6%	-2%	-3%	-3%	-3%
	2036	-9%	-11%	-12%	-12%	-4%	-6%	-7%	-8%
Quintile 4	2026	-3%	-3%	-4%	-5%	-1%	-1%	-2%	-3%
	2036	-6%	-7%	-9%	-11%	-2%	-2%	-4%	-6%
Quintile 5	2026	-1%	-1%	-1%	-2%	1%	1%	1%	0%
	2036	-2%	-2%	-3%	-4%	2%	3%	2%	1%

NHE Excess Cost Growth = 2%, All Prices

		0% Excess Medicare Cost Growth				1% Excess Medicare Cost Growth				2% Excess Medicare Cost Growth			
		65–69	70–74	75–79	80–85	65–69	70–74	75–79	80–85	65–69	70–74	75–79	80–85
Quintile 1	2026	4%	4%	4%	4%	0%	-3%	-2%		-3%	-10%	-9%	-22%
	2036	8%	8%	8%	8%	1%	-5%	-5%		-7%	-22%	-21%	-50%
Quintile 2	2026	4%	4%	4%	4%	1%	0%	0%		-2%	-4%	-4%	-7%
	2036	8%	8%	8%	8%	3%	1%	0%		-5%	-9%	-10%	-17%
Quintile 3	2026	4%	4%	4%	4%	2%	1%	1%		0%	-1%	-2%	-2%
	2036	8%	8%	8%	8%	4%	3%	3%		-1%	-3%	-4%	-5%
Quintile 4	2026	4%	4%	4%	4%	2%	2%	2%		1%	0%	-1%	-1%
	2036	8%	8%	8%	8%	5%	5%	4%		2%	1%	-1%	-4%
Quintile 5	2026	4%	4%	4%	4%	3%	3%	3%		3%	3%	2%	2%
	2036	8%	8%	8%	8%	7%	7%	7%		6%	6%	5%	4%

Source: Authors' calculations using the Medicare Current Beneficiary Survey, 2016

Health spending increases over time because of measured prices and because of growth in utilization.[19] Furthermore, because Medicare prices are set administratively, they can and do diverge from private prices, as discussed above.

Denote health spending increases in Medicare due to utilization as g, and due to prices π_M. Let the share of health spending in income for the elderly be b, and let the increase in the CPI be π. Assume for simplicity that the increase in health care utilization is the same for Medicare as for private health spending, but that prices of health spending in the CPI increase at a different rate, π_P. Finally, let the share of health care spending in income for the elderly be b, and the share for the population as a whole as measured by the CPI be x.[20] Then CPI inflation, can be written as: $= x_{t-1}\pi_P + (1 - x_{t-1})\pi_C$. Then, equation (1) can be rewritten as:

$$R_t = \frac{\frac{(Y_{t-1}(1+\pi)-b_{t-1}Y_{t-1}(1+\pi_M+g))}{(1+\pi_c)}}{(Y_{t-1}-b_{t-1}Y_{t-1})} - 1$$

$$= \frac{\frac{((1+\pi)-b_{t-1}(1+\pi_M+g))}{(1+\pi_c)}}{(1-b_{t-1})} - 1$$

$$= \frac{\frac{\left(1+x_{t-1}\pi_P+\left(1-x_{t-1}\right)\pi_C\right)-b_{t-1}(1+\pi_M+g)}{(1+\pi_c)}}{(1-b_{t-1})} - 1 \, .$$

With a little bit of algebra, this can be rewritten as:

$$= \frac{x_{t-1}(\pi_P - \pi_C) - b_{t-1}(\pi_M + g - \pi_c)}{(1-b_{t-1})(1+\pi_c)}.$$

Increases in Medicare health spending, holding constant the prices of consumption and health in the CPI, lower the growth of real non-health income. The larger the share of health spending in the household budget, the larger is the impact of an increase in health spending. An increase in overall health prices, holding constant Medicare prices, will increase income, but here it is the share of health spending in the CPI that affects the magnitude of the effect.

Notes

1. This is related to the Supplemental Poverty Rate, which subtracts out-of-pocket medical expenses from income to assess poverty.
2. State and local workers, even those not covered by social security, are typically eligible for Medicare as well. A few beneficiaries (e.g., recent immigrants) enroll in Part A by paying the Part A premium.
3. Beneficiaries only have 60 lifetime reserve days over their lifetime. (These are additional days of coverage if one is hospitalized from more than 90 days.) Once these are used up, Medicare only pays for 90 days of hospitalization for each hospitalization episode. A new hospitalization episode begins after a beneficiary has been out of hospital for 60 consecutive days.
4. In 2020, about 8 percent of beneficiaries were subject to high-income premiums. About 5 percent of beneficiaries paid a reduce premium through Medicare Advantage enrollment or through the hold-harmless provision of the Medicare B part system (CMS 2021b).
5. For example, Qualified Medicare Beneficiaries (QMBs) pay no premiums or cost sharing but they do not qualify for additional services not covered by Medicare, whereas Specified Low-income Medicare Beneficiaries (SLMBs) do not have to pay the Part B premium but are responsible for cost sharing.
6. Throughout this chapter, we focus on data through 2019, because the pandemic had significant, but probably transitory effects on both health spending and GDP. In CMS's national health expenditures accounts, health spending surged in 2020 owing to a doubling of public health expenditures and enormous federal aid (largely subsidies) to support the medical system in response to Covid. In BEA's National Income and Product Accounts, which excludes these subsidies, personal health spending actually fell.
7. The real spending estimates are derived by deflating health spending by overall GDP prices rather than health prices because it facilitates decomposing sources of growth of the health share of GDP and it provides a better measure of alternative uses of resources. We examine the role of health prices separately.
8. CBO defines excess cost growth as the difference between demographically-adjusted health spending growth and *potential* GDP.
9. It is worth noting that, in the mid-2000s, there was considerable uncertainty about whether the 1990s slowdown would persist, or whether it reflected a series of one-time factors from various health reforms, such as the shift to managed care.
10. Most analysts believe that measured health price inflation is biased upward because prices do not adequately account for improving quality of health services. See Sheiner and Malinovskaya (2016); Cutler et al. (2006); Dauda et al (2019).
11. CMS assumes income growth affects health spending over a seven-year period (i.e., income growth in 2020 affects health spending from 2020–2027), with larger effects in more recent years. To approximate CMS's lag structure, we apply an elasticity of 1.6 to the five-year average change in real GDP per capita. To get the impact on excess cost growth (which uses only current GDP) we subtract actual real GDP per capita from this estimated effect.
12. To some extent, the relatively higher level of inflation in the health care sector owes to difficulties in measuring quality changes in health goods and services. Indeed, Dauda et al. (2019) estimated that true health care prices were

actually falling, not rising. Consequently, what appears as inflation in the national accounts is likely increasing real quantities. Both factors will be captured in excess growth.

13. For example, Gruber et al. (2020) estimated a price elasticity of about 0.2, in line with the elasticity from the Rand Health Insurance Experiment (Manning et al. 1987). CMS argues, however, that a broader definition of the elasticity is necessary for time-series analysis, because prices can also affect the choice of insurance. For example, higher prices could lead consumers to choose lower-priced policies with smaller networks. On the other hand, changes in prices over time are likely capturing, to a meaningful extent, quality increases, suggesting a lower price elasticity than that derived from experiments that vary out-of-pocket costs in a particular time period.

14. This is a rough estimate that is derived from Chart 2 in Heffler et al. (2021); we estimated excess cost growth rates for Parts A, B, and D of Medicare from the graph and then weighted by CMS projected spending for each part.

15. The HRS survey data are available every two years. As such, we take the average of 2004 and 2006, 2008 and 2010, and 2014 and 2016 to compute the income adjustment factors for 2005, 2009, and 2015 respectively.

16. Consider, e.g., someone who has $80 in income in period one and spends $20 on health. In period two, income increases to $100 and health spending increases to $40. The share of health spending in income has increased from 25 percent to 40 percent, but the income available for non-health spending remains constant at $60.

17. We do not have the HRS for 2019 yet, and so begin the simulation with 2016, but we are able to use the information on health spending by age in the 2019 MCBS sample.

18. The most common pathway to Medicaid for the elderly is through SSI. According to the Office of Evaluation Services and the Social Security Administration (2018), take up for SSI is likely significantly less than 60 percent. Take up for the Medicare Savings Programs for the elderly (QMB, SLM, QI) is estimated to be less than 50 percent (Caswell and Waidmann 2017).

19. Measured health prices do not control adequately for changes in quality, and it is likely that real health price inflation is lower than that picked up in official inflation measures like the CPI. (See National Academy of Sciences, 2022, Chapter 5.) However, for our purposes, it is measured inflation that matters, since social security benefits are indexed to it. Any changes to the CPI to improve health care measurement would make decrease health care affordability for the elderly.

20. The CPI captures out-of-pocket health spending—thus it includes premiums and copays paid directly by workers and retirees, but not spending financed by employers or the government.

References

Abelson, R. (2022). 'Medicare Advantage Plans Often Deny Needed Care, Federal Report Finds.' *The New York Times*. April 28: 16.

Bureau of Economic Analysis (BEA) (2022). *National Income and Product Accounts, Table 2.4.4.* Washington, DC: BEA. https://apps.bea.gov/iTable/iTable.cfm?reqid=19&step=2&isuri=1&1921=survey#reqid=19&step=2&isuri=1&1921=survey

Carman, K.G., J. Liu, and C. White (2020). 'Accounting for the Burden and Redistribution of Health Care Costs: Who Uses Care and Who Pays For It.' *Health Services Research*, 55(2): 224–231.

Caswell, K. and T. Waidmann (2017). *Medicare Savings Program Enrollees and Eligible Non-Enrollees*. Washington, DC: Medicaid and CHIP Payment and Access Commission (MACPAC). https://www.macpac.gov/wp-content/uploads/2017/08/MSP-Enrollees-and-Eligible-Non-Enrollees.pdf

Centers for Medicaid and Medicare Services (CMS) (2021a). *National Health Expenditure Data*. https://www.cms.gov/Research-Statistics-Data-and-Systems/Statistics-Trends-and-Reports/NationalHealthExpendData.

Centers for Medicaid and Medicare Services (CMS) (2021b). *Table 4, Medicare Premiums: Medicare Part B Premium Beneficiaries and Amounts, Calendar Years 2015–2020*. Medicare Utilization and Payment Tables. https://www.cms.gov/research-statistics-data-systems/cms-program-statistics/medicare-utilization-and-payment.

Centers for Medicare and Medicaid Services (CMS) (2021c). *Projected Medicare Expenditures under an Illustrative Scenario with Alternative Payment Updates to Medicare Providers*. Centers for Medicare and Medicaid Services, August 2021. https://www.cms.gov/filcs/document/illustrative-alternative-scenario-2021.pdf.

Centers for Medicare and Medicaid Services (CMS) (2022). *Medicare Current Beneficiary Survey*. https://www.cms.gov/Research-Statistics-Data-and-Systems/Research/MCBS

Chen, A., A. Munnell, and G. Sanzenbacher (2018). 'How Much Income Do Retirees Actually Have? Evaluating the Evidence from Five National Dataset.' Center for Retirement Research at Boston College Working Paper No. 2018-14. Boston, MA: Center for Retirement Research at Boston College.

Clemens, J. and J. D. Gottlieb (2017). 'In the Shadow of a Giant: Medicare's Influence on Private Physician Payments.' *Journal of Political Economy*, 125(1): 1–39.

Congressional Budget Office (CBO) (2016). *The Long-Term Outlook for the Major Federal Health Care Programs*. Washington, DC: CBO. https://www.cbo.gov/sites/default/files/114th-congress-2015-2016/reports/51580-ltbobreakout-chapter3.pdf

Congressional Budget Office (CBO) (2021a). *The 2021 Long-Term Budget Outlook*. Washington, DC: CBO. https://www.cbo.gov/publication/56977.

Congressional Budget Office (CBO) (2021b). *The Budget and Economic Outlook: 2021 to 2031*. Washington, DC: CBO. https://www.cbo.gov/data/budget-economic-data.

Cubanski J. and T. Neuman (2018). *Closing the Medicare Part D Coverage Gap: Trends, Recent Changes, and What's Ahead*. Washington, DC: Kaiser Family Foundation. https://www.kff.org/medicare/issue-brief/closing-the-medicare-part-d-coverage-gap-trends-recent-changes-and-whats-ahead/

Cubanski, J., T. Neuman, A. Damico, and K. Smith (2018). *Medicare Beneficiaries' Out-of-Pocket Health Care Spending as a Share of Income Now and Projections for the Future*. Washington, DC: Kaiser Family Foundation. https://www.kff.org/report-section/medicare-beneficiaries-out-of-pocket-health-care-spending-as-a-share-of-income-now-and-projections-for-the-future-report/

Cutler, D., A. B. Rosen, and S. Vijan (2006). 'The Value of Medical Spending in the United States, 1996–2000.' *New England Journal of Medicine*, 355(9): 920–927.

Dauda, S., A. Dunn, and A. Hall (2019). 'Are Medical Care Prices Still Declining? A Systematic Examination of Quality-Adjusted Price Index Alternatives for Medical Care.' Bureau of Economic Analysis Working Paper No. 2019-3. Washington, DC: BEA.

De Nardi, M., E. French, and J. Jones (2016). 'Medicaid Insurance in Old Age.' *American Economic Review*, 106(11): 3480–3520. https://www.aeaweb.org/articles?id=10.1257/aer.20140015

Fiedler, M. (2022). *What Does Economy-Wide Inflation Mean for the Prices of Healthcare Services (and Vice Versa)?* Washington, DC: USC-Brookings Schaeffer Initiative for Health Policy. https://healthpolicy.usc.edu/brookings-schaeffer/what-does-economy-wide-inflation-mean-for-the-prices-of-healthcare-services-and-vice-versa/

Follette, G. and L. Sheiner (2008). 'An Examination of Health Spending Growth in the United States: Past Trends and Future Prospects.' https://papers.ssrn.com/sol3/papers.cfm?abstract_id=1997215

Freed, M., J. F. Biniek, A. Damico, and T. Neuman (2021). *Medicare Advantage in 2021: Premiums, Cost Sharing, Out-of-Pocket Limits and Supplemental Benefits.* Washington, DC: Kaiser Family Foundation. https://www.kff.org/medicare/issue-brief/medicare-advantage-in-2021-premiums-cost-sharing-out-of-pocket-limits-and-supplemental-benefits

Gruber, J., J. C. Maclean, B. Wright, E. Wilkinson, and K. G. Volpp (2020). 'The Effect of Increased Cost-Sharing on Low-Value Service Use.' *Health Economics*, 29(10): 1180–1201.

Hatfield, L., M. Favreault, T. McGuire, and M. Chernew (2018). 'Modeling Health Care Spending Growth of Older Adults.' *Health Services Research*, 53(1): 138–155.

Heffler, S., T. Caldis, S. Smith, and G. Cuckler (2021). *A Conceptual View of The Long-Term Projection Methods for Medicare and Aggregate National Health Expenditures.* Washington, DC: Centers for Medicare and Medicaid Services (CMS). https://www.cms.gov/files/document/conceptual-view-long-term-projection-methods-medicare-and-aggregate-national-health-expenditures.pdf

Manning, W. G., J. Newhouse, N. Duan, E. Keeler, and A. Leibowitz (1987). 'Health Insurance and the Demand for Medical Care: Evidence from a Randomized Experiment.' *American Economic Review*, 77(3): 251–277.

Medicare Payment Advisory Commission (MEDPAC) (2021). *Data Book: Health Care Spending and the Medicare Program.* Washington, DC: MEDPAC. https://www.medpac.gov/wp-content/uploads/2021/10/July2021_MedPAC_DataBook_Sec3_SEC.pdf

National Academies of Sciences, Engineering, and Medicine (2022). 'Modernizing Difficult-to-Measure Expenditure Categories: Medical Care.' In D. E. Sichel and C. Mackie, eds., *Modernizing the Consumer Price Index for the 21st Century.*

Washington, DC: The National Academies Press. https://doi.org/10.17226/26485

Ochieng, N. Schwartz, K., and T. Neuman (2020). *How Many Physicians Have Opted-Out of the Medicare Program?* Washington, DC: Kaiser Family Foundation. https://www.kff.org/medicare/issue-brief/how-many-physicians-have-opted-out-of-the-medicare-program/

Office of Evaluation Science (OES) and Social Security Administration (SSA) (2018). *Increasing SSI Uptake.* Washington, DC: OES. https://oes.gsa.gov/assets/abstracts/1723-Increasing-SSI-Uptake.pdf

Sheiner, L. and A. Malinovskaya (2016). 'Productivity in the Healthcare Sector.' Washington, DC: Brookings Institution. https://www.brookings.edu/wp-content/uploads/2016/08/hp-issue-brief_final.pdf

Social Security Trustees (2021). *The 2021 Annual Report of the Board of Trustees of the Federal Old-Age and Survivors Insurance and Federal Disability Insurance Trust Funds.* Washington, DC: Social Security Administration (SSA). https://www.ssa.gov/oact/TR/2021/index.html

White, C. (2013). 'Contrary To Cost-Shift Theory, Lower Medicare Hospital Payment Rates for Inpatient Care Lead to Lower Private Payment Rates.' *Health Affairs*, 32(5): 935–943.

Chapter 10

Economic Conditions, the COVID-19 Pandemic Recession, and Implications for Disability Insurance in the US

Nicole Maestas and Kathleen J. Mullen

The US Social Security Disability Insurance (SSDI) program is designed to insure American workers against earnings losses from severe, permanent disabilities. In 2019, on the eve of the COVID-19 pandemic, nearly 8.4 million disabled workers were receiving SSDI benefits (SSA 2021)—equivalent to 5 percent of the civilian labor force (BLS 2022). Including the additional 2.8 million nondisabled dependents and adult children of retired, deceased, and disabled workers, the SSDI program paid benefits to nearly 11.2 million beneficiaries in 2019 (SSA 2021). SSDI benefits are paid out of payroll tax revenue supplemented with reserves from the Disability Insurance (DI) Trust Fund, which is overseen by a Board of Trustees.

Each year the Trustees are required to provide a report to Congress on the outlook of the DI Trust Fund (as well as the Old-Age and Survivors Insurance Trust Fund). In April 2020, the Trustees' report projected that the DI Trust Fund would be depleted in 2065, without incorporating into their projections the effects of the COVID-19 pandemic, which had been declared a global pandemic by the World Health Organization (WHO) only a month earlier, in March 2020. The 2021 report updated the projected depletion date of the DI Trust Fund to 2057. In 2022, however, the Trustees projected that the DI Trust Fund would no longer be depleted within the 75-year projection period. DI Trust Fund projections rely on assumptions about several factors that affect both the size and composition of the population receiving benefits as well as the number and characteristics of the people paying into the system. These include demographic assumptions about fertility, mortality, and immigration; economics assumptions about employment, real wage growth, real interest rates, and inflation; and programmatic assumptions about DI prevalence, average benefits, and household composition of DI beneficiaries.

Nicole Maestas and Kathleen J. Mullen, *Economic Conditions, the COVID-19 Pandemic Recession, and Implications for Disability Insurance in the US.* In: *Real-World Shocks and Retirement System Resiliency.* Edited by: Olivia S. Mitchell, John Sabelhaus, and Stephen P. Utkus, Oxford University Press. © Pension Research Council (2024).
DOI: 10.1093/oso/9780198894131.003.0010

The pandemic affected all of these factors, at least in the short run, but likely at least some factors in the long run as well. In this chapter, we focus primarily on the potential ways the pandemic may have affected the DI Trust Fund through the pathway of changing DI incidence.

The SSDI Program on the Eve of the COVID-19 Pandemic

After decades of increasing numbers (since the early 1980s), the SSDI caseload peaked in 2014 and has been declining ever since. Figure 10.1 shows the numbers of SSDI beneficiaries, new awards, and exits from 2001 to 2019. From the figure we can see that the recent decline in the SSDI caseload was driven both by fewer new awards (declining since 2010) and more exits from the program. The annual number of exits has nearly doubled—mostly due to population aging—and, beginning in 2014, has exceeded the number of new awards. The number of new awards has also dropped because of population aging: as the large Baby Boomer cohort moves out of age-eligibility for the program, the next-in-line cohorts are smaller. In addition, the number of new awards may have fallen because of improving economic conditions after the Great Recession and policy changes that effectively tightened standards at the appellate level (Ray and Lubbers 2014).

Exits from SSDI may be due to one of several reasons, including death of the beneficiary (28% of disabled workers in 2019), conversion to social security benefits upon reaching full retirement age (60%), cessation of SSDI benefits due to medical improvement (4%), and cessation of benefits because the beneficiary has consistently earned more than the threshold for substantial gainful activity (6%) (SSA 2020). Figure 10.2 focuses specifically on exits due to successful return-to-work (SSA 2002–2020). Although the vast majority of exits are due to people aging out of the program at the full retirement age, there has been a surprising increase in voluntary exits from the SSDI program due to work. While work exits are rare, they nearly doubled between 2001 and 2019 (from 29,000 to 55,850).

It is possible that the strong labor market during the recent expansion (until 2020) drove the trend in work exits. Indeed, Figure 10.3 shows that employment gains among workers with disabilities were not limited to SSDI beneficiaries alone; after decades of steady decline, the employment rate among workers with disabilities started increasing in 2014 and seemed to stabilize at a rate of approximately one in five workers with disabilities by the late 2010s. By comparison, the employment rate for workers without disabilities remained roughly steady around 70 percent from the late 1980s to 2019, except for dips during recessions (denoted by the shaded areas).

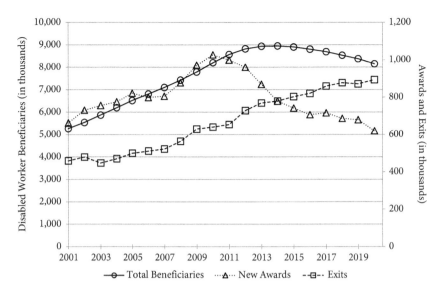

Figure 10.1 Awards into and exits from the DI program

Source: Beneficiaries in Current-Payment Status (Table 1) and *Benefits Awarded, Withheld, and Terminated* (Tables 35 and 49). Annual Statistical Report on the Social Security Disability Insurance Program, 2020, http://www.ssa.gov/policy/docs/statcomps/di_asr/2020

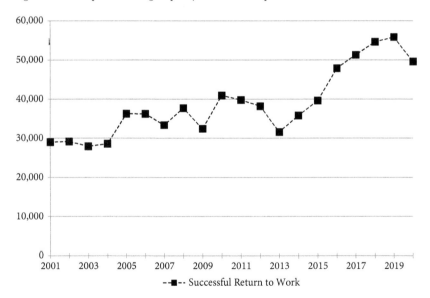

Figure 10.2 Number of DI beneficiaries with successful return to work

Source: Reason for Termination (2001: Table 39; 2002: Table 45; 2003–2004: Table 46; 2005–2020: Table 50), Annual Statistical Reports on the Social Security Disability Insurance Program.

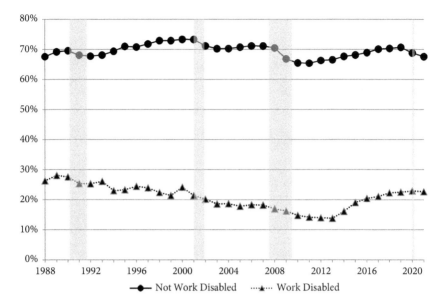

Figure 10.3 Employment rate by disability status

Source: Variables 'empstat' and 'disabwork' from Flood et al., IPUMS-CPS, University of Minnesota, http://www.ipums.org

Although speculative, this may point to structural changes in employers' willingness to hire individuals with disabilities, perhaps in response to growing labor demand pressures associated with population aging (Maestas et al. 2023).

Enter COVID

Although the SSDI program is not intended to be an alternative to labor force participation when economic conditions are weak, a robust literature has shown a negative relationship between economic conditions and SSDI applications and awards (see, e.g., Stapleton et al. 1988; Black et al. 2002; Cutler et al. 2012; Maestas et al. 2015; Charles et al. 2018; Maestas et al. 2021). For example, Maestas et al. (2021) estimated that the steep increase in unemployment levels during the Great Recession induced nearly one million SSDI applications that otherwise would not have been filed, of which 41.8 percent were awarded benefits, resulting in over 400,000 new beneficiaries who made up 8.9 percent of all SSDI entrants between 2008–2012. They also showed that recession-induced SSDI applicants had less severe impairments (and thus greater work capacity) than the average SSDI applicant during this period. Furthermore, using administrative Medicare data from 1991 to 2015, Carey et al. (2022) found that recession-induced SSDI beneficiaries had lower Medicare spending than average (an indication of better average health), and they argued that the cyclical pattern in health care spending of beneficiaries was driven by differences in the composition of new entrants rather than by poor economic conditions leading to worsening health.

Figure 10.4 shows the seasonally adjusted unemployment rate in the US between May 2002 and May 2022. Two stark differences between the Great Recession and the COVID-19 recession are immediately apparent. First, the spike in the unemployment rate at the start of the COVID recession was more than twice as large as the increase in unemployment triggered by the Great Recession. The average unemployment rate in 2007, before the Great Recession, was 4.6 percent, and the peak unemployment rate, in October 2009, was 10 percent—a difference of 5.4 percentage points, or just slightly larger than a twofold increase. By contrast, the average unemployment rate in 2019 was 3.7 percent and the peak unemployment rate of the COVID

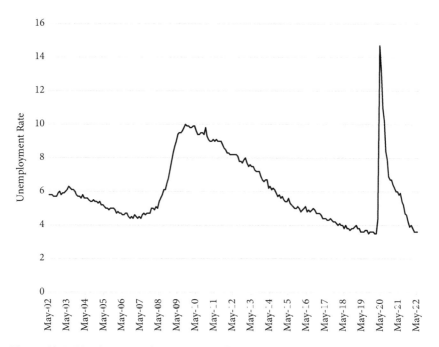

Figure 10.4 Rise in unemployment rate during COVID more pronounced than Great Recession

Source: BLS 2022 https://www.bls.gov/charts/employment-situation/civilian-unemployment-rate.htm

recession, in April 2020, was 14.7 percent—a difference of 11 percentage points, and nearly a fourfold increase.

Second, the COVID recession was much shorter (March 2020–April 2020) than the Great Recession (December 2007–June 2009), and the unemployment rate took much less time to return to pre-recession levels. By March 2022, two years after the start of the pandemic, the unemployment rate was 3.6 percent, below the 2019 average unemployment rate of 3.7 percent. By contrast, the recovery from the Great Recession took much longer; it took nearly eight years for the unemployment rate to return to within 8 percent of its pre-recession level (5%, in September 2015).

Despite these differences, certain fundamentals of the COVID-19 recession appear to be similar to prior recessions. For example, like other recessions, the COVID recession impacted the less educated the most. This is notable because disability determinations based on the medical-vocational grid take education into account. Given two applicants having the same functional impairments but one lacks a high school degree, the less educated applicant is more likely to qualify for SSDI benefits because they have fewer transferable skills than the more educated applicant. If the effects of unemployment on SSDI applications and awards are approximately linear and stable over time, then, taken together, these factors suggest the effect of the COVID-19 recession could have been about a quarter the size of the effect of the Great Recession.[1]

This has certainly not been the case. The most recent data on the number of SSDI applications and beneficiaries through May 2022, presented in Figure 10.5, show no signs of rebounding to their pre-COVID levels (SSA 2022). This is consistent with analyses of SSA's State Agency Monthly Workload Data, which show that at least one year into the pandemic (and adjusting for state and month fixed effects), there was no discernible increase in the application rate for DI benefits and, in fact, DI application rates per 100,000 people ages 20–64 *fell* in March 2020 and have remained at a lower level through at least February 2022 (Goda et al. 2021, 2022).

There are several potential explanations for the surprising lack of an application response to the COVID recession. Unprecedented unemployment insurance expansions and stimulus payments may have helped mitigate the impact of the COVID recession. In addition, unlike prior recessions, the COVID recession was the result of a global pandemic which led to massive changes in US mortality and morbidity. Whereas the effect of the mortality increase on SSDI program costs is offsetting (people die earlier than they would have absent COVID), the increase in morbidity from Long COVID could further increase SSDI applications, but likely over a longer time horizon. Finally, one very important factor unique to the COVID-19 pandemic was the widespread closure of Social Security Administration (SSA) field offices from March 17, 2020 through April 7, 2022. Deshpande

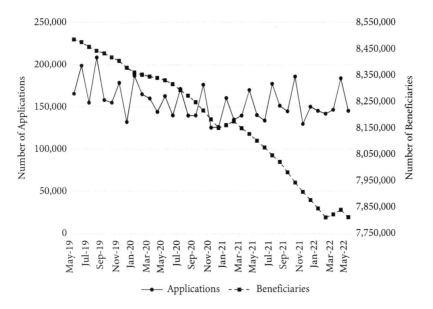

Figure 10.5 Number of SSDI applications and beneficiaries May 2019–May 2022

Source: Selected Data from Social Security's Disability Program (SSA 2022), https://www.ssa.gov/oact/STATS/dibStat.html

and Li (2019) found that, prior to the pandemic, closing an SSA field office led to a persistent 16 percent decline in the number of SSDI beneficiaries in the surrounding areas. The corresponding decrease in disability applications was only 10 percent, suggesting field office closures disproportionately affected those with more impairments. If there is pent-up demand for SSDI benefits, applications could rise as normal operations resume in 2022.

Potential Long-Run Effects

Two years after the start of the COVID-19 pandemic, the unemployment rate has recovered to 2019 levels, and there is excess demand for labor. Under these conditions, workers initially displaced by the COVID recession have likely found new employment, and therefore any pent-up demand for SSDI benefits may have dissipated by now.

An open question, however, is whether the disabling effects of Long COVID could cause a wave of disability applications in the future. As many as 30 percent of COVID-19 cases result in Long COVID—defined as experiencing at least one persistent symptom six months later (Logue et al. 2021). Current estimates imply that more than 25 million Americans may have Long COVID, although this includes mild symptoms (e.g., loss of taste or smell) as well as more severe symptoms (e.g., fatigue). It remains to be understood how many Long COVID translate to cases of disability. Figure 10.6 shows that there has been a steady increase since mid-2020 in the percentage of Americans age 18–64 who report at least one of six disabling conditions (hearing difficulty, visual difficulty, cognitive difficulty, ambulatory difficulty, self-care difficulty, and independent living difficulty) in the Current Population Survey (CPS). Whether this uptick will lead to an increase in SSDI applications and awards will depend on whether people can establish eligibility under SSDI's strict disability determination criteria.

In addition to affecting disability insurance applications and beneficiaries in the short run through its effects on the economy, the COVID-19 pandemic may also impose lasting effects on the nature of work that could affect the ability of people with disabilities to remain in the labor force. One way the COVID-19 pandemic could *enable* work is through the widespread expansion of telework, defined as the ability to work remotely from home or another location that is not the premises of one's employer. Telework is a much-needed accommodation for some people with disabilities. The

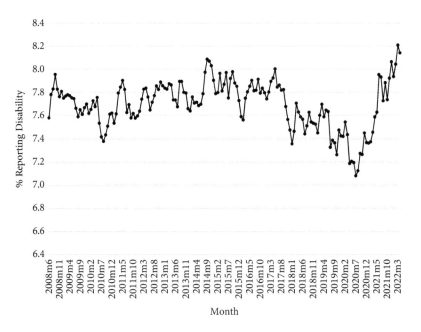

Figure 10.6 Percent reporting disability among civilian non-institutionalized population age 18–64, June 2008–April 2022

Source: Tabulations of Current Population Survey data by Hailey Clark, Nicole Maestas and Ari Ne'eman.

US Equal Employment Opportunity Commission was urged to issue guidance that telework is a reasonable accommodation under the Americans with Disabilities Act if an employer allowed it during a pandemic (Wagstaff and Quasius 2020). At the same time, telework is only possible for certain workers in certain industries, and people with disabilities tend to be concentrated in industries that require in-person work. For example, Schur et al. (2020) estimated that telework is possible for only 34 percent of people with disabilities, compared to 40 percent of people without disabilities. At the same time, they found that 13.5 percent of people with disabilities lived in homes without internet access, compared to 6 percent of people without disabilities.

At the same time, it is possible that the COVID-19 pandemic could accelerate employer automation of tasks or robotization, disproportionately affecting workers in more easily routinized jobs. Additionally, the expansions of telework and automation could both have downstream effects on job demands that intensify long-term shifts toward increasingly sedentary and cognitively demanding jobs (Lopez Garcia et al. 2020). Future research will be needed to assess long-term changes in the nature of work as a result of the pandemic.

Conclusion

COVID-19 is a novel disease that has had dramatic effects on morbidity and mortality in the US population, while launching a global economic recession. In prior recessions, there was a positive relationship between the unemployment rate and DI applications and awards. This relationship, however, did not emerge in the wake of the COVID recession. Although the COVID recession disproportionately affected less educated workers as in prior recessions, there were also unique features that may have altered the relationship between unemployment and DI incidence. These include the prolonged closure of the SSA field offices, the unprecedented expansion of unemployment insurance benefits and economic stimulus payments, and the exceptionally quick economic recovery. Although it is unlikely that there is a substantial amount of pent-up demand for SSDI benefits among workers who were displaced during the COVID recession, there could yet be a steady inflow of applications in the future from people experiencing disabling effects from Long COVID.

Note

1. The average difference in unemployment rate from 2007, over the eight years between 2008 and 2015, was 2.9. The average difference in unemployment rate from February 2020, over the two years between March 2020 and 2022, was 2.9.

References

Black, D., K. Daniel, and S. Sanders (2002). 'The Impact of Economic Conditions on Participation in Disability Programs: Evidence from the Coal Boom and Bust.' *American Economic Review* 92(1): 27–50.

Carey, C., N. H. Miller, and D. Molitor (2022). 'Why Does Disability Increase During Recessions? Evidence from Medicare.' NBER Working Paper No. 29988. Cambridge, MA: National Bureau of Economic Research.

Charles, K., Y. Li, and M. Stephens (2018). 'Disability Benefit Take-Up and Local Labor Market Conditions.' *Review of Economics and Statistics*, 100(3): 416–423.

Cutler, D., E. Meara, and S. Richards-Shubik (2012). 'Unemployment and Disability: Evidence from the Great Recession.' NBER Retirement Research Center Paper No. NB 12-12. Cambridge, MA: National Bureau of Economic Research.

Deshpande, M., and Y. Li (2019). 'Who is Screened Out? Application Costs and the Targeting of Disability Programs.' *American Economic Journal: Economic Policy*, 11(4): 213–248.

Flood, S., M. King, R. Rodgers, S. Ruggles, J. R. Warren, and M. Westberry (2021). *Integrated Public Use Microdata Series, Current Population Survey: Version 9.0 [dataset]*. Minneapolis, MN: IPUMS. https://doi.org/10.18128/D030.V9.0

Goda, G. S., E. Jackson, L. H. Nicholas, and S. S. Stith (2021). 'The Impact of Covid-19 on Older Workers' Employment and Social Security Spillovers.' NBER Working Paper No. 29083. Cambridge, MA: National Bureau of Economic Research.

Goda, G. S., E. Jackson, L. H. Nicholas, and S. S. Stith (2022). 'The Impact of Covid-19 on Older Workers' Employment and Social Security Spillovers: Evidence from Year 2.' Slides presented at NBER Conference 'The Labor Market for Older Workers, Spring 2022.'

Logue, J. K., N. M. Franko, D. J. McCulloch, D. McDonald, A. Magedson, C. R. Wolf, and H. Y. Chu (2021). 'Sequelae in Adults at 6 Months After COVID-19 Infection.' *JAMA Netw Open*, 4(2): e210830. doi:10.1001/jamanetworkopen.2021.0830.

Lopez Garcia, I., N. Maestas, and K. J. Mullen (2020). 'The Changing Nature of Work and Work Capacity.' MRDRC Working Paper 2020-415. Ann Arbor, MI: Michigan Retirement and Disability Research Center.

Maestas, N., K. J. Mullen, and D. Powell (2023). 'The Effect of Population Aging on Economic Growth.' *American Economic Journal: Macroeconomics*, 15(2): 306–332.

Maestas, N., K. J. Mullen, and A. Strand (2015). 'Disability Insurance and the Great Recession.' *American Economic Review Papers & Proceedings*, 105(5): 177–182.

Maestas, N., K. J. Mullen, and A. Strand (2021). 'The Effect of Economic Conditions on the Disability Insurance Program: Evidence from the Great Recession.' *Journal of Public Economics*, 199: 104410.

Ray, G. K. and J. S. Lubbers (2014). 'A Government Success Story: How Data Analysis by the Social Security Appeals Council (with a Push from the Administrative Conference of the United States) Is Transforming Social Security Disability Adjudication.' *George Washington Law Review*, 83(4/5): 1575–1608.

Schur, L. A., M. Ameri, and D. Kruse (2020). 'Telework after COVID: A "Silver Lining" for Workers with Disabilities?' *Journal of Occupational Rehabilitation*, 30(4): 521–536.

Stapleton, D., K. Coleman, K. Dietrich, and G. Livermore (1988). 'Empirical Analyses of DI and SSI Application and Award Growth.' In K. Rupp and D. Stapleton, eds., *Growth in Disability Benefits: Explanations and Policy Implications.* Kalamazoo, MI: W.E. Upjohn Institute for Employment Research, pp. 31–92.

US Bureau of Labor Statistics (BLS) (2022). Civilian Labor Force Level [CLF16OV], retrieved from FRED, Federal Reserve Bank of St. Louis; https://fred.stlouisfed.org/series/CLF16OV, February 15, 2022

US Social Security Administration (SSA) (2001–2021). *Annual Statistical Report on the Social Security Disability Insurance System.* Washington, DC: US Government Printing Office.

US Social Security Administration (SSA) (2022). *Selected Data from Social Security's Disability Program.* Washington, DC: US Government Printing Office. https://www.ssa.gov/oact/STATS/dibStat.html, accessed June 15, 2022.

Wagstaff, B. L. and J. Quasius (2020). 'The ADA, Telework, and the Post-Pandemic Workplace.' *The Regulatory Review.* September 7: https://www.theregreview.org/2020/09/07/wagstaff-quasius-ada-telework-post-pandemic-workplace/.

The Pension Research Council

The Pension Research Council is a research center at the Wharton School of the University of Pennsylvania committed to generating knowledge and debate on key policy issues affecting pensions and other employee benefits. For over 65 years, the Council has sponsored high-level analysis of private and public retirement security and related benefit plans around the world. Research projects are motivated by the need to address the long-term issues that underlie contemporary concerns about retirement system structures and resiliency. Members seek to broaden understanding of the complex economic, financial, social, actuarial, and legal foundations for and impacts of privately- and publicly-provided benefits. The Pension Research Council is a non-profit organization, and contributions to it are tax-deductible. For more information about the Pension Research Council please visit http://www.pensionresearchcouncil.org.

The Boettner Center for Pensions and Retirement Research

Founded at the Wharton School to support scholarly research, teaching, and outreach on global aging, retirement, and public and private pensions, the Center is named after Joseph E. Boettner. Funding to the University of Pennsylvania was provided through the generosity of the Boettner family, whose intent was to spur financial wellbeing at older ages through work on how aging influences financial security and life satisfaction. The Center disseminates research and evaluation on challenges and opportunities associated with global aging and retirement, how to strengthen retirement income systems, saving and investment behavior of the young and the old, interactions between physical and mental health, and successful retirement. For more information see http://www.pensionresearchcouncil.org/boettner/.

Executive Director

Olivia S. Mitchell, *International Foundation of Employee Benefit Plans Professor,* Professor of Business Economics/Public Policy and Insurance/Risk Management, The Wharton School, University of Pennsylvania.

Advisory Board

Julie Agnew, Raymond A. Mason School of Business, William and Mary, Williamsburg, VA
Robert L. Clark, Poole College of Management, North Carolina State University, Raleigh, NC
Julia Coronado, MacroPolicy Perspectives, New York, NY
Peter A. Fisher, Cortus Advisors, Boston, MA
Peter R. Fisher, BlackRock Financial Management, New York, NY

Fiona Greig, Vanguard, Malvern, PA
P. Brett Hammond, Capital Group, Los Angeles, CA
J. Mark Iwry, Brookings Institution, Washington, DC
Melissa Kahn, State Street Global Advisors, Washington, DC
Emily Kessler, Society of Actuaries, Schaumburg, IL
Surya P. Kolluri, TIAA Institute, Boston, MA
David I. Laibson, Department of Economics, Harvard University, Cambridge, MA
Annamaria Lusardi, Stanford Graduate School of Business, Stanford, CA
Jeannine Markoe Raymond, National Association of State Retirement Administrators, Washington, DC
Raimond Maurer, Finance Department, Goethe University, Frankfurt, Germany
Alicia H. Munnell, Carroll School of Management, Boston College, Chestnut Hill, MA
Michael Orszag, Willis Towers Watson, London, UK
Anna M. Rappaport, Anna Rappaport Consulting, Chicago, IL
Catherine Reilly, Smart Pension, Cambridge, MA
David P. Richardson, TIAA Institute, Charlotte, NC
Nikolai Roussanov, Department of Finance, The Wharton School, University of Pennsylvania, Philadelphia, PA
John Sabelhaus, Washington Center for Equitable Growth, Washington, DC
Richard C. Shea, Covington & Burling, LLP, Washington, DC
Kent Smetters, Department of Business Economics and Public Policy, The Wharton School, University of Pennsylvania, Philadelphia, PA
Jack L. VanDerhei, Morningstar Center for Retirement and Policy Studies, Washington, DC
Stephen P. Zeldes, Graduate School of Business, Columbia University, New York, NY

Members of the Pension Research Council

AARP
Bank of America
BlackRock
Capital Group
Federal Reserve Employee Benefits System
Fidelity Investments
FINRA Investor Education Foundation
International Foundation of Employee Benefit Plans
Investment Company Institute
J.P. Morgan Asset Management
The Pew Charitable Trusts
State Street Global Advisors
T. Rowe Price
TIAA Institute
Vanguard
WTW

Recent Pension Research Council Publications

Pension Funds and Sustainable Investment: Challenges and Opportunities. P. Brett Hammond, Raimond Maurer, and Olivia S. Mitchell, eds. 2023. (ISBN 978-0-19-288919-5.)

New Models for Managing Longevity Risk: Public-Private Partnerships. Olivia S. Mitchell, ed. 2022. (ISBN 978-0-19-285980-8.)

Remaking Retirement: Debt in an Aging Economy. Olivia S. Mitchell and Annamaria Lusardi, eds. 2020. (ISBN 978-0-19-886752-4.)

The Disruptive Impact of FinTech on Retirement Systems. Julie Agnew and Olivia S. Mitchell, eds. 2019. (ISBN 978-0-19-884555-9.)

How Persistent Low Returns Will Shape Saving and Retirement. Olivia S. Mitchell, Robert Clark, and Raimond Maurer, eds. 2018. (ISBN 978-0-19-882744-3.)

Financial Decision Making and Retirement Security in an Aging World. Olivia S. Mitchell, P. Brett Hammond, and Stephen P. Utkus, eds. 2017. (ISBN 978-0-19-880803-9.)

Retirement System Risk Management: Implications of the New Regulatory Order. Olivia S. Mitchell, Raimond Maurer, and J. Michael Orszag, eds. 2016. (ISBN 978-0-19-878737-2.)

Reimagining Pensions: The Next 40 Years. Olivia S. Mitchell and Richard C. Shea, eds. 2016. (ISBN 978-0-19-875544-9.)

Recreating Sustainable Retirement. Olivia S. Mitchell, Raimond Maurer, and P. Brett Hammond, eds. 2014. (ISBN 0-19-871924-3.)

The Market for Retirement Financial Advice. Olivia S. Mitchell and Kent Smetters, eds. 2013. (ISBN 0-19-968377-2.)

Reshaping Retirement Security: Lessons from the Global Financial Crisis. Raimond Maurer, Olivia S. Mitchell, and Mark Warshawsky, eds. 2012. (ISBN 0-19-966069-7.)

Financial Literacy. Olivia S. Mitchell and Annamaria Lusardi, eds. 2011. (ISBN 0-19-969681-9.)

Securing Lifelong Retirement Income. Olivia S. Mitchell, John Piggott, and Noriyuki Takayama, eds. 2011. (ISBN 0-19-959484-9.)

Reorienting Retirement Risk Management. Robert L. Clark and Olivia S. Mitchell, eds. 2010. (ISBN 0-19-959260-9.)

Fundamentals of Private Pensions. Dan M. McGill, Kyle N. Brown, John J. Haley, Sylvester Schieber, and Mark J. Warshawsky. 9th edn. 2010. (ISBN 0-19-954451-6.)

The Future of Public Employees Retirement Systems. Olivia S. Mitchell and Gary Anderson, eds. 2009. (ISBN 0-19-957334-9.)

Recalibrating Retirement Spending and Saving. John Ameriks and Olivia S. Mitchell, eds. 2008. (ISBN 0-19-954910-8.)

Lessons from Pension Reform in the Americas. Stephen J. Kay and Tapen Sinha, eds. 2008. (ISBN 0-19-922680-6.)

Redefining Retirement: How Will Boomers Fare? Brigitte Madrian, Olivia S. Mitchell, and Beth J. Soldo, eds. 2007. (ISBN 0-19-923077-3.)

Restructuring Retirement Risks. David Blitzstein, Olivia S. Mitchell, and Steven P. Utkus, eds. 2006. (ISBN 0-19-920465-9.)

Reinventing the Retirement Paradigm. Robert L. Clark and Olivia S. Mitchell, eds. 2005. (ISBN 0-19-928460-1.)

Pension Design and Structure: New Lessons from Behavioral Finance. Olivia S. Mitchell and Steven P. Utkus, eds. 2004. (ISBN 0-19-927339-1.)

The Pension Challenge: Risk Transfers and Retirement Income Security. Olivia S. Mitchell and Kent Smetters, eds. 2003. (ISBN 0-19-926691-3.)

A History of Public Sector Pensions in the United States. Robert L. Clark, Lee A. Craig, and Jack W. Wilson, eds. 2003. (ISBN 0-8122-3714-5.)

Benefits for the Workplace of the Future. Olivia S. Mitchell, David Blitzstein, Michael Gordon, and Judith Mazo, eds. 2003. (ISBN 0-8122-3708-0.)

Innovations in Retirement Financing. Olivia S. Mitchell, Zvi Bodie, P. Brett Hammond, and Stephen Zeldes, eds. 2002. (ISBN 0-8122-3641-6.)

To Retire or Not: Retirement Policy and Practice in Higher Education. Robert L. Clark and P. Brett Hammond, eds. 2001. (ISBN 0-8122-3572-X.)

Pensions in the Public Sector. Olivia S. Mitchell and Edwin Hustead, eds. 2001. (ISBN 0-8122-3578-9.)

Available from the Pension Research Council web site:
http://www.pensionresearchcouncil.org/

Index

For the benefit of digital users, indexed terms that span two pages (e.g., 52–53) may, on occasion, appear on only one of those pages.

A

Affordable Care Act (ACA), 6, 115, 161, 181, 184, 200
age discrimination, 3, 52, 99

B

Baby Boomers *see* Millennials
base wealth
  adding SSW to concept, 81–85, 88
  impact of adding DB wealth and SSW to concept of, 74
  as marketable assets minus liabilities, 3–4
  as measure of household wealth in US, 3–4
  Millennials, 76, 81–91
  and percentile point comparisons, 75–76, 88, 89–91
  SCF net worth plus DB benefits measure, 81–83, 84–88
bridge jobs, 3, 38, 40
  see also partial retirement

C

CBO *see* Congressional Budget Office (CBO)
CCP/Equifax *see* Consumer Credit Panel/Equifax (CCP/Equifax)
Centers for Medicaid and Medicare Services (CMS), 180, 184–190, 201
CMS *see* Centers for Medicaid and Medicare Services (CMS)
Coile, C. C., 3, 14, 36, 39, 45–47, 52–53, 62–65, 99, 161–162
comprehensive wealth concept, 74, 84–85

constructing measure, 77
estimating distribution and adding SSW, 76
measures used to study retirement adequacy, 74–75
need for measure, 73–74
percentile point comparisons, 88–91
and relative rank distributions, 75–76, 81–87
Congressional Budget Office (CBO), 180–181, 184, 188–189, 196–197, 201
Consumer Credit Panel/Equifax (CCP/Equifax)
  data on student loan debt, 5, 128–129
  description, 121
  evidence from, 139–141
contributions to retirement plans
  see retirement savings changes during pandemic
Coronavirus Aid, Relief, and Economic Security (CARES) Act, 100, 108
Covid-19 pandemic
  differing from past recessions, 3, 5, 157, 216–217, 219
  federal government's support in response to, 53, 157–158
  global economic decline, 97
  health concerns leading to early retirement, 53, 55–56
  as impacting lives in myriad ways, 52
  impact of health shocks triggered by, 7
  impact on Millennial workers, 14
  impact on older workers, 3, 47–50, 52, 55–56, 64, 65–67, 68 n.7

labor force participation, 3, 47, 49, 53–54, 108
lessons learned from, 7–8
Long Covid, 216–219
recessions and retirement
  data and methods, 54, 56, 59
  previous literature, 55
  results, 54, 60, 61, 63, 64, 66
  study conclusions, 67
retirements rising during, 2–3, 53, 54–56, 65, 67, 99–100
and retirement transitions 37–39, 43–50, 54, 56, 62–65
sharp rise in stock and housing market prices during, 53
similarities to prior recessions, 216
US retirees weathering better than expected, 5
see also retirement savings changes during pandemic; safety net response to pandemic; Social Security Disability Insurance (SSDI): Covid-19 pandemic; unemployment: Covid-19 pandemic
Current Population Survey (CPS), 36, 39, 44–45, 47, 54–59, 98–99, 218
Annual Social and Economic Supplement (ASEC), 160–168, 170–176

D
defined benefit (DB) pensions
bond market crisis exposing risks to, 4–5
channel for interaction of health prices and income, 194
as component of base wealth, 3–4
distributions, unable to distinguish from DC pensions, 101
employers shifting from, 2, 14, 125–127
of Millennials, 21–22
as providing steady stream of guaranteed benefits in retirement, 125–127

and student loan borrowing, 137
wealth
  context, 73–74
  cross-cohort distributions, 89–92
  data and methods, 77
  inequality, 93
  measure, 81–82, 88
  relative rank distributions, 83, 85, 87
  withdrawals, 105–107, 113, 115
defined contribution (DC) pensions
balances as rarely annuitized, 19
comparison with IRAs, 125–127
contributions, 97, 99, 101–105
distributions, unable to distinguish from DB pensions, 101
employers shifting to, 2, 125–127
withdrawals, 4–5, 100, 105–107, 113, 115
demographic characteristics
in CPS-ASEC, 156, 161, 165, 169
in Health and Retirement Study, 79–80
income differences by, 22–23
Millennials, 11–13
in Survey of Consumer Finances, 78, 121, 127
Derby, E., 4, 97
Dettling, L. J., 5, 73–74, 94 n.4, 120, 127, 128, 137, 146 n.20, 147 n.22, n.33, 148 n.34, n.35
disability insurance (DI) *see* Social Security Disability Insurance (SSDI)
Disability Insurance (DI) Trust Fund, 211
dynamic microsimulation, 12, 18, 80
Dynamic Simulation of Income Model (DYNASIM4), 18, 20–21, 23, 25, 27–30

E
Early Boomers *see* Millennials
Early Gen Xers *see* Millennials
Early Millennials *see* Millennials

earnings trends, 15
education trends, 15–16

F
financial environment, new, 3
Follette, G., 6, 115, 180–181, 183–184, 190, 200
full retirement age (FRA), 11, 40, 212

G
Goodman, L., 4, 97, 99, 101, 113, 116 n.5
Goodman, S. F., 5, 73–74, 94 n.4, 120, 123, 127, 137, 145 n.1, 146 n.20, 147 n.33, 148 n.34, n.35
Great Recession
  age discrimination as problem during, 99
  Congress providing additional emergency aid during, 159–160
  Congress providing small one-time top-up retirement benefits, 158–159
  contributions dropping during, 4, 97, 99, 101–103, 105
  effects on retirement, 53, 55–56
  employment decline during, 52, 55, 97
  and Millennial men's education, 15–16
  and Millennial women's labor force participation rates, 14–15
  new awards of SSDI falling because of improving economic conditions after, 7, 212
  poverty rate during, 6
  receipts of benefits by older population, 156–158, 161–174
  relaxation of asset tests, 158
  and retirement transitions, 37–39
  suspension of RMDs during, 100, 107–109
  and unemployment 165–173, 214–216
  withdrawals increasing during, 99, 105–107

H
Health and Retirement Study (HRS), 77, 79–80, 93, 190, 192
health costs
  context, 180–182
  data used in analysis, 189
    adjustment of income, 190
    budget shares, 190–193
    MCBS, 189–190
    out-of-pocket spending by age as share of income, 193
    real health expenditures by income quintile, 191
  evaluating changes in real income available for non-health consumption, 194
  health insurance for elderly, 182
    low-income beneficiaries, 183
  Millennials, 15, 29
  national health spending trends over time, 183
  out-of-pocket spending on, 6, 29–30, 115, 180, 182–183, 186, 191, 193, 196, 198
  recessions and mitigations, 6
  simulations to gauge importance to elderly retirement security
    additional, 202–205
    comparing different cohorts over time, 198–200
    following current 65-year-olds over time, 196–198
    overview, 195–196
    parameters, 189
  study conclusions and policy implications, 200
  vulnerability of elderly to, 6, 180
homeownership
  and student loan borrowing, 120–121, 123, 138–141
  trends, 2, 16
household debt, 17
household net worth, 17–18
household wealth

becoming more unequal over
time, 18, 73
measures, 3–4
reasons for conducting empirical
research on, 73
SSW adding to, 73–74

I
Individual Retirement Accounts (IRAs)
contributions, 101–103
aggregate, by year, 102
data on, 101
funding, 125–127
savings for college-educated
families, 138
withdrawals, 100, 105–110
asymmetric response to policy
changes, 115
close to $100,000 threshold, 111
counts, as percent of prior year
balance, 109
mean, by age, 107
probability of taking, by
age, 112–113
total, and penalized, 110
by year, 106
IRAs *see* Individual Retirement Accounts
(IRAs)

J
Johnson, R. W., 1–2, 11, 13–18

L
labor force participation
Covid-19 pandemic, 3, 47, 49, 53–54,
108
Great Recession, 53
of Millennials, 1–2, 13–15
of older workers, 36, 47, 49
labor market
disruptions due to pandemic, 52
Millennials, 15, 21, 24
recent shocks impacting on future of
retirement, 1
retiree flows back into, 37–41, 44–45,
47–50

retirement treated as permanent exits
from, 37–39
returns for students, 5, 120, 123,
139–141
service sector hardest hit during
pandemic, 3
labor market conditions
and education, 65–67
employment transitions by
gender, 64–65
as factor in retirement
decisions, 52–54, 60
sensitivity of retirement transitions
to, 63–65
Late Boomers *see* Millennials
Late Gen Xers *see* Millennials
liability-driven investment (LDI)
strategies, 4–5
lifecycle models, 79–80
Long Covid, 216–219
Longitudinal Employer-Household
Dynamics (LEHD)
as novel administrative dataset, 2–3
older workers, retirement and
macroeconomic shocks, 37–38,
40–48, 50
use examining quarterly flows
between full-time work,
partial retirement, and full
retirement, 56

M
Mackie, K., 4, 97, 99, 101, 113, 116 n.5
macroeconomic shocks
data and methodology, 37
impact on retirement transitions, 43–44, 46,
48
study conclusions, 49
Maestas, N., 7, 14, 99–100, 115, 155,
159, 173, 177 n.2, 211–215, 218
marriage trends, 16
MCBS *see* Medicare Current Beneficiary
Survey (MCBS)
McEntarfer, E., 2–3, 36, 37, 56, 62–63

Medicaid
  during Covid-19 pandemic, 162,
    164–165, 167–169
  and DYNASIM4 model, 18
  eligibility, 29–30, 156, 159–160, 183
  expenditures, 160, 175, 180
  during Great Recession, 159–160,
    167–169
  health insurance for elderly, 183,
    187, 189–191, 195–198
  as increasing during pandemic, 115
  men
    marginal effects of transfers, 166,
      170
    summary statistics, 175
    transfer program participation
      rates, 162, 164
  providing countercyclical assis-
    tance during recessions
    and at high levels of
    unemployment, 172–173
  as safety net program, 5–6, 155,
    159–160
  SSDI providing, 159
  women
    marginal effects of transfers, 168,
      171
    summary statistics, 176
    transfer program participation
      rates, 163, 165
Medicare
  62–74 age group usually in receipt of
    benefits, 169–172
  for under-age-65 people with
    qualifying disability, 159
  changes in payment policies, 115,
    181, 187, 200–201
  CMS and CBO projections, 188–189
  coverage of long-term services and
    supports, 29–30
  low-income beneficiaries, 183
  and Medicaid, 156, 159–160
  out-of-pocket spending on, 29–30,
    180, 182–183, 191
  per capita spending projection, 180
  premiums, 191–192

  projected and actual spending, 184
  simulations
    additional, 202–205
    comparing different cohorts over
      time, 198–200
    following current 65-year-olds over
      time, 196–197
    parameters, 189
  slowdown in spending
    growth, 184–186, 188, 200
    effect on retirement
      security, 194–195
  spending by recession-induced SSDI
    beneficiaries, 214–215
  structure of health insurance for
    elderly, 182
Medicare Current Beneficiary Survey
  (MCBS), 183, 189–195, 204
Mid Boomers *see* Millennials
Millennials
  assessing retirement
    prospects, 12–13, 18
  earnings trends, 15
  economic trends and demographic
    characteristics, 11–13
  education trends, 15–16
  expected retirement incomes, 2,
    12–13
  homeownership, 16
  household debt, 17
  household net worth, 17–18
  impact of social security's financing
    gap, 24–27
  income adequacy at older ages, 24–25
  income differences by demographic
    characteristics, 22–23
  income sources, 20–22
  labor force participation, 13–15
  marriage trends, 16
  method of projecting retirement
    outcomes, 1–2
  projected mean and distribution of
    per capita family income, 20
  retirement accounts, 17
  retirement preparedness, 2, 4
  risks along retirement path, 2

sensitivity to definition of adequate income, 26, 28
study conclusions, 29
wealth, 75–76, 81–93
Mitchell, O. S., 1, 56, 98–99, 124, 132, 147 n.29
Moffitt, R. A., 5, 115, 155–156, 177 n.3, 161
Mortenson, J., 4, 97, 98–99, 116 nn.4–5, 101, 107–108, 113, 155–156
Mullen, K. J., 7, 99–100, 115, 177 n.2, 211–215

N
National Health Expenditures (NHE)
excess cost growth
additional simulation, 202–204
CMS and CBO projections of excess cost growth, 188–189, 200–201
comparing different cohorts over time, 198–200
decompositions, 185–186
definition, 184–186
following current 65-year-olds over time, 196–198
impact of recent slowdown, 188
key contributors to, 186
other factors affecting, 188
parameters for simulations, 189
prices rise with overall inflation, 187, 196, 197, 199, 202–204
national health spending trends over time
CMS and CBO projections of excess cost growth, 188–189, 200–201
decompositions, 185
factors influencing spending growth, 184–186
health care prices, 187–188
implications of recent slowdown, 188
income and technology, 186
insurance, 186
other factors affecting excess cost growth, 188
projected and actual Medicare spending, 184

relative health care inflation, 187
new financial environment, 3

O
Occupation Information Network (O*NET), 58

P
partial retirement
cyclical regressions, 46, 48
flows increasing during high unemployment, 36
identifying transitions, 38–40
impact of pandemic, 49–50, 62–63
labor market returns, 48–49
timing, 3, 40
transitions and macroeconomic shocks, 43
Pre-Boomers see Millennials

R
real income available for non-health consumption, 194, 200, 202
real-world shocks, 5
Reber, S. J., 5, 73–74, 94 n.4, 120, 127, 137, 146 n.20, 147 n.33, 148 n.34, n.35
recessions
effectiveness of age discrimination protections diminishing during, 52
employment rate for workers without disabilities, 214
people affected by, 6
and SNAP, 115, 158, 172–173
and social security retirement program, 156
see also Covid-19 pandemic; Great Recession
recessions and retirement
at age 55, 60, and 62, 43
context, 52–55
data and methods, 56, 59
previous literature, 36, 55
regression results, 60–63
by age and education, 63–65
by education, 65–67

recessions and retirement (*Continued*)
  relations between, 49–50
  retirement probability, monthly, 63
  and returns to labour market
    from, 44
  study conclusions, 67
relative wealth
  adequacy across cohorts, 75, 85–86,
    88–91, 93
  drivers of decline, 93
  measures, 75
  of Millennials, 4, 76
  and retirement preparedness, 75, 93
  use of relative rank distributions, 81
required minimum distributions
    (RMDs), 98–100, 105, 107, 109
retirement
  impact of labor market shocks on
    future of, 1
  'sticky,' 3, 40, 42, 47–50
  US system, 125–127, 141
  see also partial retirement; recessions
    and retirement
retirement accounts
  and Covid-19 pandemic
    and CARES Act, 100, 108
    mean withdrawals, by age, 107
    overview of withdrawals, 115
    withdrawals, by year, 106
    workers at bottom of income
      distribution, 4
  impact of early withdrawal
    penalties, 99
  trends, 17
  see also Individual Retirement
    Accounts (IRAs)
retirement income
  adequacy at older ages, 24–25
  age, sex, and income for
    estimating, 78
  belief that economic growth will
    boost future, 12
  and borrowing, 148 n.34
  differences by demographic
    characteristics, 22–23

  impact of social security's financing
    gap, 24–27
  methodology for assessing retirement
    prospects, 18
  for Millennials, 1–2, 12–13, 29
  private sector employers reducing
    flows of, 11
  sensitivity to definition of
    adequate, 26, 28
  use of housing wealth to
    supplement, 16
  for workers experiencing weak
    labor market leading up to
    retirement, 52–53
retirement preparedness
  and adequacy, 78
  dependent on how policymakers
    address expected future social
    security shortfalls, 93–94
  government policy and private
    pension design, 7
  literature on, 73
  measures of household wealth to
    compare, 3–4
  Millennials, 2, 4
  and relative rank charts, 75
  and relative wealth approach, 75, 93
  of student loan borrowers, 122, 128,
    135, 141–143
  in United States, 1
retirement savings changes during
    pandemic
  background and policy changes, 100
  bunching, 98, 108–110, 112–113
  context, 97–100
  contributions, 4, 97, 101–105, 115
  data, 101
  required minimum distribu-
    tions, 98–100, 105, 107,
    109
  study conclusions, 115
  withdrawals, 4–5, 98, 105–115
retirement security
  decrease in retirement accounts as
    worrying sign for, 17

effect of Medicare
    slowdown, 194–195
encouraging sign for, 14
future threats to, 11, 13–14
future wage growth shaping, 29
high educational attainment as good
    for, 16, 29
implications of vulnerability of elderly
    to health cost increases, 180–181
loan forgiveness as policy to improve,
    for students, 141–142
marriage as important source of, 16,
    29
metric/measure, 181, 194
for Millennials of color, 29
in new financial environment, 3
pace of health spending growth as
    determinant of, 200–201
policy changes necessary for, 12–13
potential of future shocks to
    undermine, 7–8
simulations to gauge importance of
    health costs to, 195, 202–205
working longer proposed as best way
    to boost, 36
retirement timing, 40–42
retirement transitions
    context, 36–37
    data and methodology, 37
    effect of Covid pandemic on, 37–39,
        43–50, 54, 56, 62–65
    identifying, 38
    impact of macroeconomic
        shocks, 43–44, 46, 48
    retirement timing, 40
    study conclusions, 49
retirement wealth
    adequacy, 73, 75, 78, 91
    context, 73–76
    percentile point comparisons, 88
        10th percentile, 89
        25th percentile, 90
        50th percentile, 91
        75th percentile, 92
        90th percentile, 92
        explanation, 81

as method of comparing wealth
    distributions, 75
as pointing to contribution of social
    security, 75–76
relative rank distributions, 81
    at age fifty, 85
    at age forty, 87
    at age sixty, 83
    explanation, 81
    as method of comparing wealth
        distributions, 75
study conclusions, 93
RMDs see required minimum
    distributions (RMDs)

S
Sabelhaus, J., 1, 3–4, 18, 73–74, 94 n.3,
    77–78, 84–86, 97, 99, 146 n.20
safety net response to pandemic
    context, 155–157
    data, 160
    and other recessions, 5, 155
    results, 161
        graphical analysis, 161–165, 175
        regressions, 165–172, 175, 176
    study conclusions, 172
    in United States, and its cyclical
        responsiveness, 157
savings
    Medicare, 195, 200, 207 n.18
    retirement
        and adults who work longer, 14, 36
        estimated requirements, 29–30
        of lowest-income retirees, 47–49
        positive view of, 12, 79–80
        responsibility for, 2, 11
        women, under own names, 11
    student loan borrowers
        analysis, 129
        background, 124
        context, 120
        data and measurement, 127
        individual, 125–127
        overview, 120
        prior literature, 122
        study conclusions, 5, 141

savings (*Continued*)
  see also changes in retirement savings
    during pandemic
SCF *see* Survey of Consumer Finances
    (SCF)
Sheiner, L., 6, 115, 180–181, 183–184,
    206 n.10, 190, 200
Smith, K. E., 1–2, 11, 13–19, 80, 190
SNAP *see* Supplemental Nutrition
    Assistance Program (SNAP)
social security
  benefits as dependent on lifetime
    earnings, 11
  and comprehensive wealth, 91
  during Covid-19 pandemic, 3, 55,
    99–100, 108, 115, 162, 167–172
  data source, 101
  and DYNASIM4 model, 18–19
  eligibility age, 52–53, 63–65
  during Great Recession, 167–172
  and health spending, 180–181, 193,
    194
  importance for those at bottom of
    wealth distribution, 4
  as largest anti-poverty program in
    US, 6, 158–159
  long-term financing gap
    adjusting wealth measure for, 74
    complicating income
      projections, 19–20
    concerns about, 12
    impact of, 24–27, 29, 93–94
  and marriage, 16
  men
    marginal effects of transfers, 166
    summary statistics, 175
    transfer program participation
      rates, 162, 164
  Millennials, 2, 12–14, 16, 20–21,
    24–27, 29
  and partial retirement, 3, 40–41
  and recessions, 36, 172–173
  relative importance, 76, 84–85
  and retirement preparedness, 93–94
  rise in full retirement age, 11, 40
  as safety net program, 5–6, 156, 157

solvency, 91
and SSI benefit, 159–160, 175
women
  benefits accrued under own
    name, 11
  marginal effects of transfers, 168,
    171
  summary statistics, 176
  transfer program participation
    rates, 163, 165
Social Security Administration (SSA)
  awards into and exits from DI
    program, 212–213
  data on retirement savings
    changes, 101
  data used to look at macroeconomic
    determinants of retirement
    transitions, 36
  earnings data, 37
  field office closure, 7, 164–165,
    216–217, 219
  mortality by age and sex, 78
  payable SSW, 86–88
  SSDI applications, 216–217
  SSDI benefits, 211
Social Security Disability Insurance
    (SSDI)
  awards into and exits from, 213
  countercyclical assistance for
    disabled, 173
  Covid-19 pandemic
    during, 7, 99–100, 159, 162–165,
      167, 169–173, 211
    on eve of, 212
    long-run effects, 217, 219
  description, 159, 211
  employment rate by disability
    status, 214
  evidence of countercyclical
    effects, 172–173
  expenditures, 175
  during Great Recession, 7, 162–164,
    167, 172–173
  men
    marginal effects of transfers, 166,
      170

summary statistics, 175
transfer program participation
rates, 162, 164
Millennials, 13–14
number of applications and
beneficiaries, 217
number of beneficiaries with
successful return to work, 213
percent reporting disability, 218
rise in unemployment rate during
recessions, 215
as safety net program, 156–157
some countercyclicality, 159
women
marginal effects of transfers, 168,
171
summary statistics, 176
transfer program participation
rates, 163, 165
Social Security Trust Fund, 2–4, 12
social security wealth (SSW)
adding to household wealth, 73–74
data and methods, 77
distributional effect, 74
expected, 77, 84
inclusion in comprehensive wealth
concept, 74, 76, 81–82
net worth plus DB and, 83, 85, 87
overall dominance at every
age, 88–89
payable, 3–4, 19–20, 24–27, 74, 76,
86–91–92, 93–94
relative importance of, 76, 84–86
scheduled, 3–4, 12–13, 19–20, 24–27,
29, 86–92
SSDI *see* Social Security Disability
Insurance (SSDI)
SSI *see* Supplemental Security Income
(SSI)
SSW *see* social security wealth (SSW)
student loan borrowing
analysis
aggregates by age, 144
by college-educated families, 136
comparisons with
non-borrowers, 137–139

credit report characteristics, by
status, 140
evidence from
CCP/Equifax, 139–141
family characteristics by presence
of student debt, 133
general trends, 129–135
imputing history from
SCF, 135–137
share of families with student debt
by age, 130
student debt and college
attendance by age group, 132
wealth and retirement preparation
for college-educated families, by
status, 138
background
individual saving and US retirement
system, 125–127
loan facts, 124–125
wage income and wealth by
debt-holding status and
education, 126
context, 120
data and measurements
CCP/Equifax, 5, 128–129
Survey of Consumer Finances
(SCF), 126
loan forgiveness, 125, 128
overview, 120
prior literature, 122
student debt as largest component of
non-housing debt, 5
study conclusions, 141
Supplemental Nutrition Assistance
Program (SNAP)
during Covid-19 pandemic, 5–6,
155–156, 161–167, 169–173
description, 158
expenditures, 160, 175
during Great Recession, 158,
161–167, 169–173
men
marginal effects of transfers, 166,
170
summary statistics, 175

men (*Continued*)
transfer program participation rates, 162, 164
during recessions, 115, 158, 172–173
responsiveness, 156, 158
as safety net program, 5–6, 155, 157
transfers at household level, 160–161
women
marginal effects of transfers, 168, 171
summary statistics, 176
transfer program participation rates, 163, 165
Supplemental Security Income (SSI)
during Covid-19 pandemic, 162, 164–165, 167–169, 172–173
cyclical responsiveness, 159, 173
description and eligibility, 159
and DYNASIM4 model, 19
expenditures, 160, 175
during Great Recession, 159–160, 167–169, 172–173
lack of response to unemployment rate, 173
men
marginal effects of transfers, 166, 170
summary statistics, 175
transfer program participation rates, 162, 164
Millennials, 21–22
as of more relevance to older population, 156
as safety net program, 5–6, 155, 159–160
some evidence of countercyclical effects, 172–173
SSDI providing, 159
women
marginal effects of transfers, 168, 171
summary statistics, 176
transfer program participation rates, 163, 165
Survey of Consumer Finances (SCF)
base wealth figures from, 3–4

in retirement wealth study, 73–74, 77–79, 81–82, 88
student loan borrowing, 121–122, 125–127, 130, 132–133, 138–141, 144
data and measurements, 127–128
imputing history from, 135–137
limitation in using to study lifecycle outcomes, 139, 142
Surveys of Income and Program Participation (SIPP), 18, 161

T
technology, 186
telework, 54, 58–67, 218–219
transfer programs
analysis restriction, 161
marginal effects of transfers
for men (age 50–61), 165–169, 172
for men (age 62–74), 169–172
for women (age 50–61), 168–169, 172
for women (age 62–74), 169–172
participation rates
for men (age 50–61), 162
for men (age 62–74), 164–165
for women (age 50–61), 163–164
for women (age 62–74), 165
trends in real spending among adults, 175

U
unemployment
Covid-19 pandemic
comparison with Great Recession, 215–216
comparison with prior recessions, 219
rates declined for older workers, 3
rates returned to pre-pandemic levels, 3, 217
and retirement, 39, 47, 49, 54, 55, 57, 62–67
and safety net system, 155, 157–158, 165–173, 175–176
sharp employment decline not fully translating into higher, 3

sharp increase in, 115
and SSDI program, 216–217, 219
and Great Recession, 165–173,
   214–216
as high during Millennials' early
   careers, 13
probability of retirement increasing
   with, 52–54
and retirement flows, 36, 39, 45–49
state, 165–167, 168, 170, 171,
   175–176
unemployment insurance (UI)
and contributions to DC
   plans, 103–105
Covid-19 pandemic versus Great
   Recession, 167, 169
drop in SSDI applications linked to
   increases in, 99–100
eligibility requirements, 157–158
expenditures, 160, 175
federal government expanding
   eligibility for benefits, 53
as important for less educated
   older population of men and
   women, 172–173
income, 111–112
as increasing during Covid-19
   pandemic, 97, 108, 115
   possibly helping mitigate
      impact, 216–217, 219
labor market returns, 48
and LEHD data, 37, 39
men
   marginal effects of
      transfers, 166–167, 169–172
   summary statistics, 175
   transfer program participation
      rates, 162, 164–165
as most cyclically sensitive
   program, 161–162
older workers not yet retired, 156
prior research on, 98
responsiveness of, 155–156

retirement and partial
   retirements, 46
as safety net program, 5–6, 155
and withdrawals from retirement
   plans, 98
women
   marginal effects of
      transfers, 168–172
   summary statistics, 176
   transfer program participation
      rates, 163–165
Utkus, S. P., 1

V
Volz, A. H. 3–4, 18, 73–74, 94 n.3, n.4,
   77–78, 84–86, 123, 125–127, 146
   nn.19–20

W
wealth *see* comprehensive wealth;
      household wealth; relative
      wealth; retirement wealth; social
      security wealth (SSW)
wealth accumulation
   difficulty in linking student borrowing
      to, 121
   as feeding into retirement
      wellbeing, 141
   SCF containing measures of, 128
   and student debt, 120, 134–135,
      141–142
   student loan borrowers
      following trajectories of other
         college attendees, 122
      largely resembling
         non-borrowers, 142
wealth inequality, 73, 75, 82–84, 91–93
withdrawal from retirement plans
   see retirement savings changes
      during pandemic

Z
Zhang, H., 3, 14, 39, 47, 52, 99, 161–162
Ziliak, J. P., 5, 115, 155–156, 177 n.3,
   161